BLACK PRISON INTELLECTUALS

UNIVERSITY PRESS OF FLORIDA

Florida A&M University, Tallahassee
Florida Atlantic University, Boca Raton
Florida Gulf Coast University, Ft. Myers
Florida International University, Miami
Florida State University, Tallahassee
New College of Florida, Sarasota
University of Central Florida, Orlando
University of Florida, Gainesville
University of North Florida, Jacksonville
University of South Florida, Tampa
University of West Florida, Pensacola

Black Prison Intellectuals

Writings from the Long Nineteenth Century

Andrea Stone

UNIVERSITY PRESS OF FLORIDA

Gainesville/Tallahassee/Tampa/Boca Raton
Pensacola/Orlando/Miami/Jacksonville/Ft. Myers/Sarasota

Cover: Letter from James Foster to the governor on penitentiary stationery, September 5, 1901. Courtesy of Alabama Department of Archives and History.

This book will be made open access within three years of publication thanks to Path to Open, a program developed in partnership between JSTOR, the American Council of Learned Societies (ACLS), University of Michigan Press, and The University of North Carolina Press to bring about equitable access and impact for the entire scholarly community, including authors, researchers, libraries, and university presses around the world. Learn more at https://about.jstor.org/path-to-open/

Publication of this work made possible by a Sustaining the Humanities through the American Rescue Plan grant from the National Endowment for the Humanities.

Copyright 2025 by Andrea Stone
All rights reserved
Published in the United States of America

30 29 28 27 26 25   6 5 4 3 2 1

Library of Congress Cataloging-in-Publication Data
Names: Stone, Andrea, 1971– author.
Title: Black prison intellectuals : writings from the long nineteenth century / Andrea Stone.
Description: Gainesville : University Press of Florida, 2025. | Includes bibliographical references and index. | Summary: "Recovering critical, understudied writings from early archives, this book calls into question the idea that the Black prison intellectual movement began in the twentieth century, tracing the arc of Black prison writing from 1795 to 1901"— Provided by publisher.
Identifiers: LCCN 2024018809 | ISBN 9780813079202 (hardback) | ISBN 9780813080833 (paperback) | ISBN 9780813070933 (pdf) | ISBN 9780813073613 (ebook)
Subjects: LCSH: Prisoners' writings, American—History and criticism. | African American authors—History and criticism—19th century. | African American prisoners—History—19th century. | African Americans—Intellectual life—19th century. | BISAC: LITERARY CRITICISM / American / African American & Black | HISTORY / African American & Black | LCGFT: Literary criticism.
Classification: LCC PS153.P74 S86 2025 | DDC 810.9/920693—dc23/eng/20240528
LC record available at https://lccn.loc.gov/2024018809

The University Press of Florida is the scholarly publishing agency for the State University System of Florida, comprising Florida A&M University, Florida Atlantic University, Florida Gulf Coast University, Florida International University, Florida State University, New College of Florida, University of Central Florida, University of Florida, University of North Florida, University of South Florida, and University of West Florida.

University Press of Florida
2046 NE Waldo Road
Suite 2100
Gainesville, FL 32609
http://upress.ufl.edu

For Ken

I was ordained for some great purpose. . . . [It] had been said of me . . . that I had too much sense to be raised, and if I was, I would never be of any use to any one as a slave.

                    Nathaniel Turner, *Confessions* (1831)

CONTENTS

List of Figures   xi
Acknowledgments   xiii

   Introduction: Rethinking Outside and Inside through the Early Black Prison Intellectual   1
1. Gallows Death and Political Critique: Abraham Johnstone's *Address, Dying Confession, and Letter to His Wife* (1797)   16
2. Lunacy and Liberation, Black Crime and Disability: Antislavery Argument in the *Dying Confession of Pomp* (1795)   45
3. Nineteenth-Century Counter/Terrorism: Black Prison Intellectual Nathaniel Turner's *Confessions* and the Southampton Revolt (1831)   73
4. Nearly Six Months Imprisoned: Celia's Textual and Embodied Intellectualism in Missouri's Callaway County Jail (1855)   102
   Interlude: Postemancipation Criminality and Enmity in the *Christian Recorder* (1861–1901)   126
5. Dear Governor: The Parole Request as Literary Genre in James Foster's Letters (1901)   141
   Conclusion: Early Black Prison Intellectual Legacies   167

Notes   171
Works Cited   183
Index   195

FIGURES

1.1. Title page of Johnstone's pamphlet   19
1.2. Execution sermon with iconography   29
1.3. Execution sermon with emphasis on the crime   30
1.4. Broadside confession and dying words   31
1.5. Map of New Jersey   38
2.1. Pomp's *Dying Confession*   46
2.2. "Lord" Timothy Dexter   67
2.3. Jonathan Plummer   67
5.1. Foster's published first letter   149
5.2. Letter from Foster on penitentiary stationery   157
5.3. *Happy Will* by Foster   160
5.4. Untitled photograph by Foster   161
5.5. Untitled photograph by Foster   162
5.6. Untitled photograph by Foster   163

ACKNOWLEDGMENTS

Initial thinking about *Black Prison Intellectuals* began in a summer seminar on Black intellectuals led by Brent Hayes Edwards at the School of Criticism and Theory, Cornell University, in 2006. I continued to develop the project during the yearlong Kahn Institute project "Renaissances" at Smith College in the academic year of 2011–12, under the direction of Nalini Bhushan and Jay Garfield. I want to thank the leaders of these two seminars and all participants for stretching my thinking and providing stimulating intellectual environments with great support and laughs. Thank you to Sara Cohen for critical insights at later stages and Jessica Hinds-Bond for expert copyediting. Any mistakes are mine. Thank you also to participants in the seminars I taught at Smith on Black prison intellectuals, as well as my research assistants: Audrey Davis, Rhys Vulpe, Linea Kay, Juliet May, and Candace Russell.

Major support in myriad ways from members of the Celia Project, a research collaboration on the history of slavery and sexual violence, especially from Crystal Feimster, Ariela Gross, Martha Jones, and Hannah Rosen, was invaluable for this book. You all make my world better in every manner. Thank you. Also, thanks to Ariela Gross and Martha Jones for the invitation to serve as a commentator on a prison studies paper at the 2022 Law and Humanities Workshop for Junior Scholars at the Georgetown Law Center in Washington, DC. It was a pleasure engaging with Emily Hainze's essay and discussing my work with other commentators.

I want to thank American studies graduate students at Harvard University for their invitation to present my work and speak with them about new directions in the discipline. Your comments on an early stage of this book's second chapter were tremendously helpful.

Four conferences in particular offered me the opportunity to test ideas from this book internationally in the United Kingdom, France, and Poland. Thank you to my interlocutors at each (in descending chronological order): the ninth annual Conference on Madness, University of Oxford; the Conference on Problematizing the Self in Eighteenth-Century Autobiographical Writing in English at the Université de Paris Diderot 7; the International Interdisciplinary Scientific Symposium on the Birth of Mental Illness at Jagiellonian University in Kraków; and the Association for the Study of Law, Culture and the Humanities annual conference at Birkbeck, University of London. Particular thanks to co-panelist and great friend/colleague David Caudill for his always brilliant critical insights and sense of humor. Also, thank you to Gwen Bergner for inviting me to present early work from this book on a special panel on the (non)human and biopolitics of bare life at the Modern Language Association annual convention. The conversations that followed were most helpful.

I want to acknowledge my ongoing intellectual and personal relationships with friends and colleagues: George Elliott Clarke, Jeannine Marie DeLombard, Arlene Keizer, Robert S. Levine, Arthur Redding, and Steven Winter. Thank you also to Robert Levine for the invitation to present early work from this book's fourth chapter as part of the Local Americanists lecture series of the Department of English at the University of Maryland.

Archivists and collections at the American Antiquarian Society, the Alabama Department of Archives and History, and Smith College Special Collections were invaluable to my research for this book. In the Smith Collections, I want to thank Shannon Supple for her work with my seminars, which also helped my research.

This book would not have been possible without the excellent work of senior editor Sian Hunter—what a pleasure it was working with you again!—the anonymous reviewers, and the staff at the University Press of Florida.

My colleagues and friends at Smith College deserve special thanks for their insights and for all of our conversations over the years and leading up to the publication of this book: Marnie Anderson, Nalini Bhushan, Nancy Mason Bradbury, Brigitte Buettner, Floyd Cheung, Carrie Cuthbert, Craig Davis, Rick Fantasia, Susan Faludi, Michael Gorra, Lily Gurton-Wachter, Ambreen Hai, Yona Harvey, Alice Hearst, Alexandra Keller, Gillian Murray Kendall, Jina B. Kim, Elizabeth Klarich, Daphne Lamothe, Naomi Miller, Richard Millington, Christen Mucher, William Allan Oram, Ruth Ozeki, Melissa Parrish, Douglas Lane Patey, Cornelia Pearsall, Kate Queeney, Loretta J. Ross, Kevin Rozario, Russ Rymer, Marilyn Schuster, Michael Thurston, Lester Tomé, Susan Van Dyne, Steve Waksman, Frazer Ward, and Louis Wilson.

I offer deepest thanks to my dear, dear friends, some dating back to my childhood. First to my oldest friends and their families: Mark, Lisa, Ally, and Meg Mitchell; Kathy Sitak-Pickard and Dave and Elliot Pickard; Brent Wilde, Nikki Peters, and Alec and Dhillon Wilde; Brad Smith; Todd McDaniel; Steve and Karen Stone; Liz and John Baker; Gemma and Gary Robinson; Sharon and Chris George; and Marilyn and Gord Fair. To my beloved friends in (or from) my beloved Toronto: Dan, Jen, Shealyn, and Darcy Blaik; Vincent Barbee; Ian Gogolek; Lesley Grant; Don MacGregor; Raji Singh Soni and Ralph Callebert; James Sommerville; Mary Jo Smith and Paul Brown; Cheryl Suzack and Neil McIntosh; and Giovanna Riccio. To my close friends I met in western Massachusetts: Amy Campbell and Lisa Woods; Will Cassini; Caroline Christie and Chet Mitchell; Justin Crumbaugh; Liz Elder; Randall Griffey; Josh and Nicole Jones; Jennifer and Gary Kmetz; Robin Longo; Tom McCormick; Janet Simeone and Chris Yurko; Mike Wall; Donna Webster; and Emily Wojcik-Thurston. To my dear friends in (or whom I met in) Greece, who have listened to me think through this book over the years: Liza Bellett; Steve Burke; Miles and Shirley Davis; Ken Hall; Deborah and Jon Hobson; Georgia and Kostas Keheyas; Martin and Brenda Kerry; Tristan O'Donnell; Alan Ormston; and Martin and Harriet Rapley.

I also want to offer huge thanks to my extended family for their love and support over the decades: Dianne and Mike Melitzer; Rachel, Chris, Trent, and Jayce Dobson; Colleen and Henry Piotrowski; Helena and Sam Trabulsi; Derek, Barbara, and Louise Hodson; Sarah, Neil, Catherine, and Rachel Hallett; Charles and Linda Gray; Bob and Mary Gray; Duane, Nancy, Braeden, and Alyssa Gray; Bobbie Lynn, Christian, and Logan Powers; Grant, Jennifer, Alexa, and Owen MacDonnell; Dan Gray, Sue Brocklebank, Jamie, and Clara; Colleen Gray and David Lynch; and Jim and Gloria Ross.

And to my parents, David and Edith Gray. Thank you for your love, support, and wit, and for keeping me grounded, always. Your insights into just about everything are always brilliant, and I love you.

Finally, my deep thanks to Ken Ross, to whom this book is dedicated. Thank you for your patience and sharp ideas, and for being the best partner I can imagine. And, of course, enormous thanks to our excellent little listeners and critics: the late-great Grimsby and Ricky and Violet.

Introduction

Rethinking Outside and Inside through
the Early Black Prison Intellectual

"When I was in prison, I read an article—don't be shocked when I say that I was in prison. You're still in prison. That's what America means: prison." Malcolm X made that proclamation in his 1963 speech "Message to the Grass Roots," but his missive rearticulates Black ancestral thought from two previous centuries. *Black Prison Intellectuals* analyzes the emergence, influence, and cultural significance of Black prison intellectual work in the United States from early gallows literature of the late eighteenth and early nineteenth centuries through to the prison correspondence of the early twentieth century. The book's chapters include close readings of the work of early imprisoned Black people, ancestors in this tradition: Abraham Johnstone, Pomp, Nathaniel Turner, Celia, and James Foster. Besides Turner, the other four people are relatively unknown. *Black Prison Intellectuals* illustrates how the works of these individuals serve as the foundation for the explosion of output from more recent figures in the Black prison intellectual movement—Eldridge Cleaver, George Jackson, Bobby Seale, Angela Y. Davis, Assata Shakur, and Mumia Abu-Jamal, to name a few. These ancestors' theories about Blackness, incarceration, violence, and state control also help us theorize and comprehend our own time as part of this long and enduring context.[1]

Black Prison Intellectuals is an interdisciplinary project situated at the crossroads of law, literature, politics, and print cultures. Emphasis on the early Black prison author as intellectual distinguishes this book from other studies in three ways.[2] First, it broadens the concept of the intellectual and counters historically white determinations of what constitutes intellectual life and work. The book questions who qualifies as an intellectual and what it means to expand that category to read the figures studied here through that lens, and to see their work as critique on individual, community, and state levels. Second, it emphasizes that the intellectual work Black people have produced in US jails and prisons has a history as long as that of the United States itself and therefore is not exclusively a tradition beginning in the twentieth century, even though most scholarship on Black intellectuals tends to focus on figures from this time and after. Reading and interpreting the long history of the Black prison intellectual figure highlights the important predecessors to more recent traditions we rely on in our critical thinking today regarding systemic oppression and prison studies in the United States. Third, it demonstrates the collapse of the putatively distinct categories of criminal and enemy in the historical US context. Perhaps the most important contribution these prison intellectuals make in exposing this collapse of criminal/enemy is revealing how the United States, since its inception, has waged an undeclared war against Black people. In an effort to demonstrate the long past of this important intellectual history, this book seeks to reframe the study of early violations of Black people's rights and reveal the trajectory of Black intellectual labor emerging from incarceration that at times coincided with as well as followed the enslavement of Black people in the United States.

Drawing together scholarship from, for example, Khalil Gibran Muhammad, who identifies and traces the criminalization of Black people, Caleb Smith, who articulates the prison's role in shaping the American imagination (*Prison*), and Jeannine Marie DeLombard, who analyzes the importance of the Black imprisoned person's early print persona in the creation of Black civic authority (*Shadow*), this book attempts to uncover what incarcerated Black people's literary and philosophical work teaches us about white supremacy, state regulation, civic life, and racially motivated suppression of civil and human rights from the early republic to the aftermath of Reconstruction. The outlawed Black intellectual, over time, not only exposes the fiction behind the rhetoric of the Revolutionary War, but also demonstrates how such rhetorics continue to inform those of safety and security, which increasingly justify the confiscation of civic and human rights and freedoms of US citizens in general, and of Black people in particular.

Black Prison Intellectuals is most concerned with the ways in which the figures featured here critique and at times welcome and appropriate the status of the Black internal enemy as well as the role of the jail or prison/penitentiary in shaping their discourse (jail typically being a more local and temporary carceral space, and the penitentiary being a longer-term place of incarceration and nineteenth-century iteration of the jail). Close reading of works as diverse as Abraham Johnstone's *Address, Dying Confession, and Letter to His Wife* (1797), the *Dying Confession of Pomp* (1795), Nathaniel

Turner's *Confessions* (1831), Celia's recorded depositions and printed confessions, and her actions in a Missouri county jail (1855), and James Foster's parole request letters from Alabama's convict leasing program (1901), all produced from the confines of their own cells, highlights the state's enmification of Black criminality and expands Black imprisoned people's theories and critiques of enmity, incarceration, enforced labor, and the justice system. Their exposure of Black enmity as a component of criminality in the long nineteenth century can deepen our moral, political, and legal philosophical debates about imprisonment, carceral labor, and white supremacy more broadly. Additionally, taking a break from close readings, *Black Prison Intellectuals* offers an interlude between analysis of Celia's and James Foster's work to demonstrate shifts and consistencies in the role of the Black person deemed criminal and enemy in the years leading up to the Civil War and after emancipation.

Such are dynamics that Foster's complex early twentieth-century intellectual efforts highlight. He prompts us to consider his parole request letters more deeply, and this book reads them closely. I see Foster's requests for parole as an important new literary-critical genre, and encourage further study of such Black-authored letters to the state for what they can teach us about the individual writer, their specific critique of jails and prisons, and the people and systems that support these institutions.

Imprisonment shapes the contours of Black intellectual labor in the United States. Indeed, the prison has historically been a rich source of Black intellectual work—as much as universities and colleges, Black churches, and other voluntary civil associations. Supplementing close readings of selected Black imprisoned people's texts (performed and printed), book history and print culture methodologies reveal the relation between incarceration and the development, circulation, and influence of Black thought and knowledge.

Black orality and action defy literate-centric notions of intellectualism, and the predominance of the body in these texts complicates what has been understood as the intellectual's preoccupation or association with the "life of the mind." The book conceives a notion of embodied intellectual work that brings the mind and body together as a framework to contextualize the relation between un- or postconventional bodies, their printed texts, and their cultural/intellectual interventions at a time when enslaved and incarcerated Black figures, as thinkers and as holders and producers of knowledge, were not recognized as intellectuals.[3]

Black Prison Intellectuals focuses on early US jails and prisons as sites where incarcerated people theorized Blackness and injustice as central in their own time, an idea that resonates through to today. In political theorist Joy James's edition of twentieth-century imprisoned peoples' writings from different parts of the globe, the author argues in the introduction that "the imprisoned intellectual is a public intellectual who, like his or her highly visible and celebrated counterparts, reflects upon social meaning, discord, development, ethics, and justice. Prisons function as intellectual and political sites unauthorized by the state" (3–4). This argument applies as well to those who preceded the authors in James's collection, even across diverse US temporal and geopolitical contexts. Reading eighteenth-, nineteenth-, and early twentieth-century incarcerated figures as proto–public intellectuals demonstrates the ancestral, even inaugural reflections James refers to that can help us understand the historical relation between Blackness and imprisonment from the beginnings of what became the United States.

Intellectualism and Imprisonment

Beyond the influential theories of intellectualism from twentieth-century thinkers such as Antonio Gramsci, Julien Benda, Edward W. Said, and Michel Foucault, a good place to begin to particularize thought about Black intellectual history is in the work of Black studies scholar Abdul Alkalimat. He argues, "Black intellectual history is often portrayed as the history of the texts of the Black intelligentsia. But these ideas and values also have deep resonance within the popular consciousness of the broad masses of Black people, and frequently even originate with them. It is necessary to draw attention to this tradition, because it helps to contextualize Black Studies as the unfolding of collective intelligence. It counters the mythology of the singular genius of any given member of the academic elite" (63). Just as the academic intellectual in our time is often distinct from the public intellectual, theorists have imagined the academic as distinct from the intellectual more broadly. In conversation with bell hooks, Cornel West, for example, states: "An academic usually engages in rather important yet still narrow scholarly work, whereas an intellectual is engaged in public issues that affect large numbers of people in a critical manner" (29, and see 34). It is only relatively recently that academia has taken more seriously the academic as public intellectual. The thinkers/actors featured in *Black Prison Intellectuals*—Abraham Johnstone, Pomp, Nathaniel Turner, Celia, and James Foster—are not academics. But they function as intellectuals in the ways that West and James describe.

The works of these early Black prison intellectuals critique tenets central to the founding of the republic, institutions of enslavement, imprisonment, law, and politics, and form a foundation for subsequent works about institutional and personal injustice. Read together, they also highlight the state's enmification of Black people, generally, and demonstrate the consequences for those also deemed criminal. They reveal the stakes of occupying the official statuses of enslaved and criminal, and the unofficial one of enemy. As far as we know, all but Foster were executed by the state amid this exact engagement with public issues.[4] In the same conversation with West, hooks refers to a previous moment when West understood "the vocation of the intellectual as trying to allow suffering to speak" (34). For those studied in this book, suffering comes to the fore in their work, and in four of five instances their state-sanctioned death punctuates their suffering.

Reading Johnstone, Pomp, Turner, Celia, and Foster as intellectuals underscores the long history of Blackness and institutional and individual racism, as well as the role of jail and prison in shaping Black intellectual discourse in the United States. For each, the jail or prison seems to allow space and time to theorize critical issues. The connection between spirituality and intellectual work, according to hooks, requires time spent alone in thought. Johnstone, Pomp, Turner, and, to an extent, Foster find time on their own, "where one's mind becomes a workspace," to contemplate religious teachings and their spiritual lives (hooks and West 80–81), some before and during their imprisonment, and some after incarceration. Malcolm X exemplifies the kind of "intellectuality" to which hooks refers, and the thinkers/actors here represent forerunners of this deep tradition. But as hooks emphasizes, the mind is not a discrete entity in this intellectual context.[5] The connection between the body and the ability to love and defend this body (Pomp, Turner, and Celia) features in important ways as the people studied here confront and illuminate how, as West states, "white supremacist discourse associat[es] Black being with Black bodies . . . [without] minds [and without] intelligence" (hooks and West 86). The Black prison intellectuals here challenge such discourse and remove demarcations of body and mind.

I realize the work I'm doing here does not cohere entirely with the definitions and theories of intellectualism that hooks and West describe, and I'm not trying to map their theories onto those I study. But I want to demonstrate how the people in this book have propelled the trajectory of intellectual work through legacies that inform theories of what it means to be an intellectual, and, particularly, how they have helped shape the Black intellectual tradition through their navigation and theorizations of race, particularly Blackness, and imprisonment. Thinkers from many disciplines and subject positions have theorized intellectualism for millennia. I don't intend to give an overview of that history per se. But I do want to highlight some ideas that complement or give voice to how I understand Johnstone, Pomp, Turner, Celia, and Foster as doing intellectual work. Through their theories and actions, and writing from within their own historical, geopolitical, and cultural contexts, they situate themselves as antecedents of a continuing trajectory of intellectualism that emphasizes and challenges systemic racism, violence, and injustice—and they do this from physical places of literal imprisonment, revealing the fragile, even fictional democracy on which the United States is built.

Many theorists of Black intellectual history over time have argued against white and Eurocentric definitions of what it means to be an intellectual—and specifically a Black intellectual—as well as narrow understandings of the spaces wherein intellectual work takes place. Philosopher Charles W. Mills's enormously influential *The Racial Contract* (1997) presents the long, global history of desperate white supremacist and colonial methods of producing "the desired outcome of confirming nonwhite intellectual inferiority" (60). The authors here analyze these very methods. The edited volume *Toward an Intellectual History of Black Women* (2015) demonstrates how "Black women have rarely worked out of the academy or research institutes [and rather work] from the intimate spaces of parlors, where epistolary exchanges were produced, to highly public podiums, where oral expressions of ideas often mixed with the material demands of communities" (Bay et al. 5). *Black Prison Intellectuals* aims to demonstrate that the jail, particularly for Celia, pushes our understanding of where such labor takes place and how Black women's intellectual history can encompass this space, which is so central to that work and is yet separated even further from academic or research institutions than are the private parlors and public podiums.

Thinking through *Toward an Intellectual History of Black Women*, Black studies scholar La TaSha Levy notes the ways in which Black intellectual traditions not only "[disrupt] Eurocratic conceptions of who counts as an intellectual and what constitutes intellectual work," but also look beyond canonical Black intellectuals to a multitude of other figures who have "[explored] contention, conflict, and controversy as well as Black folks' miraculous ways of being—in spite of, and beyond, racial domination." Even further, editors and contributors to the recent volume *New Perspectives on the Black Intellectual Tradition* (2018) have expanded that tradition to include "those with little to no formal education" and writers in the genres of autobiography and slave narratives, articulating the "enduring quest for social justice" as a "key—although often vaguely defined—ingredient of the black intellectual tradition" (Blain et al. 4–5; Dagbovie 133). *Black Prison Intellectuals* builds on these and other definitions and genres of intellectual work through close readings of early texts from incarcerated Black thinkers/actors who were not formally or traditionally educated. The book centers US jails and prisons as crucial spaces of Black intellectual production, particularly about racial injustice, underscoring the thinkers' critical theories as vital to and defining of their own time, not to mention invaluable for an understanding of our present.

For this book, intellectual work involves thinking and acting in ways that reveal and underscore injustice, particularly injustice against Black people from the early days of the republic through to post-Reconstruction. Reading and analysis of perhaps-unconventional intellectual figures helps decolonize intellectual work and highlight how, in Mills's words, "From the inception . . . race is in no way an 'afterthought,' a 'deviation' from ostensibly raceless Western ideas, but rather a central shaping constituent of those ideals" in the "unnamed global political structure—*global white supremacy*" (14, 125). Recognizing this white supremacist global frame and focusing on early US historical periods when the jail or prison might seem an unlikely site for Black intellectual thought allows us to rethink the contributions of lesser-known figures and pay close attention to their trailblazing work. Further, their groundbreaking activity helped clear the way for the reckoning that has taken shape since: the realization that Black intellectual traditions are part of the very fabric of US history, with much to tell us about white supremacy and US democracy.

The term *Black prison intellectuals* denotes a historically enmified intellectual group in a racially stratified nation—one that has systemically and disproportionally oppressed, imprisoned, and sanctioned the deaths and even murders of members of its Black population.[6] Despite oppression and imprisonment, even the imminence of execution, Black prison intellectuals in the United States have produced a rich body of critique from within carceral institutions. Recasting criminals, enemies, and intellectuals, the term *Black prison intellectuals* asks us to reframe the discussion about unjust carceral practices and the function of US justice. Expanding on the work of scholars who have argued that Black people in the United States are routinely criminalized, this book reveals the deep historical enmification of perceived Black criminality that shapes US culture, and it illuminates the theories Black prison intellectuals produce about the institutions and their supporters central to that culture.

Criminals and Enemies

As Michel Foucault has influentially argued, it is institutions that turn the person who commits a crime into a criminal, and it is institutions that create enemies. Within these categories, which are mapped onto people, several factors distinguish the criminal from the enemy. Historians, literary critics, and theorists have long understood the criminalization of Blackness from the early national period to the present in the United States. Angela Y. Davis, H. Bruce Franklin, Khalil Gibran Muhammad, Jeannine Marie DeLombard, and Michelle Alexander—to name just a few important contributors—have demonstrated the perceived relation between Blackness and criminality, as well as the state-sanctioned racialization of crime throughout US history. This book, however, argues that far more insidiously, the state's enmification of Black people starts with suspected criminal activity. Within white supremacist culture, these suspicions are fraught with racist biases and presumptions of guilt. The works of the Black prison intellectuals featured here theorize the United States' approach to and treatment of imprisoned Black people as beyond simply criminals. Rather, individually as well as collectively, the intellectuals in this study demonstrate that the state regards Black people charged with crimes as unofficial and at times official public enemies.

Writing or narrating from within carceral spaces after having been convicted of crimes ranging from theft and larceny to conspiracy to rebel and murder, Johnstone, Pomp, Turner, Celia, and Foster demonstrate the United States' racialization of crime in the production and discipline of the Black enemy. The thinkers/actors here theorize enmity, at times situating themselves and the state as enemy combatants. Whether detailing false arrest and conviction, recounting the killing of an enslaver, calling for revolution, fomenting revolt, conspiring to escape jail, or requesting parole, these Black prison intellectuals conceptualize and critique a foundational problem in the republic that haunts us to this day: the persistent enmification of Black people suspected of or charged with criminal activity in the United States. The figures in this book also question what constitutes criminal behavior and reveal the racial imbalance of the US scales of justice.

The examples in this book lay bare the state's efforts to quell criminalized violence and maintain the perception of Black violence as individual and criminal. They also illuminate how the state's perceived threat of collective violent Black action is always present, allowing for the enmification of the Black person seen as criminal. A succinct distinguishing factor between criminality and enmity comes from Paul Kahn's 2011 essay "Criminal and Enemy in the Political Imagination." In it, he argues, "The criminal is not the enemy; the enemy is not the criminal. The enemy can be killed but not punished" (148). He continues, "Criminals have no right of self-defense against the police. The force of law is asymmetrical. For this reason, we think of the violence of law—policing—as 'depoliticized.' There is a corresponding depoliticization of the violence of crime: it is not political threat but personal pathology. Law enforcement aims to prevent the violence of the criminal from becoming a source of collective self-expression. Were it to become so, we would confront an enemy" (149). The example of Nathaniel Turner in this book could serve as the poster image for the "depoliticization of the violence of crime [into] personal pathology." Individuality and collectivity, pathology and politicization, punishment and killing, all these concepts Kahn explains are those that Turner and others in this book use to distinguish criminal from enemy.

This book's objective is to demonstrate how the state's punitive treatment of Black people charged with crimes consistently blurs this distinction between criminal and enemy. The enslaved people who kill their enslavers (even if in self-defense) and the leader of the revolt who gathers together a collective to overthrow the authority of slave codes or Reconstruction-era Black codes, for example, commit political acts and, through the criminal justice system, are treated more like enemies than like what the state calls criminals. Furthermore, their criminal punishment typically takes the form of state-sanctioned execution (whether legal or not), at times with torture as part of the process.

The enslaved, fugitive, imprisoned, and Black noncitizen persons all occupy a state of exception. Political theorist Achille Mbembe argues, "the state of exception and the relation of enmity have become the normative basis of the right to kill. In such instances, power (and not necessarily state power) continuously refers and appeals to exception, emergency, and a fictionalized notion of the enemy. It also labors to produce that same exception, emergency, and fictionalized enemy" (16). Mbembe's analysis concerns a twenty-first-century crisis, but his rubric represents a long-standing thread in US political and social thought. The perceived (or at least promoted) sense of Black incompetence for self-sustainment, the possibility of revolt, and the fear of Black crime all produce a narrative of emergency against which white society needs protection and through which Black people (enslaved, fleeing enslavement, and imprisoned) emerge as Mbembe's "fictionalized enemy."[7]

Except for Abraham Johnstone and James Foster, the individuals studied in this book admitted to following through on actual threats to their white victims, but as a group—under the more general rubric of Blackness and even before they committed their legally inscribed criminal actions—they represented to the dominant society the *potential* for threat. Psychologist Ofer Zur argues, "'enemy' can be defined as a person or a group of persons perceived to represent a threat to or to be hostile toward the perceiver" (350). White supremacist lawmakers and enslavers promoted the perception of Black threat or hostility to justify enslavement. Zur further outlines seven types of enemies in existence from the fourth millennium BCE to the late eighteenth century, with one of these types the "withholding enemy." In a US context, in some ways, this enemy still exists. Zur details the withholding enemy as "viewed . . . as one who deprived us of our physical and psychological needs. The enemy was not to be destroyed, but to be exploited, enslaved, and used to fulfill the greedy needs of the group and its individuals" (347). This type of enemy in Zur's estimation is an enemy in a time of European warfare, but the premise augments the racial warfare that has been part of the fabric of US culture from its beginnings. With reference to the founding of the United States, and borrowing a word from Thomas Paine's *Common Sense* (1776), scholar of rhetoric Jeremy Engels argues that "enemyship produced [national] identity through antithesis" (*Enemyship* 31). The perception and confrontation of enemies gave the United States a sense of national identity against the confronted others, whether British, Indigenous, or Black.

In many ways, for Johnstone as well as for his legal, moral, and literary descendant David Walker, who penned the provocative 1829 *Appeal to the Coloured Citizens of the World*, naming of the enemy is a response to what was effectively the early republic's undeclared war against enslaved Black people and those charged with crimes. Drawing on Carl Schmitt's work on "the political" and his notion that "all collective political bodies, all peoples, are premised on an antagonism between friend and enemy"—as well as Jacques Derrida's response that knowing how to identify an enemy is a difficult matter of *"practical identification"*—Engels focuses his attention on the early US republic to the early nineteenth century ("Friend" 40). He argues, "Slavery was a system premised on the logic of the political. Thomas Jefferson's writings on slavery in the 1780s, and David Walker's response to Jefferson's *Notes on the State of Virginia* and Walker's attempt to unite slaves in a revolution to overthrow the enemies in the late 1820s, both contained the complicated rhetorical task of naming the enemy in different ways" ("Friend" 40–41). Here is an example of Zur's notion of perception and the perceived threat posed by a potential enemy. Walker, as did Johnstone a little over two decades previous, wrote about how white supremacists identified Black people as their enemies and concentrated on white people's actions as they made that identification. Engels further argues that even though there were other enemies of the early republic, "slaves were an important and enduring foe and thus Jefferson and others talked up the antagonism between white and black in order to constitute a white American 'people' united by their whiteness. Although slavery was the negative face of the race war that threatened to destroy society, it was also constitutive of it" ("Friend" 44). State disciplinary treatment of the figures in this book, as well as their response to this treatment, underscores the enmification of Black, particularly enslaved, criminality.

Black Prison Intellectuals: Enmity and Criminality in the United States, 1795–1901

The first chapter, "Gallows Death and Political Critique: Abraham Johnstone's *Address, Dying Confession, and Letter to His Wife* (1797)," demonstrates how Johnstone's pamphlet recasts the definition of enmity by recalibrating revolutionary rhetoric to emphasize what Johnstone refers to as the deceptive, deceitful, hypocritical, and, therefore, unstable foundations of New Jersey politics and the new republic in general. Johnstone's pamphlet was published in Philadelphia, a major publishing center at the time. His *Address* not only undoes the criminalization of Black civility as Jeannine DeLombard has argued, but also identifies a false white civility as the enemy that represents the greatest threat to state and national security in New Jersey, Pennsylvania, and the broader early republic.[8]

Chapter 2, "Lunacy and Liberation, Black Crime and Disability: Antislavery Argument in the *Dying Confession of Pomp* (1795)," reads aspects of Pomp's confession in Ipswich, Massachusetts, within the broader genres of street and gallows literature to reveal how his text and the addenda from his amanuensis, Jonathan Plummer, complicate rehabilitative discourses inherent in the dying words genre and in early nationalist impulses more generally. Highlighting the nexus here of disability, intellectualism, and the Black prophetic tradition, the chapter hinges on Pomp's critique of slavery and uncovers the forces that translate the Black disabled criminal into legal person, only to identify him as a public enemy and eradicate him from the social body.[9]

Chapter 3, "Nineteenth-Century Counter/Terrorism: Black Prison Intellectual Nathaniel Turner's *Confessions* and the Southampton Revolt (1831)," builds on chapter 2 in the context of Black-led revolts in Haiti and the United States and investigates perceptions of mental distress, Black prophecy, and health as it turns to a consideration of probably the most well-known antebellum US revolt. This chapter analyzes print production surrounding the 1831 Southampton slave revolt, which saw the massacre of some sixty white people and indiscriminate retaliation that resulted in the deaths of approximately two hundred people, a number of them tried and executed for their participation, others killed merely on suspicion of having supported the revolt. In many ways, Nathaniel Turner, who led the revolt, is the prototypical radical Black prison intellectual, a precursor to those like Malcolm X who would come to prominence in the years leading up to the US civil rights movement. Key characteristics include Turner's intellect, dedication to reading, and devotion to prayer.

Turner's *Confessions* (particularly the parts in the voice of local lawyer and amanuensis Thomas Gray) and the newspaper coverage of the event both emphasize Turner's mental state. Extending from the previous chapter's discussion about Pomp's mental distress and its relation to his violent actions, this chapter highlights how Turner draws out the perceived need to connect Black protest and insanity—the pathologization of Black dissent and Black prophecy—and by contrast underscores the white supremacist factors prompting Black violence. The chapter reveals how Turner's intellectual work, his status as noncitizen, his printed *Confessions*, Virginia slave law, and newspaper accounts of the revolt all underscore the period's fraught conceptions of enmity and criminality, which for many white people prompted a need to racialize madness in the wake of the realization of Turner's prophecies. Turner's status as a radical Black intellectual critiquing the state from outside and inside the jail, as well as his emphasis on enmity and terrorism, resonates to this day, and provides a crucial template for reading Black resistance throughout US history.

Chapter 4, "Nearly Six Months Imprisoned: Celia's Textual and Embodied Intellectualism in Missouri's Callaway County Jail (1855)," looks to another rebellious nineteenth-century figure, the woman at the heart of the trial *Missouri v. Celia, a Slave*, a nineteen-year-old enslaved woman who killed her sixty-year-old enslaver after years of sexual abuse. Turning the focus from Celia's case toward her time in jail, this chapter analyzes contemporary prison and jail memoirs, county records, newspaper articles, photos, and histories. The chapter puts these materials about her physical conditions into conversation with her printed confessions and depositions to continue her story and depict as accurately as possible the continued abuses Celia would have encountered in the county jail as a young, pregnant woman awaiting trial and ultimately execution. Here analysis of the interrelation between physical action and printed words as intellectual acts builds on the significance of the work of Nathaniel Turner. The chapter's attention to her direct involvement in at least three jailbreaks, including her own and that of a young enslaved boy, offers a new dimension to Celia's character beyond that of the sexually abused and unjustly imprisoned enslaved woman. She is also part of the tradition of the Black rebel outlaw.

Next, *Black Prison Intellectuals* provides an interlude amid the close readings. This interlude, "Postemancipation Criminality and Enmity in the *Christian Recorder* (1861–1901)," addresses the concepts of criminality and enmity leading up to the Civil War and into the post-Reconstruction period. Highlighting Black responses to the Civil War, emancipation, prison, crime, enmification, convict leasing, the Thirteenth Amendment, the Ku Klux Klan, and lynching (among other concerns), this section of the book reads the *Christian Recorder*, the era's leading Black newspaper. The interlude reveals the ways in which the newspaper and its correspondents understood and critiqued these concepts, practices, and institutions and their supporters. As a bridge between chapters, the interlude underscores the enmification of Black people across the long nineteenth century, both before and after emancipation.

Following this interlude, chapter 5 seeks to open literary studies to a new genre of Black prison writing that appeared after emancipation: the parole request letter. "Dear Governor: The Parole Request as Literary Genre in James Foster's Letters (1901)" focuses on a particular form of Black political critique. The source material for this chapter comes primarily from the Alabama Department of Archives and History in Montgomery, which contains prison correspondence produced during the time when convicted Black people were leased to coal mining and other companies, for which they were forced to perform hard labor. Alabama was not the only state to use such enforced and inhumane labor practices, but it was the last one in the country to end this particular form of exploitation of imprisoned Black people. Parole request letters illustrate an important form of Black testimony and theory about white supremacy, Blackness, incarceration, injustice, and politics, particularly convict leasing and the Thirteenth Amendment. They reveal the realities of imprisonment in post-Reconstruction Alabama as well as the literary techniques imprisoned Black people used in their attempts to secure parole. In these respects, the Black-authored parole request letter is a literary critical genre in its own right, one deserving of close attention.

This chapter focuses on an early example of this genre—parole legislation passed in Alabama in 1897, only four years prior—with a fascinating duo of letters from James Foster, an older man and professional photographer. "Dear Governor" features his remarkable letters to the governor as well as an analysis of his photos of fellow inmates. Foster's letters theorize and critique Alabama's parole laws, the state's handling of his own case, the governor's role, and the justice system more broadly. Foster's work highlights shifts in prison populations, the realities of Black imprisonment and enforced labor, and the continued enmification of Black criminality after the Civil War. As early US gallows literature, dying words, confessions, and so forth have become recognized for their centrality to Black print expression—expanding literary-historical study of antebellum Black literature beyond the genres of the exhortation, poems of virtue, and the slave narrative—so too I hope Black parole request letters will reshape the ways in which scholars and students of literature, history, law, and culture understand the value of this genre as an important mode of Black critique and a critical source of Black intellectual work.

These chapters uncover and showcase work we can think of as the foundation to the better-known theories from Black prison intellectuals at the dawn of the twentieth-century civil rights movement and extending into our own time with the continued undeclared war against Black people. The book's conclusion, "Early Black Prison Intellectual Legacies," traces the contributions of these early examples of Black prison writing/oration as they manifest in the published and recorded works of figures like George Jackson, Angela Y. Davis, Eldridge Cleaver, Assata Shakur, Rubin "Hurricane" Carter, and Mumia Abu-Jamal. These later generations of imprisoned writers and activists explicitly draw on the criminal/enemy distinction in the United States, and the racialization of that putative demarcation. They characterize themselves as political prisoners and declare the United States their enemy and a fascist state. *Black Prison Intellectuals* concludes with a bleak but telling extension of the history of Black criminalization turned enmification, a history that is as deep as the nation's roots.

From the eras of slavery through post-Reconstruction, Black carceral expression tells a revelatory and cautionary story about racialized criminality and the history of Black enmity in the United States. The Black intellectual work emerging from incarceration offers an important source of insights into and theories about the US justice system. Whereas many white intellectuals got their start on the campuses of colleges and universities, the thinkers here got their start—and sometimes also met their end—in a starkly different institution. For many Black people in this country, the prison has long shaped and continues to shape intellectual labor. For us now, at a time when the United States still imprisons more people, and particularly more people of color, than any other nation worldwide, these early writings/orations provide a central understanding of the crisis of incarceration and the racial animosity and violence that continue to define the United States today.

1

Gallows Death and Political Critique

Abraham Johnstone's *Address, Dying Confession, and Letter to His Wife* (1797)

One of the earliest forms of printed Black testimony in what became the United States was the criminal confession or dying words genre, which has in the past three decades or so increasingly attracted scholarly attention, largely due to the work of Jeannine Marie DeLombard, Frances Smith Foster, Karen Halttunen, Donna Hunter, Richard Slotkin, Caleb Smith, and Daniel E. Williams, among others.[1] This genre, authored and orated by both Black and white individuals, was in its own day popular reading. The pamphlets and broadsides were produced cheaply, and over time they became more and more secular and sensational. We might think of the popularity of today's true crime genre. Valid anxieties about the genre's potential to substantiate notions of Black criminality, as well as a corresponding desire to promote examples of Black people's virtuous and respectable conduct in the early republic, made the field of Black literary studies initially and understandably uneasy about focusing on what could be interpreted as Black vice. Since then, however, the field has expanded well beyond study of the genres of the slave narrative and poems of virtue to look closely at what the criminal confession might reveal about notions of criminality and justice, as well as the interior lives of incarcerated Black people legally forbidden to testify in court against white people. The genre has proven invaluable for its insights.

As this book demonstrates, the Black intellectual output from the inside, as it were, is as illuminating in its descriptions, criticism, and theories as that produced from within other US institutions such as universities, colleges, churches, and medical and law schools. The work of Black intellectuals in such institutions throughout history is the subject of much scholarly interest. This chapter and those that follow analyze the ways in which Black people imprisoned in the United States have long been producing intellectual work through the prisons and jails that seek to suppress their ideas and the meaning of their actions. Their discussions of incarceration; interventions in understandings of jails, prisons, and penitentiaries; and ideas about religion, individual and community conduct, truth, and justice all contribute in important ways to the Black intellectual tradition. Though not learned in the formal, traditional sense, the figures featured here rethink and retheorize legal and political concepts of criminality and enmity and are the forerunners of a robust intellectual trajectory and practice that continues into our own time.

In the early national period, carceral institutions were not what we think of when we think of jails or prisons today. Today's prisons are rooted in the model of the penitentiary, a nineteenth-century phenomenon that did not replace or eliminate local jails. In contrast, the late eighteenth-century prison, jail, or gaol—the terms were used somewhat interchangeably—held people temporarily. People in jail included debtors, those awaiting trial for more serious crimes, and the condemned. The country's founders saw capital punishment as undemocratic, more ideologically related to a monarch's power over a subject's life and death than to a "'logic of republicanism,' which sought to limit the government's powers and in which a citizen's inalienable right to life was sacrosanct" (Barton 244). Nevertheless, the practice of executing people convicted of serious crimes existed at the republic's inception and has continued throughout US history. The United States retains the punishment to this day, alongside fifty-six other countries ("Which Countries"). Through the genre of the dying words and amid a context of political incongruence around capital punishment and the disproportional execution of Black people, the thinkers in the first four chapters of this book interrogate categories of criminal and enemy, with specific attention to Blackness. The subject of this chapter is a groundbreaking 1797 pamphlet printed in Philadelphia of a Black man condemned in New Jersey.

Of the extant examples of dying words or criminal confessions that Black people produced from within local jails in the early national period, this publication is unique for multiple reasons, not least of which is its reworking of the genre. Paramount for this book's purposes, however, is its reorienting and retheorizing of the criminal/enemy paradigm. The distinction between criminal and enemy was essential in the new republic to creating a national identity through antithesis, and Johnstone refigures the status of each (see Engels, "Friend"). This pamphlet, in its rethinking of the state's rubric, argues what Black prison intellectuals would continue to voice in the lead-up to the civil rights movement nearly two hundred years later and through to today. The 1797 *Address, Dying Confession, and Letter to*

His Wife of Benjamin/Abraham Johnstone is not a confession but rather a declaration of innocence. Furthermore, it serves in part as a critique of a legal system vulnerable to false oath taking and perjury. Through this argument, Johnstone, rather than accept his state-sanctioned role as criminal and unofficial enemy of the state, instead defies it and recasts enslavers, slavery supporters, liars, and hypocrites as the real enemies of the republic. According to Johnstone, these enemies contravene early national ideals, yet are backed by policy and law, particularly the laws of New Jersey, where he is about to be hanged.

Johnstone explains that he was enslaved from the time of his birth in Delaware, and that he had five enslavers until his last, James Craig, manumitted him sometime around 1790. He changed his name from Benjamin to Abraham (his brother's name) as the executors of Craig's will wanted to sell him into slavery in Georgia. Before his execution in New Jersey for the murder of a friend, the enslaved man Thomas Read, he lived in Maryland and Pennsylvania. He was in Philadelphia during the 1793 yellow fever epidemic. He married Sarah Johnstone, whom he called Sally and whom he addresses in his *Dying Confession* and letter to her, both of which accompany his *Address*. An apparent dispute with a Samuel Huffsey on whose farm Johnstone lived led Huffsey to enlist Read to steal Johnstone's lease so that Johnstone (being later unable to provide this lease) would have to leave the farm. After Read disappeared and was presumed murdered, Huffsey's friends served on the jury that convicted Johnstone of murder.

The three-part work taken down on the eve of his execution signifies, in Gatesian fashion, on the genres of autobiography (internally focused) and memoir (externally focused), both well established by his time (see Egerton 235–37). It is historically, politically, and religiously informed, at once a project of self- and community-making and one of enemy identification. He executes or brings into being a new definition of enmity that recalibrates revolutionary rhetoric to emphasize the deceitful, hypocritical, and, therefore, unstable foundations of New Jersey politics and, by extension, their resonance in Philadelphia (the pamphlet's place of publication) and the new republic in general.[2]

The uniqueness of Johnstone's work lies primarily in its reworking of the gallows genre into a pronouncement of his innocence, despite the title page's ambiguous description of "his dying confession or declaration" (see figure 1.1). Literary scholar Jeannine DeLombard contextualizes Black people's contributions to gallows literature: "Of the roughly two hundred works offering 'sermons, moral discourses, narratives, last words, and dying say-

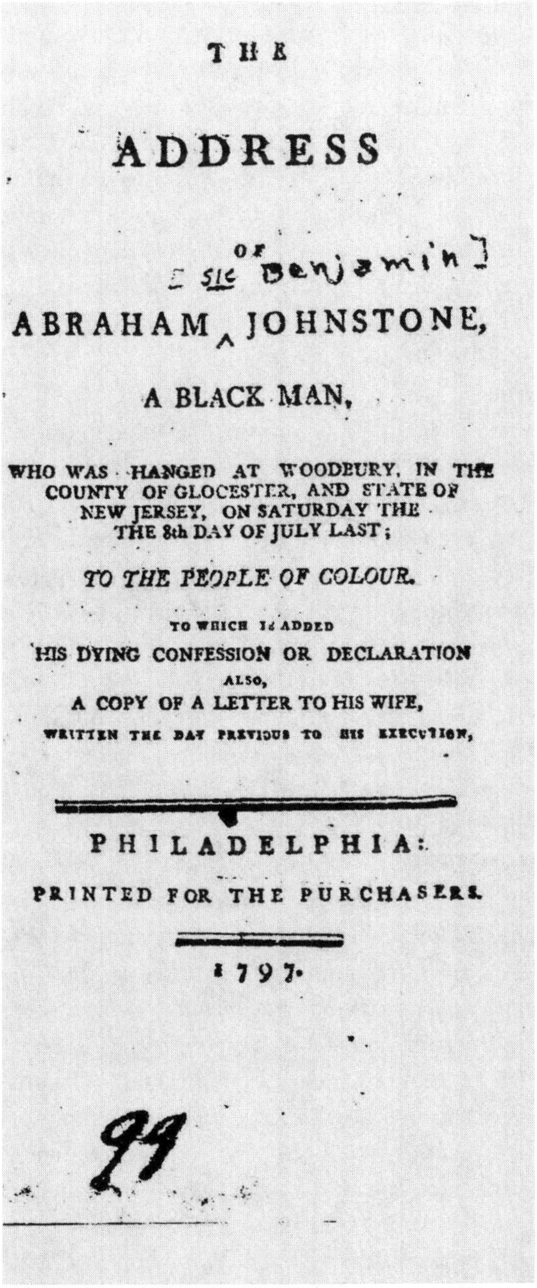

THE

ADDRESS

[sic *or Benjamin*]
ABRAHAM JOHNSTONE,

A BLACK MAN,

WHO WAS HANGED AT WOODBURY, IN THE
COUNTY OF GLOCESTER, AND STATE OF
NEW JERSEY, ON SATURDAY THE
THE 8th DAY OF JULY LAST;

TO THE PEOPLE OF COLOUR.

TO WHICH IS ADDED
HIS DYING CONFESSION OR DECLARATION
ALSO,
A COPY OF A LETTER TO HIS WIFE,
WRITTEN THE DAY PREVIOUS TO HIS EXECUTION.

PHILADELPHIA:
PRINTED FOR THE PURCHASERS.

1797.

Figure 1.1. Title page of Abraham Johnstone's pamphlet, 1797. Available from America's Historical Imprints.

ings, and poems written for, by, and about persons executed for criminal activity' published from 1674 to the Civil War, at least sixty featured criminals of African heritage" ("Apprehending" 95). As far as we know, Johnstone's work represents the only Black declaration of innocence in the genre's substantial pre–Civil War history. Yet the pamphlet heralds a later tradition in US Black prison writings of asserting innocence or non-culpability for the crime, and, more foundationally, of questioning the categories of criminal and enemy in the state imaginary. In this latter respect, Johnstone's *Address* blazes a trail of critical inquiry not only around penal procedure but also about the very demarcations that purport to distinguish criminals from enemies.[3] For all these reasons, Johnstone's text opens this book's inquiry and sets the stage for the readings that follow.

DeLombard's comprehensive and groundbreaking analysis of gallows literature in terms of race and civic identity contradicts Daniel A. Cohen's assessment that Johnstone "exhort[s] his fellow African Americans to adopt conventional virtues of bourgeois Christians" ("Social Injustice" 516). DeLombard argues, rather, that "even as the *Address* appears to join the chorus of black and white reformers admonishing African Americans to prove their eligibility for citizenship through performances of virtue, its gallows perspective reveals that the persistent misapprehension of Black civil activity as criminal behavior renders such civic displays not only futile but dangerous" (*Shadow* 121–22). In fact, as I argue, Johnstone's distinguishing of the categories of criminal and enemy and his deployment of the rhetoric of enmity not only highlight the "racialized logic of citizenship and criminality that ensured the continuity of Black political exclusion" (*Shadow* 122), but reverse the dangerous categorization of enemy, which the new nation conferred on the Black person convicted of a crime, particularly one convicted of murder. Johnstone's gallows delineation of a new national enemy exposes an ethos that would only become more entrenched over time, one that relegated Black people convicted of violent crimes to a nefarious category that marked them as unfit for political participation and, worse, as threatening to national security.[4] State emancipation bills, the 1793 Fugitive Slave Law (with its implications for free Black men and women), abolitionist conventions' turn toward directing free Black conduct, and negative responses to Black people's assistance during the yellow fever epidemic provide the backdrop to Johnstone's pamphlet. In it, I argue that he not only undoes, if rhetorically, the criminalization of Black civility but also details the enmity of a sham white civility that he argues poses the greatest threat to state and national security (see DeLombard, *Shadow*, ch. 3; Otter, ch. 1).

The 1797 *Address of Abraham Johnstone, a Black Man, Who Was Hanged at Woodbury in the County of Glocester, and State of New Jersey, on Saturday the the [sic] 8th Day of July Last; to the People of Colour. To Which Is Added His Dying Confession or Declaration Also, a Copy of a Letter to His Wife, Written the Day Previous to His Execution* questions the distinction between "enemy" and "criminal," which the new government was meant to secure. The pamphlet refashions the narrator as simultaneously both and neither. Johnstone highlights how the relocation of sovereign power in collective government confuses such boundaries, but more importantly, in alleging that his accusers have committed perjury, he identifies the enemies of the new republic, and New Jersey in particular, as part of the newly formed democratic process, which itself drew on discourses of enmity to define and promote a free republic against a tyrannous Britain. From the confines of prison, on the eve of his execution for murder, Johnstone hybridizes the popular print genres of the execution sermon and the criminal's dying words and casts the republic as a necropolitical order, which subjugates life to the power of death—its subjects as much in bondage as they were under the previous imperial governance. Worse, according to Johnstone, the enemies are located within the infrastructure of the state meant to protect them, and they fear not even the absolute sovereignty of God.[5]

The Pamphlet

The pamphlet becomes increasingly intimate as it proceeds from section to section. Maintaining the objectives and contexts of each section, the analysis here will follow Johnstone's own structure and preserve his sections as both independent and interdependent. Johnstone's *Address . . . to the People of Colour* draws heavily from the 1796 appeal *To the Free Africans and Other Free People of Color in the United States*, drafted by the Convention of Delegates from the Abolition Societies. Like its predecessor, Johnstone's *Address* employs the rhetoric of respectability, which, James Brewer Stewart argues, "connoted the possession of the intellectual and literary skills necessary to allow African Americans to contribute their own authoritative political voices as equals to the nation's ongoing civic discussions" (quoted in DeLombard, *Shadow* 135). Within this seemingly typical structure, though, Johnstone creates suspense in the opening pages, almost anticipating the genre of the murder mystery. He refers particularly to the scaffold and spectacle, builds a sense of intrigue about the circumstances of his conviction, and delays revelation of his innocence (this first appears on page 5 of the thirty-one-page *Address*). This first part of the pamphlet functions as an execution sermon, "usurp[ing] the clergyman's role," wherein he calls for emancipation and exhorts African Americans to be aware of the double standards of white scrutiny and behave accordingly (DeLombard, *Shadow* 120). Johnstone's *Address* represents a hybrid confession genre, employing Enlightenment rhetoric to chastise white as well as Black, and crafting a distinctive definition of the enemy threatening both populations in the new republic, specifically in New Jersey and (through publication) in Philadelphia.

The second part of Johnstone's pamphlet, the *Dying Confession*, gives the history of and context surrounding the criminal accusations made against him and recounts his arrest and conviction for the murder of an enslaved man named Tom. This part of the gallows narrative is conventionally where the condemned person accepts responsibility for the crime, but here Johnstone uses the space to declare his innocence. Furthermore, he names his accusers and, in turn, accuses them of having committed perjury, the "crime of Blackest dye." Johnstone's *Dying Confession* instantiates the condemnation of lying, false or cavalier oath taking, and perjury that he professes in his *Address . . . to the People of Colour*. He provides a potential rationale and explanation for his having been framed for the crime of murder and, as if to underscore his innocence of that offense, he admits to a different indiscretion, adultery, "the only crime [he fears] will hurt [him] in the sight of God" (40). His admission of cheating on his wife demonstrates his humanity and honesty as he admonishes others for lying.

The third and final part of Johnstone's pamphlet directly addresses his spouse. The *Letter to His Wife* presents him in intimate terms and emphasizes his enemy thesis about liars and betrayers as national foes. The handful of scholars who study Johnstone tend to subordinate this portion of the pamphlet to its other sections, perhaps because of the letter's seemingly private purpose. However, the overlooked political significance of this marital missive emerges when Johnstone advises his wife (and by extension us) to read three chapters from the apostle Luke. The letter confirms his political ideals through biblical intertext and allusion, by humbly acknowledging that the story of Christ's betrayal by his friend Judas, his rejection of Caesar's corrupt authority, and his ultimate execution at the hands of the enemy represented by Pontius Pilate all signify a far greater sacrifice than Johnstone himself faces. The comparison nevertheless bleakly pulls together the political, legal, and moral failure of the republic in general and New Jersey in particular to realize their revolutionary and republican ideals. Furthermore, Johnstone implicitly compares these governments to that of the Roman Empire, whose leaders caused Christ's death as they saw him and his rejection of their politics as a threat to their control.

Johnstone's text is a critique of republican ideals, of US institutions of government, law, and slavery, and of the power of these institutions to execute people. His work, through the use of literary strategies such as irony, indirection, and signifying, is also a project of construction, of community and self-creation, just as he is about to die—another irony he exposes and complicates about the genre and the laws governing condemned Black people in this period. As he executes or calls into being the enemy, he engages in an act of self-construction just before his execution. The twofold usage of the word *execute*, coupled with Johnstone's definition of enmity, demonstrates the potential of the confession genre to intervene in, even cut through—if only rhetorically—a necropolitical paradigm in order to subjugate death to the power of life, physically/materially or metaphysically through print publication and beyond, into an enduring cultural consciousness.

"Ravages Committed by the Enemy": Enmity in Eighteenth-Century New Jersey

In the late eighteenth century in what became the United States, and in New Jersey more particularly, the rhetoric of enmity and revolution attempted to distinguish patriots both from the British and from loyalists to the empire (Gigantino 36, 39; section heading from A. Barnes). In keeping with Sun Tzu's extraordinarily influential aphorism on knowing one's enemy, revolutionary-era print culture took pains to define and reinforce the threat of that entity. At the same time, aptly, the incongruity between the practice of slaveholding and the ideals of republican freedom became increasingly severe, as some states enacted gradual emancipation or abolition bills and others did not, or did so more slowly. Furthermore, the deployment of that selfsame rhetoric of revolution for abolitionist purposes, Black and white, gained traction with enslaved and free Black people, thereby stoking the fears of proslavery patriots.

The hypocrisy of maintaining both a commitment to individual freedom and a practice of slaveholding became a common trope in nineteenth-century Black and white abolitionist literature and print culture more generally. The particularity of its use in the years leading up to and following the Revolutionary War reveals the emergence of the concept of Black enmity in the new republic. As patriots emphasized Britain's enslavement of colonial subjects at the same time that this enemy was also offering freedom to enslaved people in colonial America and urging Black participation in loyalist militias, and as the contradictions between the patriots' practice of slaveholding and the revolutionary project became clear, the rhetorical demarcation of the Black person as a kind of proto–national enemy emerged. Furthermore, the perception of Black incapacity for citizenship and by extension the criminalization of Black civility not only proscribed Black political participation but undergirded laws enacted to limit or eradicate the perceived threat Black people posed to state security. This rhetorical and political/legal rubric is the precise paradigm that Johnstone's *Address, Dying Confession, and Letter to His Wife* reconfigures, even reverses.

In the early part of the eighteenth century, white New Jerseyans found themselves reeling in the aftermath of the New York slave revolt of 1712, in which nine white people were killed and six others injured, and after which twenty-one Black people were convicted and executed. In response to white fears, New Jersey enacted a new slave code in 1713–14, which included penalties for anyone found harboring another's bondsmen and women, for any enslaved person found five miles or more from the enslaver's home, and for enslaved people from other provinces found in New Jersey without written permission. The new code also reiterated that freed bondsmen and women could not own property. Furthermore, the new law stipulated that "it is found by experience, that Free Negroes are an Idle Sloathful People, and prove very often a charge to the Place where they are," and therefore enslavers who manumitted their enslaved people were required to pay two hundred pounds to the Crown and twenty pounds yearly to the "Negro or Mullatto Slave, during their Lives" (statute 14). This fear of freedpeople becoming a "charge" to the city/state is something that resonates in the early part of the twentieth century, when James Foster requests parole from prison and highlights his ability to support himself through his photography business.[6]

Furthermore, the early eighteenth-century white fear of slave revolt, combined with the perception that enslavement reduced the inevitable financial burden Black people would pose to the place where they reside, provides the backdrop for the attitudes that would spread in the postrevolutionary era, coinciding with Johnstone's arrest, conviction, and execution. The 1779 supplement to the slave code emphasized the perceived danger Black people posed to patriot efforts; rang with phrases like, "several Negro Slaves, belonging to Persons residing within Places under the Power of the Enemy," and "it may be dangerous to the Community to permit such Negroes to reside near the Enemy's Lines"; and stipulated corporal punishment for "Negroes [who] presume to return to any Part of the State adjoining the Enemy's Lines after such Removal" (statute supplements 6, 8). Historian James J. Gigantino II argues, "While it was rooted in the revolutionary belief of individual freedom, the Revolution in New Jersey did not heighten support for black liberty. On the contrary, the war reinforced slavery by highlighting the dangers white New Jerseyans would face if they supported abolition" (6). This contradictory logic of the purported value of individual freedom and a coexisting fear of freed Black people created (or at the very least demonstrated) New Jerseyans' association of Blackness, particularly free Blackness, with enmity and treachery.

The *New Jersey Journal* printed proslavery articles in the years leading up to the revolution, with one author "claiming that even the discussion of liberty for slaves could 'stimulate servants to insurrection'" (Gigantino 28). The combination of a fear of Black insurrection and British enticements for Black people to fight for a loyalist cause drew an association in the white New Jerseyan imagination between Black people and British enemies. During the same period, "emphasis on the hypocrisy of enslaving one race while fighting for freedom from the British, spread to other abolitionists and became a repetitive cry in abolitionist tracts.... The proslavery voices that rose in protest were largely motivated by fears of slaves harnessing this abolitionist rhetoric for their own purposes" (Gigantino 27–29). The revolutionary rhetoric of freedom became central to the abolitionist cause, and enslaved Black people drew heavily on it in conversations with their enslavers.

By the time Johnstone's *Address, Dying Confession, and Letter to His Wife* appeared in print, the logic of proslavery ideology had grown reliant on the continued association of Black people with enmity. This association reflects a postrevolutionary shift in the definition of enmity, removing it from the British and mapping it onto the formerly enslaved person and free Black person deemed criminal. "Reports of ex-slaves murdering, raping, and pillaging their former hometowns delayed serious discussions of abolition as many Jersey whites believed themselves under attack by a ruthless and uncontrollable enemy. The institution of slavery provided security and control over blacks in the insecurity of war, which encouraged lawmakers at the end of the Revolution to not free the vast majority of confiscated loyalist slaves" (Gigantino 33). Some used this shift from the British to the Black person presumed criminal to rationalize or justify continued enslavement of Black people in the North. Abraham Johnstone's characterization of enslavers and proslavery supporters, particularly perjurers, as the real enemy lurking within the infrastructure of the new republic makes an explicitly Black rejection of revolutionary racism and the fiction of republican freedom.

Extending and further supporting Johnstone's agenda here is the pamphlet's publication in Philadelphia in the aftermath of the 1793 yellow fever epidemic, which saw the deaths of many Black Philadelphians (presumed immune to the disease and therefore able to attend to the sick), and that same year's substantial influx of refugees from the Haitian Revolution—particularly white enslavers and their enslaved people (the latter also perceived to have brought the epidemic to the city). Johnstone's pamphlet, taken down on the eve of his execution, countered perceptions of Black enmity and exposed the hypocrisy of white revolution in ways particular to the contexts of both his home state and his text's place of publication.

"Enemies of Freedom and Our Colour"

Theoretically, execution in the late eighteenth century functioned also as an act of national self-making and the creation of state sovereignty. Legal scholar Paul Kahn explains that "punishment was once a display of sovereign power—the spectacle of the scaffold. That display cast the criminal as the enemy" (148; section heading from Johnstone 14). In Johnstone's example, we see his eve-of-execution words reworking this rubric. The spectacle of his execution that he anticipates, and which may have cast him as the enemy of republican sovereignty, becomes, in his *Address, Dying Confession, and Letter to His Wife*, an example of the state's inability to distinguish between criminal and enemy. Rather, he presents a project of enemy identification through his analysis of the state's and by extension his own personal vulnerability to perjury, which ultimately results in his wrongful execution. Furthermore, the racism behind false oaths underscores the hypocritical republican construction of individual freedom and corresponding rejection of Black freedom.

In contrast to what Johnstone's readers would have expected from the criminal confession genre, the author signifies on the execution sermon to define "the low minded illiberal and sordid persons who are the enemies of our colour, and of freedom" (7). In the history of the execution sermon, the assumption that crimes of individuals reflected the degeneration of the community lent the genre two particular purposes: first, to correct behavior, and second, to assert the power of religious and secular authorities (Hunter, *Dead Men* 6–7). Hangings in Johnstone's time were public, well-attended displays of state violence, and offered a symbolic reintegration of the condemned back into society that signaled that "the community was back to normal" (Banner 32). Execution sermons, which preceded crime narratives, functioned as ceremonies to restore order. What Johnstone does, ultimately, is undermine the validity of the very social order the sermon was meant to restore and question the value of the "normal" the execution was supposed to reestablish.

His *Address*, assuming the sermonic purpose traditionally fulfilled by the clergy, follows the typical sermon structure to a degree, but uses the platform radically differently. Rather than make an example of himself and his crimes, he demonstrates the process by which his brethren have become vulnerable to state hypocrisy, lies, and perjury. The execution sermon format, which would have been familiar to readers—particularly in the earlier part of the century, before the increased secularization of gallows literature—generally included reference to a scriptural quotation, explication of doctrine, application of that lesson of the text to the congregation, and a warning to the audience about their own sinfulness. From there, it generally concluded with a description of the crime and the criminal, a condemnation of the criminal acts, an admonishment to repent, and, finally, the criminal's dying words. Instead of following this pattern, however, as DeLombard points out, Johnstone's *Address* seems to take as its model the abolitionist appeal *To the Free Africans and Other Free People of Color in the United States*, which was printed in Philadelphia the year before Johnstone's pamphlet was published. On the surface, his *Address* appears to do the work of the typical execution sermon, referencing scripture, warning the audience about their own sinfulness, and offering advice for proper comportment, but, as DeLombard argues, "The signal difference is that the *Address*, while conceding 'there are some very bad' black people, leaves no question that the nation, rather than its black inhabitants, must take responsibility for moral improvement" (*Shadow* 151). It is in this difference and in the context of increased racialization of sin and crime that Johnstone's identification and redefinition of the enemy surfaces.

According to William E. Nelson in *Americanization of the Common Law*, "criminal law served the function of enforcing puritanical religious and moral standards that continued to linger in the province as a whole and of reintegrating those who had violated the standards into the existing community structure" (40). In enforcing religious and moral standards and bringing violators back into the fold, published crime narratives and public executions had an instructional function. Beyond their didacticism, they also supported the period's increased racialization of sin and the growing association of Black people with religious and moral transgressions. Richard Slotkin argues, "blackness was used as a metaphor to describe class and generational disobedience (sin)" (quoted in Hunter, *Dead Men* 82). Black people came to symbolize sin and its consequence for white audiences and readers, as crime narratives, implicitly or otherwise, warned enslavers against treating enslaved people too leniently. After 1750, amid the swirl of rumors about uprisings, building fears leading up to the Haitian Revolution, and a seeming obsession with the threat of Black violence across much of society, crime narratives began to depict Black people as degenerate (Harnett 154). Accounts of rape appeared more frequently, specifically of Black men raping white women. "Slotkin argues that these racialized fears about the rebellious and even monstrous violence of blacks began to coalesce at the close of the eighteenth century around 'the idea that all black crime is implicitly revolutionary,'" and therefore, I would add, explicitly political (Hartnett 154; see figures 1.2–1.4).

In the most comprehensive treatment of Johnstone's *Address* so far, DeLombard argues compellingly, "Characterized by a temporal consciousness that highlights narrative's historicizing and projective functions—functions that also link individual, race, and nation in and through time—[Johnstone's particular] penality also exposes the racialized logic of citizenship and criminality that ensured the continuity of black political exclusion, from slavery through the nominal freedom enacted by the First Emancipation, to today's incursions on African Americans' Fourth Amendment rights" (*Shadow* 122). However, Johnstone's narrative exposes more than the racialized logic of citizenship and criminality that DeLombard identifies; it exposes the United States' racialized logic of enmity, which cast the Black person deemed criminal as an even greater threat, an enemy of the state. In exposing this particular logic, Johnstone problematizes the state's characterization of the Black self as at odds with civic responsibility and authority. His narrative underscores a radically different enmity embedded in the structures of early US civic responsibility and authority.

The *Address* opens with a seeming avowal of the success of the legal process that determined his guilt and condemned him to death. But this opening is perhaps ironic, as it sets the stage for the critique to follow, which dismantles that perception of the system's soundness and demonstrates its

The Power and Grace of Christ display'd to a dying Malefactor.

A

SERMON

Preached at Worcester

October the Twentieth, 1768.

Being the Day of the Execution of *ARTHUR*,

A Negro of about 21 Years old, for a RAPE.

By THADDEUS MACCARTY, A. M.
Pastor of the Church in Worcester.

"When Lust hath conceived, it bringeth forth Sin: And Sin when it is finished, bringeth forth Death".
                                                          Apostle JAMES.
"The Blood of Jesus Christ his Son, cleanseth us from all Sin".
                                                          Apostle JOHN.

BOSTON: Printed and Sold by KNEELAND and ADAMS, next to the Treasurer's Office, in Milk Street. MDCCLXVIII. 1768

Figure 1.2. Title page of an execution sermon with skull and bones iconography. *The Power and Grace of Christ Display'd to a Dying Malefactor*, by Thomas Maccarty, Boston, 1768. Available from America's Historical Imprints.

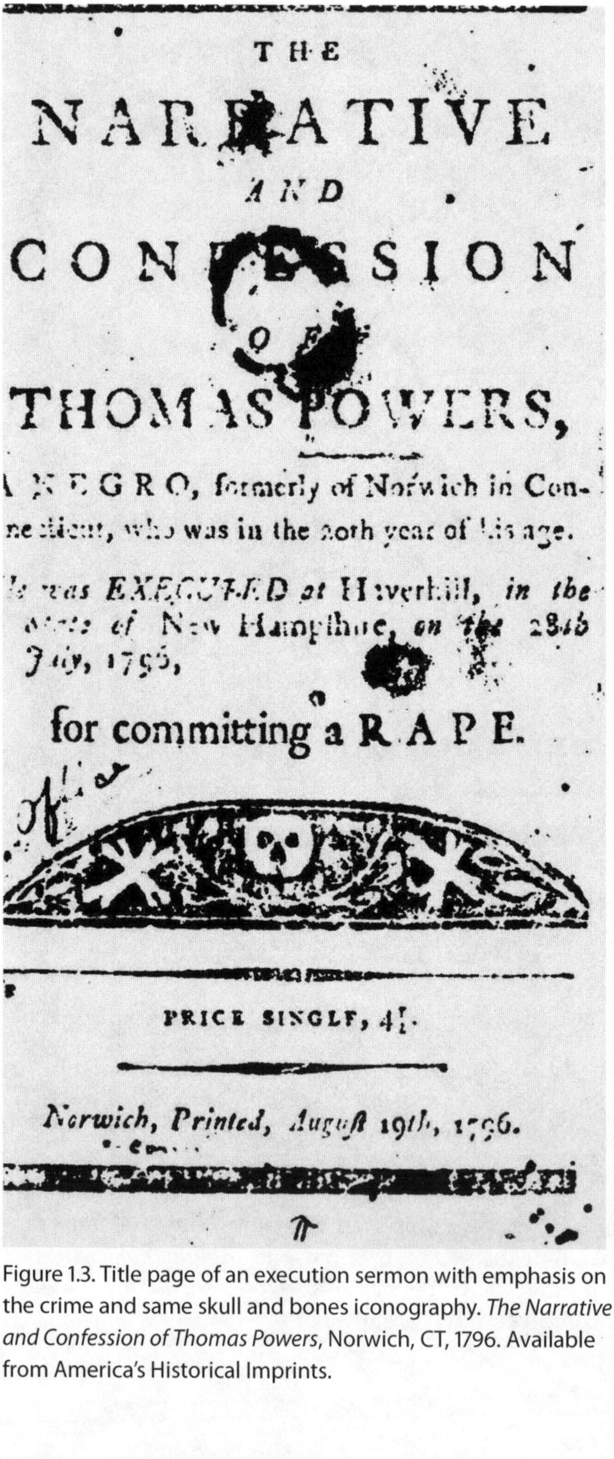

THE
NARRATIVE
AND
CONFESSION
OF
THOMAS POWERS,
A NEGRO, formerly of Norwich in Connecticut, who was in the 20th year of his age.

Was EXECUTED at Haverhill, in the State of New Hampshire, on the 28th July, 1796,

for committing a RAPE.

PRICE SINGLE, 4½.

Norwich, Printed, August 19th, 1796.

Figure 1.3. Title page of an execution sermon with emphasis on the crime and same skull and bones iconography. *The Narrative and Confession of Thomas Powers*, Norwich, CT, 1796. Available from America's Historical Imprints.

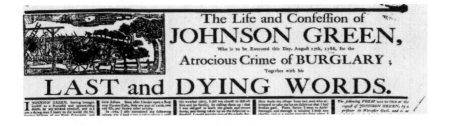

Figure 1.4. A broadside of a confession and the condemned's "last and dying words." *The Life and Confession of Johnson Green*, Worcester, MA, 1786. Available from America's Historical Imprints.

inherent flaws. Preserving the lengthy sentences of the *Address*, commensurate with literature of the period, I'll quote the passage in full:

> Being now a devoted victim to the just resentment of the laws of my country and the rules of society—just resentment—because, after a candid and impartial trial I have been convicted of a jury of my peers, twelve truly good and worthy men whose integrity and love of truth I so well know that had they not conceived themselves clear of all doubts and scruples, they would not have consigned a fellow creature to death, and to so ignominious a death—therefore their verdict having established a *presumption of* my guilt and my having not only

transgressed the positive rules of society, but committed a crime of the Blackest dye, a crime justly hateful odious and horrid in the sight both of God and man, I am to suffer death. (3–4)

Such an affirmation of the system is typical, almost a trope of the confession genre, but Johnstone's following assertion of his innocence despite his having been tried in "a candid and impartial trial" implies that the pamphlet might function ironically from the start. Jodi Schorb, literary scholar, sums up how "just a page earlier, an anonymous preface directly challenged the evidence used to find Johnstone guilty and demanded that he be given an overdue opportunity to offer a 'full and impartial account of himself'" (65). Furthermore, literary scholar Ian Finseth argues for the importance of "moments of irony . . . as they recruit the reader into a subtle alliance with the narrator; they articulate between the narrative problems of artfulness and sincerity; and they reflect an essential indeterminacy in language, thus seriously complicating the narrated relation between 'black' identity and 'white' philosophical or ideological discourse" (33). And yet, the three parts of the pamphlet produce their own philosophical and ideological discourse to reveal and reinforce, rather, the failure of "the laws of [his] country and the rules of society." Furthermore, the italicized emphasis on the "verdict having established a *presumption of* my guilt" highlights the miscarriage in his trial of the burden of proof intrinsic to criminal law. Irony is just one of Johnstone's critical methods.

One theory about the case is that Johnstone didn't murder the alleged victim, Tom, whose body was never found, but that rather he helped the man escape from slavery. Johnstone himself was no longer enslaved when he was arrested and convicted. If he did help Tom escape from slavery and is now about to hang for the man's supposed murder, Johnstone's real crime would have been helping an enslaved man flee, a humane act and a punishable offense. Perhaps to underscore the contradictory logic of republican slavery, Johnstone points out the racism inherent in assumptions about Black people and crime, particularly violent crime. He argues that a "vast majority of whites have died on the gallows when the population is accurately considered"; they are "capable of being equally as depraved" (7). Legal historian Stuart Banner observes of Johnstone's *Address* that "social commentary was a rare commodity on the scaffold" (44). We can see how Johnstone, assuming the role of social commentator, takes a few approaches in his critique. He signals to readers to not take him as an example of the Black violence they have come to expect and fear, and rather identifies his situation as the product of a morally deficient citizenry and an unjust system vulnerable to perjury. The white population feared Blackness, regardless of examples of white-perpetrated violent criminal acts. This fear, in turn, rendered Black people more vulnerable to the perjury that Johnstone points out actually threatens what he refers to as the country's laws and society's rules.

Johnstone reminds his readers that by an act of Congress, the United States was "declared sovereign free and independent"; to that, he says, "we may ascribe our present dawning hopes of universal freedom," that "freedom, liberty, and the natural rights of mankind" are the promise of the republic (10). Kahn observes: "Violations of law—crimes—do not threaten sovereign identity because law only represents the absent sovereign. Enemies, on the other hand, threaten the sovereign, even as they might agree with the content of [the] law" (153). Murder, for example, as an individual as opposed to political act, is a crime, not a threat to the sovereign identity. Johnstone's discourse on enmity and his polemic on perjury cohere with Kahn's theory of enmity. In Johnstone's estimation, liars, racists, and supporters of slavery are enemies to the sovereignty of the nation.

Johnstone's six uses of the word *enemy* in the first twenty-two pages of his *Address* depict the hypocritical and, frankly, foolish character of the new republic, a nation doomed to fail if it doesn't change its ways. Using Enlightenment rhetoric, Johnstone describes "enemies . . . to an open freedom of thought . . . averse . . . to the admission of ideas they were not before made acquainted with," but thanks "God in this enlightened age there will not be wanting men of genius, spirit and candour . . . some that cannot but with indignation see reason stoop to the controul [*sic*] of prejudice, and adopted principles" (14). Here Johnstone connects racism with small-mindness. The real enemies are unimaginative thinkers susceptible to pressure from others who are prejudiced. Johnstone warns of the dangers of consensus— his trial serving as an example.

Johnstone's arguments against consensus and against the status quo would have resonated with the era's readers, who were keen for "descriptions of deviant and defiant individuals . . . especially popular in American literature [as] the criminal, the clever rogue in particular, became both hero and anti-hero, both epitome and parody of the American character" (D. Williams 6). The country had recently defied authority. Though Johnstone does not spend much time depicting his own character until the *Dying Confession* and *Letter to His Wife*, in the *Address* he does draw on the popular sense that uncritical devotion to any institution is dangerous. Furthermore, he highlights the hypocrisy of capital punishment in a postrevolutionary context. As literary scholar Kristin Boudreau points out, "it might of course be argued that, by 1797 [the year Johnstone's pamphlet was published], the public sentiment toward executions was changing, especially in a republic that defined itself in opposition to British tyranny" (32). She then cites the account of a condemned white man that may have functioned "to turn public sentiment not against the law breaker, erected in front of the people as an example of improper conduct, but against the lawmakers who conspired to put him there. The precise target is not merely a particular law—which may, of course, be reformed—but an entire government, represented here as tyrannical and heartless" (32). Furthermore, the late eighteenth century saw "more and more spectators . . . translate their sympathy for the condemned prisoners into opposition to capital punishment generally" (Banner 31). Johnstone goes beyond attempting to deflect attention away from the lawbreaker, however, wanting to focus on the deeper hypocrisies he sees operating through the lawmakers, their laws, and the entire governance structure, particularly when Blackness is a factor.

In order to identify the enemy of sovereignty and critique the individuals who testified against Johnstone for purposes of personal vindication—and whose actions actually hold a much greater political significance—he theorizes that perjury is the worst crime of all, even worse than murder, the crime for which he is about to hang. As literary scholar Samuel Otter points out, "Johnstone links perjury to pestilence, as he imagines the fate of his accuser: 'Perjury, like poison, most certainly destroys the guilty taker . . . instead of health, rottenness will seize his bones, every chronic disease, and every fierce malady will afflict him . . . and sickness, sorrows, and all the catalogues of human plagues will sink him to the grave' . . . According to Johnstone, false stories infect and consume" (43, quoting Johnstone 25). This language of infection and pestilence is key for Johnstone, who was writing in the wake of the yellow fever epidemic, an illness he believed himself to have contracted in New Jersey.[7] Turning attention directly to the sickness and sin of lying, Johnstone names perjury as the real threat to sovereignty and therefore national security. Johnstone's move from a critique of lying to his discourse on perjury is based on the premise of state protection. It seems that Johnstone's *Address . . . to the People of Colour* is as much a critical address to and about white people, an example of what literary scholars refer to as "active double-voice discourse" (see Bakhtin)—just as his dying words in the criminal confession genre actually declare his innocence.[8]

Implicitly connecting definitions of the criminal and the enemy, he refers to the dishonest when warning the nation against treason. He writes, "we can lock up from a thief, but cannot from a liar" (21). His contention is that ideas, words, and published texts are, when untruthful or hypocritical, a greater threat than physical violence. He continues, "It should therefore never be a maxim inviolably sacred with all men, never to disclose the secrets of private conversation . . . for, to conceal any immoral purpose which, to disclose is to disappoint, any crime which to hide is to countenance, or any character which to avoid is to be safe; as it is compatible with virtue, and injurious to society, can be a rule or law only, among those who are enemies to both" (22–23). In other words, those who hide the immorality of others because they think it is the virtuous thing to do are actually inflicting injury on society and are thus acting as enemies to that society and to virtue. For Johnstone, consensus based on falsehood, collusion, and corruption, regardless of whether it actually presents a physical threat, is a present political danger.

Johnstone highlights the relationship between sin and criminality in his discussion of lying, which he argues leads to "that most dreadful of all crimes, perjury" (23). He explains, "laws and rules of every society wherever the [C]hristian faith is professed, presume that oaths will be kept sacred, and that no man will perjure himself; therefore faith is given to an oath; and all judgments as well upon the lives as the properties of the citizens or subjects respect are founded upon oath" (23–24). Invoking law, rule, and the sacred, Johnstone situates perjury as the crime that deposes all three. Perjury is worse than murder "because that abominable crime must in many cases, be hidden from, and escape the judgment of mankind, and be known only to the heart of the criminal and to God whose holy name he has prostituted and made subservient to injustice" (24). Thus, he reveals that under the invisibility of perjury, the criminal and sinner remain an unexposed, twofold threat to sovereign security: "this . . . horrid crime is become too general in this country, for it to offer any security for either life or property" (26). Perjury threatens the self-evident truths of the Declaration of Independence that the government is to secure. In a republic wherein "even radical abolitionists supported the death penalty when it threatened national security," and in which grounds for capital punishment were becoming increasingly secular, "legal-procedural," and "patriotic," Johnstone suggests that the threat of perjury to the course of justice is especially glaring (Cohen, *Pillars* 111; see also Hartnett 209).

Johnstone's use of the rhetoric of security in his discussions of perjury and the promise of revolution implicates his accusers as enemies of the state—those who take oaths lightly, and "upon whose testimonies the estates and lives of their fellow-citizens depends" (26). Beyond the estates and lives of individuals, such as his own, Johnstone emphasizes the political implications of false oath taking. He argues, "And surely, if it be viewed only in a political light, it is the interest of every state to render oaths as inviolable as words and ceremonies can make them, and must be highly and essentially necessary for the government to keep up the sanctity of an oath in the opinions of men" (26). For Johnstone it is the state's responsibility to ensure that its citizens fully recognize the crucial inviolability and sanctity of oaths, because oath taking is both a political and individual act and the foundation of national sovereignty. Johnstone's *Address* and indeed his own example demonstrate the failure of the republic to keep its subjects safe, as its enemy has infiltrated the mechanisms installed to secure the democracy it claims to want. Indeed, Gigantino demonstrates the national importance of oath taking as he points out, "The revolutionary government in Trenton demanded that residents take loyalty oaths to affirm their standing within the new American body politic" (57). Breaking such an oath, then, is tantamount to treason.

Dying Confession

Just as the execution sermon follows a standard form that Johnstone reworks for his own purposes, the dying words genre, too, tends to follow a formula, one that he similarly alters (Pomp, too, engages with this genre, as the next chapter discusses). Typically, the convicted person's dying words include an admission of guilt, followed by a conviction for the narrator's sinful nature, and finally a demonstration of the speaker's repentance. Frances Smith Foster notes that crime narratives represent the first instances in which "the black person as statistic or subject gave way to the black person as narrator" (*Witnessing* 36). Most such narratives include execution sermons written by clergy, with the narration of the crimes then being attributed to the convicted. Cotton Mather's 1721 *Tremenda* serves as a canonical example of the execution sermon. In this genre and through the process of confessing, the confessor becomes a positive model for the community, not just a negative representative. The confession entails the evacuation of the autonomous, distinct self for an ideal of the Christian self. The narrator is usually thankful for being fortunate enough to have people to help with the preparation for death. "Thus, while the commission of a capital crime gave these convicted criminals access to a forum from which to express their individual will, the genre demanded that they, in the end, condemn their agency, and replace it, through conversion, with the will of God and the laws of man" (Hunter, "Race" 81). Access to a public forum for the testimony of the convicted person accompanied spiritual conversion and state-sanctioned physical death.

By the time of Johnstone's conviction and his pamphlet's publication, the dying words genre had already become more secular and sensational, typically omitting the sermon altogether and often being printed as a broadside, as we'll see in the next chapter. Yet, Johnstone's work includes a sermon and appears in pamphlet form. In three ways at least, the *Address* defies convention. Johnstone includes the sacred aspect, but he, rather than a clergyman, authors it. Also in the *Address*, he resists the secularization and sensationalized aspects of the more typical late eighteenth-century confession—though there is a bit of that in the *Dying Confession*. And finally, as mentioned, he does not confess to the crime of murder for which he has been convicted. In the *Dying Confession*, instead, Johnstone details how he prevented his enslaver's murder.

The inclusion of his heroic act attests to his good character, perhaps even his loyalty to his enslaver, as well as his general (Christian) value of human life, but it also implicitly addresses white fears of revolts by enslaved Black people, and more particularly, the enslaver's dread of being murdered by his property. In 1779, less than twenty years before the publication of Johnstone's pamphlet, an enslaved man named Cuffee in Hopewell Township, New Jersey—two counties north of Woodbury, where Johnstone was hanged—stabbed his enslaver, Daniel Hart, "with a penknife dozens of times before ultimately killing him with an ax" (Gigantino 48). Rather than face capture, Cuffee hanged himself.

The story became lore, emblematic of fears among white New Jerseyans that their bondsmen and women were being encouraged to kill them. "British efforts at creating an atmosphere conducive to slave revolt caused owners to not only fear mass plots but individual slave action as well," and indeed authorities discovered a British-designed plot urging enslaved people to kill their enslavers in nearby Elizabethtown (Gigantino 48; see figure 1.5). A local balladeer versified Cuffee's tale in order to warn the enslaved population about the consequences of such acts. Therefore, Johnstone's mention in his *Dying Confession* of the risk he took with his own life to protect that of his enslaver counters the stereotype of the "murderous slave" (even though it was another enslaved man who threatened Johnstone's enslaver). Johnstone's portrayal of his willingness to risk physical harm, perhaps even

Figure 1.5. Map of New Jersey, with Woodbury indicated near the Delaware River, just south of Philadelphia. *United States Gazetteer*, Philadelphia, 1795. Courtesy of New York Public Library.

death, to prevent his enslaver's killing appears rather heroic as he is about to be wrongfully hanged for the crime of the murder of Tom.

But the anecdote does more than simply disrupt the popular narrative of the mortal danger all enslaved people posed to their enslavers and instead presenting Johnstone in heroic terms. It also offers another example of his use of rhetorical shifts, here disrupting the categories not only of enemy and criminal (as he does in his *Address*) but also of slavery and mastery.

He explains how he told the attacking bondsman that "he must bury the knife in me before he should hurt my master, who all that time stood in amaze at seeing the fellows knife. He and I wrestled and fought sometime, but having got the knife away, I mastered him at last and got him fairly under" (33). His use of the word *mastered* marks a shift in his identity from enslaved man to master as he subdues another enslaved man. His usage here may give the reader pause—with Johnstone adopting the rhetoric of mastery over another enslaved man (even if a threatening one)—but his diction in this scene denotes the beginning of his process of manumission. This is not to say that Johnstone becomes an actual master over another human being, but rather that he gains mastery over himself. He explains, "My master owned that he owed his life to me, and ever after held me very high in esteem, and told me that after such a time I should be free, shortly after he sold my time to myself, and gave me a considerable length of time to pay the money" (33). Johnstone's use of the rhetoric of ownership, of owning up, combined with the rhetoric of debt, linguistically mimics the temporarily reversed power differential that the incident reveals, and that ultimately led to his manumission. At the same time, Johnstone, in saying that his enslaver "sold my time to myself," acknowledges that ultimately the enslaver still came out ahead financially and interpersonally, even after his rescue from mortal danger. We'll see something similar in James Foster's description of the crime he committed and the marked distinction between his punishment and the victim's compensation. In the time Johnstone worked to pay for his freedom, he explains, his enslaver died drunk in a Dover jail. The man's "executors then wanted to have [Johnstone] a slave, but being informed of my master's agreement with me, they did not then attempt it" (33). Johnstone's use of *mastery* to describe his prevention of murder and eventual acquisition of self-mastery emphasizes the irony of his becoming a spectacle of the scaffold for the very criminal act he previously thwarted.

These multiple ironies embedded in Johnstone's account of his foiling the attempted murder by "the black . . . esteemed the stoutest man in all that county, and a very vicious bad man" only to find himself years later about to hang for murder provide the backdrop for the author's condemnation of lying and false oath taking continued from his *Address* (33). Recollection and emphasis of these ironies heighten the injustice of the system, which is so reliant on honesty and yet so vulnerable to dishonesty. Disregarding the conventional format of the dying words genre (which would require him to repent for his sinful nature), Johnstone instead proceeds to catalog the sins of those who have maliciously accused him and committed perjury, all acts ultimately responsible for his conviction and impending execution. Referring to Richard Skinner, the "Guinea negro" who "swore to a falsehood" against Johnstone, he concedes that the accuser's status (as stated) and his "not speaking the English language well" meant that "it could not be expected that he knew the nature of an oath" (36). Implicit in this statement, especially taken together with his discourse on oath taking in the *Address*, is his critique of those (white) people who, though having a command of English and possibly an education and therefore being in a position to know better, swear false oaths and thereby represent "enemies to both" rule and law, the foundations of the new democracy (23).

Taken together, Johnstone's *Address* and *Dying Confession* do not so much emphasize the perceived prerevolutionary relation between Black people and the enemy British, as reveal that the real and present threat is the deliberately false oath taker, with whom no aspect of social or political security can be trusted. In order to instantiate the severity of oath breaking, the *Dying Confession* turns its attention to Henry Ivens, "whose evidence caused [Johnstone's] conviction." The author contends, "I never since I had existence, nor at any time, told Henry Ivens either the whole, nor any part of what he declared on oath I did" (37). Following Johnstone's logic and New Jersey's revolutionary government's reliance on the practice of oath taking, Ivens becomes an example of a potentially treasonous threat. If he could view so lightly the taking of an oath when a man's life is at stake, how could anyone guarantee that he would not take equally lightly the security of the new nation? Johnstone's *Dying Confession*, far from following the conventions of the criminal confession genre in which he writes, thus instead builds on the political treatise of his *Address* about the fallibility of the new democratic government, resulting from the immorality and self-interest of its individual (white) citizens. This scaffold revelation demonstrates the racialized exclusion of Black people, and especially those enslaved, from citizenship and political participation. It underscores the new republic as dangerously vulnerable to the lies and false oaths of the citizens to which it entrusts its safety and security.

In keeping with Johnstone's commitment to honesty—the foundation of democracy, as he articulates it—he cannot lie in his *Dying Confession*. He partially fulfills the criminal confession's admission of guilt, however, by submitting to the "crime" of lust. He acknowledges, "nor is there any crime of great enormity wherewith I can justly charge myself, except a too great lust after strange women, and that is the only crime that I fear will hurt me in the sight of God" (40). This declaration not only emphasizes the severity of his punishment, given his guiltlessness of the conviction for which he is about to hang, but also substantiates the veracity of the rest of the pamphlet. Johnstone does not portray himself as a saint, but he's of far better moral and legal character than those who have perjured themselves in accusing him. He's not above (or below) confessing to "crimes" he committed, but he will not admit to acts he did not commit.

Johnstone's *Dying Confession* reiterates his definition of enmity and prepares the reader for the intimate yet intensely (if allusively) political *Letter to His Wife* to follow. He states, "I most fervently pray that God may bless Messrs. Stockton, and Person, my two lawyers, the Sheriff, and all the people in this jail, and all mankind; and bless and forgive my *enemies*, and grant them grace to repent and die his holy love and fear, I with heartfelt gratitude, bless them" (41, emphasis mine). Johnstone's forgiveness of his "enemies"—following the contents of his discourse of enmity in his *Address* and his marking of false oath takers in his *Dying Confession* as at worst actually treasonous and at best a potential threat to democracy—links those individuals who had perjured themselves to secure his criminal conviction with those citizens who are the real menace to the democracy of New Jersey and the new nation, and who, perhaps unjustly, share not his march to the gallows.

Letter to His Wife

Following the *Dying Confession* and Johnstone's characterization of the injustice he has suffered, the opening of the *Letter to His Wife* draws a parallel between the narrator and probably the most famous example in Christian history of one unjustly executed. This implicit parallel between Johnstone and Christ says much about the political and judicial structures responsible for their unmerited executions; ultimately, he parallels the new government with the empire of Caesar. Johnstone explains to his wife, Sally: "I am perfectly innocent, and therefore am perfectly resigned to death, and satisfied to quit this world, for like a lamb led to the slaughter house, shall I go in a few moments to my death" (42). His reference to the archetypal lamb to slaughter might be a general figurative expression to denote any innocent unjustly sacrificed, but his following advice to Sally to read certain chapters in Luke indicates that he means to draw a more particular and critical comparison, one that reveals a blunt similarity between the practice of treason in democratic and imperial governments. He asks her to read Luke 22–24 in order to console herself, but of course, at this point we know that he has confessed to cheating on Sally and that she has not visited him in jail, so one might wonder how serious her need for consolation actually is at this point. At any rate, he explains, "You will see there how . . . every species of ignominy and infamy was heaped on the divine immaculate [lamb]" (44–45).[9] Here he alludes to his previous reference to the lamb and indicates that the comparison is meant to obviate his own suffering in light of Christ's. Nevertheless, he also reveals the letter's deeper purpose of political critique.[10]

The parallel accounts of Christ forgiving his enemies and Johnstone's own similar pardoning of his, combined with the history expounded in Luke, speak to the greater political agenda of the *Letter to His Wife*. Johnstone argues, "His life was taken away by false swearing, (Alas! So is mine,) He prayed for and forgive his enemies, (so do I most freely forgive mine,)" (45). Johnstone's reiteration of *enemy* at the end of the pamphlet recalls his theories of enmity from the *Address* and *Dying Confession*: the use of *enemy* here in the letter (alongside the reference to the chapters from Luke) emphasizes the government's vulnerability to treason by citizen enemies of the state. In this analogy, he and Christ are less alike for their virtue and more for their shared status as victims of unjust governance. Whether the unjustice is foolish or malicious, the intertextual picture he paints is grim.

The chapters Johnstone specifies from Luke depict Judas's betrayal of Christ, the crowd's overruling of Pilate's objection to charges against Jesus, and, ultimately, the Savior's crucifixion and resurrection. The parallels between Judas's lie (a form of treason), the unjust condemnation of Christ determined by the crowd gathered for the crucifixions, and the context of Johnstone's conviction and pending execution underscore justice's vulnerability to lies and false charges. Furthermore, the drastic consequences of such vulnerability are writ large in Johnstone's example from Luke. Chapter 23, in particular, reads, "And they began to accuse him, saying, We found this *fellow* perverting the nation, and forbidding to give tribute to Caesar, saying that he himself is Christ a King" (*New American*, Luke 23.2). Christ is a public threat, charged with inciting a rebellion, an enemy refusing to submit to authority. Johnstone implicitly draws a parallel between this example and revolutionary ideology, the rejection of tyranny, and the demarcation of the enemy Britain. However, if we understand Johnstone as analogous to Christ in this story, the government becomes the tyrannous counterpart to Caesar's rule. The enemy now becomes the flawed and therefore unjust government that ultimately will execute the Son of God. And what's worse, it will execute him based on false testimony and by the decision of an uninformed and bloodthirsty public. Johnstone's suggestion that Sally read these chapters of Luke functions much more as a political critique than as a consolation to her that her husband's sufferings at least were not as severe as Christ's. That he would have a readership in Pennsylvania as well, and hoped his words would live on forever, emphasizes the letter's political function. These chapters read analogously reveal the failure of justice that is founded on oath taking and dependent on the word of an ignorant or vengeful public. The enemies to freedom are no longer the British or the Black people whom white New Jerseyans mistrusted, but rather the citizens who pervert the course of justice. They are the early national citizen enemy.

Executing the Enemy, Executing the Self

The multivalence of the word *execute* signals the gallows literature genre's complicated project of self-making on the eve of execution. Historian Stephen John Hartnett considers the twofold understanding of *execute*, analyzing its operation on the state level as it both condemns individuals to death and executes laws, for example. This twofold meaning also functions in Johnstone's portrayal of the individual. To execute means to kill as well as to carry into effect or bring into being; it also connotes performance or spectacle. There are both destructive and constructive elements to the word *execute* or *execution*. As Johnstone is about to be executed by hanging, he also executes or brings into being a concept of the enemy that challenges the era's relegation of Black people, particularly those suspected or convicted of crimes and those who are loyalists, to that category. His *Address, Dying Confession, and Letter to His Wife* execute (or carry into effect) the redefinition of the enemy and the self, these dual meanings functioning almost as an extended metaphor or conceit throughout the pamphlet's three sections.

Johnstone is explicit about the effect that he imagines his thoughts, printed on his death, will have on his readers: "for as the water by continual and incessant dropping makes an impression on the stone, so will these my admonitions make an impression on your minds by frequent readings and recourse to them" (31). He is hopeful that his words will have a generative or productive effect after his death. Johnstone's hope may not have been in vain. Banner notes with reference to the genre in general, "By the time the last pamphlet was sold, several months might have passed since the criminal had been sentenced to death. He had been the object of hatred, then fascination, and then sympathy, and all the while in the eye of a public much larger than the crowd that attended his execution" (51). And, indeed, more of us are reading Johnstone more than two hundred years after his publication. His pamphlet figuratively condemns the state that has literally condemned him. His critique charges his community and the state to recognize the real enemy, the real threat to state and national security, and emphasizes the injustice of his conviction and death sentence, resulting from the state's failure to recognize that threat.

Johnstone's most direct, if perplexing, invocation of the complicated entendres of *execute* appears in his *Letter to His Wife*, when he says that if the tables were turned and she, Sally, were about to face the gallows, "[I would] executingly embrace you even in death" (43). I suspect here he means that he would make a show of his love, possibly one that would rival the spectacle of the scaffold. The three parts of his eve-of-execution pamphlet, then, are a project of enemy-, self-, and lovemaking. Kahn argues that "[the] original act of killing tells us who are the enemies: they are those who threaten the order of love" (165). The spectacle of the scaffold, symbolic of the state's sovereign right to kill (and itself a disingenuous institution in the republic as a spectacle of monarchical sovereignty) relies on the real enemies of the state: false oath takers. It is that enemy who threatens the order of love—scriptural, political, social, and romantic.

Johnstone reveals how the hypocrisies of slavery and capital punishment in the new republic render him both an individual example and a political example of the failure of the promise of freedom the revolution was meant to produce. He prompts us to think about not only inequities in the justice system throughout history, but also the way we understand, construct, create, and respond to enmity. The next chapter will travel just a couple of years back in time from 1797 to 1795—and geographically from New Jersey/Philadelphia to Massachusetts—to consider the final words of Pomp and his broadside's engagement with the state's racialized creation and destruction of enmity through slavery, criminality, and mental distress.

2

Lunacy and Liberation, Black Crime and Disability

Antislavery Argument in the *Dying Confession of Pomp* (1795)

> Insanity is the saddest and most terrible of all diseases,—the most pitiable and helpless of all the states and forms of human helplessness. And yet it is a condition to which all men are liable, and into which any man may at any time fall with or without premonition. In its relation to crime it presents one of the darkest and most mysterious problems of medical and criminal jurisprudence.
>
> *Legislation on Insanity* (1884)

In 1795, an enslaved Massachusetts man named Pomp confessed to having murdered his enslaver, Captain Furbush, with an axe while the man lay asleep in bed and after voices told him to do it.[1] Pomp's firsthand account was published in the broadside *Dying Confession of Pomp, a Negro Man, Who Was Executed at Ipswich, on the 6th August, 1795, for Murdering Capt. Charles Furbush, of Andover, Taken from the Mouth of the Prisoner, and Penned by Jonathan Plummer* (see figure 2.1). Whereas Abraham Johnstone uses his pamphlet to theorize criminality, enmity, and hypocrisy in the new republic as he declares his innocence of the murder conviction, Pomp freely admits in his broadside to having killed a man after a considerable time experiencing "fits and lunacy" and ultimately the voices that would urge him to take up the axe.[2]

Pomp's enslaved and criminalized/enmified presence as a historical and literary figure in the gallows literature genre offers a perspective that intermingles individual transgression, self-protection, and state-defined categorization as a criminal turned enemy. Pomp's work anticipates the collective action led by Nathaniel Turner (ch. 3), and the bridging of individual and collective resistance we see in Celia's work (ch. 4). Pomp's "fits and lunacy" serve as an example of disability in the early nation and simultaneously as an early US instantiation of the Black prophetic tradition. The violent

Figure 2.1. Pomp's *Dying Confession* broadside, 1795. Available from America's Historical Imprints.

actions of this former Revolutionary War soldier also anticipate later acts of armed Black resistance and revolution, while underscoring the early US national period's relation between sanctioned revolutionary violence and perceptions of racialized national enmity, whether violent or not.

Radically different than Johnstone's work (which marries execution sermon, criminal confession, and letter to his wife), and seeming at first glance to adhere to early national crime narrative generic conventions, Pomp's testimony on closer look offers more than a personal account of his actions the night he killed Furbush; it also offers a unique perspective on foundational problems plaguing the new republic. Similar to Johnstone, Pomp and his amanuensis, Jonathan Plummer, underscore the difficulty the state has in maintaining the demarcations of enemy and criminal that it relies on for a sense of national selfhood. Pomp is enslaved, mentally distressed, convicted of the murder of his enslaver, and positioned as an unofficial public enemy; and he highlights the complexities and incongruities of all four categories. Pomp's murderous act and his consideration of it reveal both the potential for and the cause of Black revolutionary violence in a postrevolutionary national context.

In Pomp's *Dying Confession*, readers get a portrayal not only of Black criminality/enmity but also of Black disability in the early republic, responses to both highlighting the long history of racialized early national othering from within national borders.[3] Pomp's narrative and confession highlight Furbush's drastic attempts to abuse Pomp and demonstrate the period's registering of the outlawed Black person as enemy—an even deeper threat than the criminal—his disability underscoring fears of social degeneration. In his *Dying Confession*, before admitting to the killing, Pomp first critiques Furbush's disreputable and abusive character as well as his ineptness as a farmer, contra Pomp's expertise, and recounts the floggings Pomp received at his enslaver's hand after various attempts to run away. Pomp's confession serves as an admonishment of Furbush and slavery more broadly, and Plummer's subsequent reading of the narrative offers an analysis of the social circumstances that had led to Pomp's actions against Furbush and the influential fiction of Black enmification.[4]

This chapter's reading of Pomp's *Dying Confession* first interprets his fits and voices as suggesting at once disability and liberatory prophecy, particularly the Black prophetic tradition, extending and anticipating Turner's example in 1831 Southampton, Virginia. Second, it situates the confession in the context of early national anxieties about the loss of personal and national control/reason. And third, it supplements the reading with research into Pomp and his amanuensis, Jonathan Plummer—the significance of which is rendered visible against the horizon of the era's print cultures more broadly. The broadside complicates rehabilitative discourses inherent in the dying words genre and in early national notions of criminality. Pomp's text and Plummer's paratext, through gallows and street literatures, demonstrate how forces transform the Black, disabled, enslaved Pomp—deemed criminal—into the category of legal person, only to then identify him as a public enemy and eradicate him from the social body. In the Black prison intellectual tradition, the text and paratext leave readers with a prison-penned, powerful antislavery argument.

"Fits and Lunacy"

Pomp's depiction of his "fits" underscores the relation between his sociopolitical status and his mental distress. The fits Pomp describes commence when his "old master," Mr. Abbot, informs Pomp of his enslaved state, explaining that he is not free to leave his enslaver. Pomp notes, "About this time I was seized with convulsion fits which continued to oppress me at times ever after, to the fatal night that I murdered Capt. Furbush." The fits become increasingly severe, often coinciding with experiences of physical abuse, and they culminate in his hearing of voices, which urge him to kill Furbush. The voices whisper to him: "now is your time! kill him now! now or never! now! now!" Pomp is arrested and sentenced to hang.

Pomp's "fits and lunacy" and his hearing of voices denote disability and prophecy. Potential responses to the trauma of mental and physical abuse, these differential mental conditions provide liberatory states (if temporary) from the brutality of enslavement. The fits and voices also lead to his final liberation from Furbush; though still enslaved, he no longer resides on the Furbush farm, but finds warm and welcome companionship, perhaps surprisingly, in jail. By contrast to his life with Furbush, the jail is a communal and intellectually generative place, which Pomp seems to prefer, despite knowing that it will be the site of his execution—an execution that is also brought about by the fits and voices.

The "fits and lunacy" Pomp describes lead him, a former Revolutionary War soldier, to reclaim through violence the freedom that has been stolen from him. In this way, Pomp prefigures on a smaller scale the 1831 revolt of Nathaniel Turner, the subject of the next chapter. Turner's *Confessions* depicts the role of prophecy in revolt: "And on the appearance of the sign, (the eclipse of the sun last February) I should arise and prepare myself, and slay my enemies with their own weapons. And immediately on the sign appearing in the heavens, the seal was removed from my lips, and I communicated the great work laid out for me to do, to four in whom I had the greatest confidence" (48). The taking back of stolen property (freedom) in both cases offers only temporary liberation, but its connection to differential mental states is worth further investigation for what it reveals about Black prison intellectuals' theories of Blackness, disability, and criminality.

The relation of disability and prophecy viewed through a critical disability studies lens reveals in Pomp's confession the multiple legibities of such states and moments. In keeping with this book's objective of tracing the ancestry of the Black prison intellectual history, Pomp's *Dying Confession* also underscores the long history of disability in this tradition. This chapter takes up a question I posed in 2012: "How can disability and crip theory help us understand how the injured, ill, scarred, amputated, and/or blind slave body, for example, might have occupied or inhabited liberatory states of being within slavery as they resisted white constructions of normalcy and the transatlantic marketing of slavery, abolition, and emancipation—and their 'rehabilitative' narratives?" ("Black Atlantic" 824). How might Pomp's articulation of disability reveal the complex relation between Blackness, slavery, disability, crime, and liberation that both highlights and challenges deep-seated cultural anxieties about the disruption of the normal, controlled, and autonomous self? How might a critical disability studies lens—which seeks "to unsettle entrenched ways of thinking on both sides of the putative divide between disabled and non-disabled, and to offer an analysis of how and why certain definitions are constructed and maintained"—help enrich our reading of Pomp as a person who comes into legal being through a criminal act, as a narrator in the genres of street and gallows literature, and as a threat to national stability and security (Shildrick, "Critical" 35). How might his narrative, reconsidered as an intellectual product, underscore the broader political implications for his individual actions as he demonstrates to readers the connections between thoughts and events and unsettles distinctions between the hierarchical categories of human life that his era sought to entrench.

In Pomp, disability as creative resistance produces liberatory (albeit temporary) states. His *Dying Confession* supports the ideological contradictions inherent in a slaveholding New England that enslaved and abused a former Revolutionary War soldier, misunderstood his mental condition, isolated him, and ultimately convicted and executed him for murder, an act for which he may not have been legally responsible.[5] The broadside reveals that disability exacerbates the already assumed connection between Blackness and criminality and renders Pomp even less fit for national belonging than other enslaved people and thus more of an enemy within. Pomp's violent response to injustice (whether that response is conscious or not) and his printed documentation of this response is an early example in the Black prison intellectual tradition that underscores the paradoxical colonial, revolutionary, and republican ideology of a nation that saw itself enslaved by England and in need of enslaved Black labor but that ultimately deemed Blackness, and emphatically here disabled Blackness, radically incompatible with national belonging. Pomp's general critical obscurity means that important documents related to his life and broadside have also been overlooked. Uniquely for this genre, in which typically little is known about the confessors' lives leading up to the publication of their dying words—Johnstone is a good example here—we have some of Pomp's personal history, which helps contextualize and emphasize the contradictions and ambiguities of his situation and the details of his confession.

In Pomp's confession, we see how the Black disabled person convicted of a crime further emphasizes the distinction between what literary critic Caleb Smith, referring to eighteenth-century Italian philosopher Cesare Beccaria, calls the "full humanity of the rights-bearing citizen and the monstrous, marked body of the enemy" (*Prison* 32). Pomp reveals, quite literally, this monstrous marking. A sensationalistic account of his "fits" and murderous hallucinations gives readers an encounter with the print performance of Black madness.[6] But Pomp's crime narrative and his amanuensis's supplement resist a tropological rendering of the crazed Black murderer as they testify to the abuses he suffered and offer insight into his understanding of his condition. Even as the texts demonstrate Pomp's shift from legal nonperson in slavery to criminally liable person in jail to marked enemy in execution—as other Black-authored/orated crime narratives do—description of his disability reveals his even deeper perceived incompatibility with national belonging. Compared with nondisabled Black narrators convicted of crimes, Pomp represents a more dangerously uncontainable threat. It is in this way that his narrative works at what literary scholar and crip and queer theorist Robert McRuer calls the challenges of crip theory—of "always imagining subjects beyond . . . disability visibility, tolerance, and inclusion; the challenge of shaping movements that, regardless of how degraded they are, can value the traces of agency, resistance, and hope that are as legible where identity disintegrates as where it comes together" ("Submissive" 108–9). The complex and shifting configurations of Pomp's identity, though not representing a "movement" per se, in this light prompt us to interrogate the significance of the relation between (in McRuer's words) degradation, agency, resistance, and hope in the early national period.

Pomp's descriptions underscore the complex layering of difference that threatens the national and individual ideal self. On the one hand, Pomp's narrative suggests the dominant and nondisabled or temporarily able-bodied fear of each individual's "disabled other who cannot be acknowledged" yet whose lurking, threatening proximity to the dominant ideal requires continual physical as well as psychological distancing from it (Henri-Jacques Stiker, quoted in Shildrick, *Dangerous* 4). On the other hand, the narrative also emphasizes the ready early national cultural impetus to acknowledge, reform, and even eradicate the more comfortably distant rubric of the disabled Black criminal other. Pomp's narrative, by articulating his differential mental states, reveals the ways in which power produces hybridity or difference that it then must fold back into its structural schema in order to maintain control. We can read Pomp as "cripping" the "compulsory able-bodiedness" of the US early national period, which defined itself in relation to a white normative masculine ideal (McRuer, *Crip Theory*). He demonstrates the possibility of "creative forms of resistance generated within and around cultural locations of disability" (McRuer, "Disability" 170). At the risk of generalizing: the terms *disability* and *mental distress* here are deliberately chosen descriptors for Pomp's "fits and convulsions," in lieu of terminology that might identify his disability.[7] Rather than attempting retroactively to diagnose Pomp's condition, which could range from epilepsy to schizophrenia, for example, this chapter is more interested in exploring how the narrator represents and interprets his symptoms, and what they reveal about the relation of Blackness, crime, enmity, disability, intellectualism, and print cultures.[8]

Notably, the relation between Blackness, criminality, and disability in Pomp's example potentially reinforces stereotypical associations of Black and disabled people and crime, Black confessors being disproportionally represented in the eighteenth-century crime narrative genre and disabled people more generally and historically having been associated with criminal behavior.[9] Furthermore, the relation between abuse and the onset of disability as Pomp describes it potentially reiterates negative notions of disability as deficiency or excess, as something to be avoided, corrected, or cured. Nevertheless, Pomp's articulation of the connection between crime and disability also functions as critique of the abusive environment of late eighteenth-century northern slavery. Moreover, the narrative details the centrality of the complex interrelation of Blackness, disability, and crime in the state's flawed recognition of Pomp as an enemy requiring eradication from the social body (on citizenship and disability, see Baynton).

As the introduction and chapter 1 of this book outline, the genre of the Black criminal confession in the antebellum United States served as a central register not only for Black print expression but for the assertion of Black civic authority as well (see DeLombard, *Shadow*). Growing out of the larger execution sermon and dying words traditions of the colonial period, late eighteenth-century iterations of the genre tended to be more secular and sensational than their colonial counterparts, and, as Jeannine Marie DeLombard (perhaps most thoroughly) and others explain, offered a mode not only for Black testimony but for the print performance of legal personhood as well (see also Cohen, *Pillars*; F. Foster, "Narrative"; A. Gross; Hunter, *Dead Men*; Halttunen). As the law understood enslaved individuals to occupy the mixed character of both person and property, it allowed only the former designation in criminal contexts. In short, criminality for the enslaved secured their legal personhood (see Madison; chapter 1). Gallows literature offered readers examples of "print performance[s] of black authorship" and a look into first-person depictions of Black crime (DeLombard, *Shadow* 37). That Pomp's realization of his enslavement coincides with the onset of his mental distress invites the reader to draw a causal connection between the revelation of his lack of freedom and the mental condition that would eventually culminate in the murder of his enslaver. As much as the broadside is a confession of a crime, it also offers an explanation that calls into question the confessor's legal culpability.

The *Dying Confession of Pomp* demonstrates the link between knowledge of the narrator's enslaved condition and the onset of his mental distress. At the very least, implicitly, the connection functions to critique both slavery and late eighteenth-century US legal jurisprudence. His confession commences with an account of his mother giving him away to "Mr. Abbot of Andover" and then of him deciding to live with one of the man's sons. "With young Mr. Abbot I lived not long, before I grew uneasy with the place. I told him that I meant to leave him soon, but he informed me that I was not free." This is the first instance of several that indicate Pomp's ignorance of his social condition and the laws that bind him, and it coincides with the emergence of his disability. He reveals, "About this time I was seized with convulsion fits which continued to oppress me at times ever after, to the fatal night that I murdered Capt. Furbush." The laws that determine Pomp's enslaved condition thus contribute to or at least coincide with his changed mental condition, which finds expression in fits, convulsions, instructive voices, and violent behavior. In the slave narrative genre of the nineteenth century, narrators retrospectively account for their childhood pain as commensurate with new knowledge of their enslaved status, a marked shift from the previous and relative bliss the unaware child experienced.[10] In Pomp's instance, he is not a child, but his mental state changes radically as he comes into awareness of his lack of freedom—the revolutionary promise for which he as a soldier fought. Isolation from other Black people in Massachusetts and from discussions about Black enslavement could easily explain how as an adult he could be naive about his status. Considered property under civil law, Pomp became a legal person under criminal law, only to be executed shortly after (see DeLombard, *Shadow*; A. Gross).

Despite Pomp's admission of guilt, he portrays himself as a more complex person than the criminal designation he receives under law. In the confession, he is a man of agricultural expertise and piety. With the selectmen's permission, Pomp left the service of the young Mr. Abbot and went to work for Captain Furbush. He explains: "Furbush had a considerable farm and when I first began to live with him did some work himself, but I did not like the way he carried on his business, and after a while he left off work entirely, and by my desire left the whole management of the farm to me." Pomp's presentation of himself as a skilled and efficient farmer contra his enslaver establishes him as a sort of Gramscian organic intellectual, terrifically knowledgeable about agriculture and in possession of managerial skills, one "distinguished less by [his] profession, which may be any job characteristic of [his] class, than by [his] function in directing the ideas and aspirations of the class to which [he] organically belong[s]" (Gramsci 3). Pomp continues, "I performed nearly all the work that was done on the place, cut all the hay, and with a trifle of help from the boy, whom my master desired to assist me a few days in the season, raised an hundred and seventy bushels of corn in a year." Not only was Pomp a skilled farmer, but he managed another worker, and produced an impressive harvest as well.

This section of the narrative also establishes Pomp's virtuous character, again in contradistinction to his wicked enslaver. He explains that despite his successful physical work and tireless ethic on the farm, Furbush did not permit him time to nourish his soul. "But my master still continued unkind to me, never letting me to meeting on Sundays, and forcing me to clear out the cattle on those sacred days." Pomp expressed a desire to pray and belong to a Christian community, but instead he had work on the Sabbath. These details portray enslaver and enslaved as oppositional not only in knowledge, skill, and diligence in farming, but in overall strength of character as well.

In a Saidian intellectual sense, Pomp's confession situates the narrator in his own time as someone who is "capable of resisting [mass politics of representations embodied by the information or media industry] only by disputing the images, official narratives, justifications of power circulated by an increasingly powerful media—and not only media but whole trends of thought that maintain the status quo, keep things within an acceptable and sanctioned perspective on actuality—by providing what [Charles W.]

Mills calls unmaskings or alternative versions in which to the best of one's ability the intellectual rises to tell the truth" (Said 22). Pomp may not have fancied himself as such an intellectual, but it's precisely the sort of work his narrative does.

The Black prison intellectual's disruption of official narratives promoted through media justification of the status quo is a common thread that runs through every chapter of this book. In many ways, such disruption distinguishes these figures as unique in their time, whether they were writing in the genres of the confession (Johnstone, Pomp, Turner) or the parole request letter (Foster), or responding to oppression and abuse with violence (Pomp, Turner, Celia). For example, whereas many of Pomp's contemporaries in the criminal confession genre generally accounted for their crimes, some expressing remorse, others sensationalizing, even boasting of them, this figure emphasizes his virtuous character through his intellectual pursuits of agriculture and religion and critiques the power structures that produce his disability and criminality.[11] He counters stereotypical narratives of the inherently depraved Black criminal who requires self- or community rehabilitation, if not removal from the community altogether through condemnation. He refuses to stand as either the unruly, uncontainable result of a lenient enslaver, or the roguish character whom US readers of crime narratives had begun to crave. Pomp serves as a warning against exploitation and abuse and reveals—as Johnstone does, but in a very different way—the faulty logic behind enslavement and republican ideology, the notion of an ideal national self, and the stereotype of Black incapacity for civic participation.

By representing his own virtue, Pomp provides a rationale for his criminal behavior, even as he describes his *ir*rationality brought on by the fits.[12] His mistreatment at the hands of Furbush brings about his convulsions. As a preamble to discussion of his fits and long-term suffering of abuse, Pomp describes Furbush in even more critical terms:

> I thought I found that he was a bad man, and a cheating horse jockey, and finally being unable to like him, I ran away from him, but was pursued, found, and brought back, and severely flogged, by him for my pains. I afterwards ran off again but again met with the same fate. In this manner I went on ten or a dozen years, not liking my place, and not able to get away from it. I was frequently troubled with convulsion fits and sometimes crazy in such a degree, that I was generally bolted in to a chamber every night, in order to hinder me from getting into the chamber where my masters daughters slept.

This marks Pomp's second articulation of his disability. He details the physical abuses he suffered from Furbush for more than a decade, his attempts to flee the family, and the Furbushes' perhaps paradoxical refusal to release him, even though they perceived him as such a threat to their daughters' safety that he required locking up in his room at night. Based on this description, it is perhaps not surprising that in the actual jail, as opposed to the de facto jail of Furbush's home, Pomp finds some relief. It is this repressive and abusive environment, Pomp implies, that breeds the legally criminal behavior that lands him in jail, awaiting execution as an internal public enemy.

In recounting how he was refused time to go to church, routinely flogged, and locked up in his room each night, Pomp implies a connection between isolation, the prohibition of practicing religion, physical abuse, and disability. Early American medical historian Rebecca Tannenbaum explains:

> Colonial era people of European descent put disorders such as mental illness, epilepsy, and intellectual disability into one category. In their view, people with these disorders all lacked "reason" and could be showing a sign of sin or God's displeasure. . . . Similarly, neurological disorders such as stroke and paralysis were categorized as having a religious as well as a physical component. . . . In European American culture, scientific changes during the eighteenth century caused a shift in perceptions of mental illness. Rather than a divine or spiritual affliction, physicians redefined mental illness as a physical illness that required physical treatment. (135)

Whether Pomp understood his mental disability as a spiritual or physical affliction is uncertain, but the organization of his narrative reveals the possible interrelation of both. Furbush prevents him from practicing his religion and severely flogs him—spiritual deprivation and physical abuse both potentially bringing on Pomp's fits and convulsions.

With Pomp's spiritual, physical, and mental condition in context, the reader sees the environmental factors underlying his eventual act of killing. Pomp gives no account that Furbush ever had a doctor examine him, and there is no indication that his mental distress was a consideration in his imprisonment and execution. Therefore, not only does his condition go unexamined and untreated, but Pomp also implies Furbush's exacerbation of it through both spiritual deprivation and physical abuse. Without explicitly saying so, Pomp rhetorically inverts the roles of victim and criminal in the dying words print genre, which depends on his professed guilt. Such rhetorical inversion is unique to the genre in this period and anticipates, perhaps even influences, the nineteenth-century US slave narratives that conventionally and rhetorically put the institution of slavery and its supporters on trial and positioned readers as metaphorical jurors.

Pomp's *Dying Confession* demonstrates how far he would go to claim the rights promised by the revolution in which he had fought. The confession calls into question the putative value of deliberate, conscious action in contexts of physical and mental abuse, particularly as experienced during enslavement and by someone hearing voices. Interwoven into Pomp's self-description as victimized and oppressed are signs of the defense mechanism through which he retaliates. His disability becomes more severe, to the extent that he begins to hear voices telling him to end the life of his oppressor. Attention to this mechanism reveals the emergence into personhood that Pomp's text effects. The interrelation of physical, mental, and spiritual abuse and affliction builds toward Pomp's reclamation of the freedom stolen from him through the institution of New World African slavery.

Pomp's act of killing Furbush transforms him from legal property into legal person, and his disability provides the means through which he commits the transformational act. He describes the lead-up to the killing, which followed an instance during which he escaped the farm and managed to stay away for one week before Furbush caught him and returned him to his property. There the captain stripped Pomp, tied him up, "and unmercifully flogged" him. Pomp states that it was an evening in the fall, and Furbush left him outside in the "cold, frosty, icy weather" until morning. This event precipitates Furbush's murder. Pomp explains, "My sufferings during the tedious hours of this lengthy night, by reason of cold and nakedness, a sore back and wounded spirits, were extremely great, and while under this torture, I thought it likely that my master would sometime or other feell the effect of his cruelty. My conjectures were so far right that it was the last time, that Furbush ever struck me."[13] In a rhetorical move anticipating that which Frederick Douglass would make famous a half century later, Pomp implicitly proclaims his transformation from slave to man through the killing of Captain Furbush.[14] This transformation is both rhetorical (in the dramatic revelation that Furbush would never strike Pomp again) and literal.

The idea to kill Furbush comes from Pomp's intense desire not only to be free of his cruel enslaver, but also to take the man's place as owner of the farm and husband to his wife. Justifying the murder in these terms, the narrative enacts this desire to take over and performs Pomp's emergence into personhood historically, diegetically, and rhetorically. This section of the narrative marks the first instance in which Pomp indicates that his fits also signal for him a form of misinterpretation. He explains, "My master used to tell me I might stay as long as I pleased at his house, adding that he should not stay in the world forever. From this I entertained an idea that Mrs. Furbush and the farm would be mine, after the death of my master." This misunderstanding leads Pomp to consider the idea of murder: "The hopes of being master, husband and owner, on one hand, and the cruel treatment I had received from Furbush on the other, prompted me to wish for his death and produced an idea of hastening [illegible] by [illegible] my self." As becomes a staple in nineteenth-century Black male–authored literature of slavery (personal narratives and fiction), Pomp expresses the desire of the enslaved man not just for freedom, but for a sort of manhood that means having a wife, dependents of his own, and property as well (see Carr; Reid-Pharr; Wallace). The personal pride of intimate partnership, however flawed, that Johnstone suggests in his *Letter to His Wife* also recalls the aspects of romantic love and sexuality central to humanity. Here, Pomp's desire is so strong that he believes that if he murders Furbush, he will acquire all that the undeserving enslaver had. Instead, however, the manhood Pomp acquires through crime is legal personhood and state-sanctioned execution.

The connection between Pomp's intent to kill Furbush and his mental distress intensifies as the instructional or perhaps prophetic voices attend his fits. This section of the narrative reveals Pomp's connection to the tradition of spiritual influence. Jennifer C. James argues that "prophecy has appealed to African Americans precisely because it offers a source of empowerment and hope. . . . It is easy to understand how blacks would evaluate an emancipatory war in prophetic terms. . . . To be sure, the American Revolution had long held a place of symbolic significance in African-American political discourse. From the moment it became clear that the North American colonies were poised to shed tyrannical rule, free and enslaved blacks began to weave the Revolutionary War and anti-imperialist discourses into arguments for their own independence" (171). Pomp's role in the Revolutionary War, like his narrative, highlights this interrelation between prophecy and emancipation, empowerment, and hope.[15]

However, as noted earlier, medical understanding of mental illness and cognitive disability shifted during Pomp's time, with such conditions increasingly attributed to physical rather than spiritual causes. There was also an established belief that the public had a duty to care for those afflicted. Tannenbaum explains that a law to this effect was in place as early as 1694 in Massachusetts; it "addressed the problem of caring for the mentally ill (as well as those with cognitive disabilities). It obligated towns to 'take care and make necessary effectual provisions for the relief, support and safety' of those who were unable to care for themselves" (146). During Pomp's time, as Tannenbaum further explains, "The public began to view mentally ill people as overwrought, potentially violent victims of their own passions" (147). It may be possible to read a glimpse of sympathy here into Pomp's enslaver through the narrator's characterization of him. Furbush's explanation to Pomp that he could stay on at the farm after Furbush's death indicates that his fears about Pomp's violence may have subsided to an extent, and that perhaps he had some understanding of his condition and felt that the family, and perhaps even Pomp, was able to manage it. Instead, however, the one potentially kind gesture Pomp describes his enslaver making brings about the man's murder.[16]

Pomp explains waking the next day in the same "state of mind," imagining himself replacing Furbush after hastening the man's death. He begins, "I arose considerably disordered having a great singing noise in the ears, and something whispering strange things to me I however went about my work as usual, cut up bushes all the day, near where there was another man to work but revealed nothing concerning my designs to him, at night went home, eat a beef steak for supper, and went to bed. Soon after I was seized with a fit, bit my tongue almost through, and after coming out of the fit, was delirious. I continued not long after this in bed, being impressed with an idea that I must get up and kill Capt. Furbush." The onset of these particularly violent convulsions following his flogging and his night spent naked out in the cold potentially substantiates the historical correlation between physical abuse and an increased severity of fits. Medical historian Dea H. Boster explains that "for centuries, epilepsy had been linked to trauma to the head, neck, and extremities, as well as overwork" (285). Furthermore, Pomp's description of the voices whispering to him and the violent fit that caused him to bite his tongue suggests his understanding that somehow the thought that Furbush put into his head about attaining freedom, owning the farm, and having his wife is directly connected to the increased severity of Pomp's fits, to the point that voices begin to accompany them. If we recall that his fits began with the knowledge of his enslavement, Pomp suggests here a correlation as the fits intensify with the belief that he might become free. The voices suggest a mental state wherein another party apart from himself participates in his plan, urging him to fulfill it. Though Pomp does not suggest that the voices come from God or any other spiritual entity, we can read his description of his actions as part of a larger tradition of literary accounts of spiritual influence or perhaps cognitive disability, extending back from his time to a figure like Anne Hutchinson and forward to Nathaniel Turner. In this trajectory of potentially prophetic guidance in resistance to oppression, Pomp's disability produces a liberatory state in which he, if briefly, takes back his freedom.

The severity of Pomp's distress signals the liberatory character of his differential mental state, as he indicates an inchoate sense that things improve for him after the murder and as a consequence of the voices. Pomp invokes God when, taken aback by the voices that convince him to kill Furbush, he momentarily ponders the gravity of his situation. He explains,

> The Lord a massy! said I to myself what is a going to take place now! The door of my chamber not being bolted as usual, I left my apartment and went down to the fire place. I was struck with horror by my reflections; but something still kept whispering in my ear, that now is your time! kill him now! now or never! now! now! I took an axe and went softly into the bed room of my master, and the moon shining bright, distinguished him from my mistress, I raised the ax before he awaked and at two blows, I so effectually did the job for him, that he never after even stretched himself.

The singular reference to God at this point in the narrative perhaps signals a moment wherein Pomp questions, through an apostrophe to the Lord, the morality of his proposed actions. Nevertheless, the voices urge him on. Whether Pomp understood the voices as divinely inspired remains uncertain, but his invocation of the Lord suggests, at the very least, that in his mind there was a divine presence either accompanying him or beckoned by him on the verge of Furbush's killing. Whereas Marcus Wood argues that Pomp "acts as a divine instrument, his violence is a revolutionary gesture sanctioned by God in opposition to a wicked system and its wicked representative," I think the lens of disability complicates this interpretation, revealing an interplay of cognitive awareness and self-consciousness at work (161).

Pomp's recounting of these combined factors—God, voices, and his own questioning of what would follow the murder—implies a justificatory element, whether divine or marked by insanity and therefore an incapacity for culpability. The insanity defense has a history dating back to ancient times, and as late as four years prior to Pomp's conviction at least one attempt at a pardon occurred in Massachusetts. "A layman pleading for a pardon for his convicted son in 1791 on the grounds of insanity argued that he was 'shattered in his brain' because he had 'suffered his passions to rule over his head'" (Jimenez 33).[17] Furthermore, the shift in ideas about madness from religiously to physically motivated corresponded with changing social structures that provided ways of responding systematically to those considered insane after the Revolutionary War (Jimenez 34–35). Pomp's account of hearing voices occurs at the crossroads of this shift in ideas about madness and structural social change. So far, we have no evidence that the insanity defense was a factor in Pomp's case. As his narrative details that he immediately admitted to killing Furbush, it is doubtful that his case went to trial. Regardless of the potential of the voices to provide Pomp with a legally justifiable defense, he indicates that they are at least personally significant. Pomp's curious and exclusive use of dialect in this scene corresponds with the only example of spoken dialogue from him in the narrative. Pomp's readers only "hear" him speak to God, potentially emphasizing his isolation from the rest of the family and community as an enslaved man and as one of very few Black people in the area, which his amanuensis discusses in an addendum to the confession. All his other conversations, Pomp simply describes. We only hear his words and the words of the voices urging him to kill, perhaps signaling that there were two or more parts of himself in conversation or that he was in communion with some spiritual force prior to the killing. Regardless, the two examples of dialogue suggest that Pomp may have favored these direct quotations as particularly significant.[18]

Another potential indication of the severity of Pomp's mental distress or cognitive disability comes through his ignorance of the consequences of his actions and the impending reinstatement of the order he disrupted. The "wild beast" legal concept in place at the time held that people who had no more understanding of the ramifications of their behavior than a wild beast could not be held responsible for their actions. Yet this test appears not to have been applied to Pomp's legal situation (see Hallevey). He explains how he remained at the scene of the killing and "did not try to escape not knowing that there was any necessity of it. I was told that I had but to go up to my chamber, I went there and perceived that somebody had bolted the door after me." Furthermore, once Pomp hears that he will be hanged, he expects that the execution will take place straight away.[19] As Plummer later notes, Pomp's expectation corresponds with his understanding that punishment follows punishable behavior immediately—as it did with the floggings he received after previous attempts to escape. Pomp seems to have had no knowledge of legal procedure or practice, or even the idea that he would be punished for his actions. He continues, "Company soon began to croud [*sic*] into the house, and I was soon told that I should certainly be hanged. I was now very much frighted, nnd [*sic*] expected to be hung immediately, but my grief wore off considerably w [illegible] found that I was not to be hung there." The scene Pomp anticipates is less a legal process and more something akin to the horror of lynching. His relief both on discovering that he will not be hanged immediately and on being moved to jail reveals the sort of liberatory experience that differential mental states might have produced in late eighteenth-century slavery, even though in Pomp's case his disability ultimately contributed to a chain of events including his exercise of violence, Furbush's death, and Pomp's own execution.

Pomp makes known that his time in jail is preferable to life with Furbush not only because of the absence of abuse but also because he finds, there, companionship and prayer through which he cultivates a new life, if briefly. Pomp tells of being "brought to this Jail," where he "enjoy[s himself] considerable well." Contrary to accounts of Pomp's counterparts institutionalized a half century later for their mental distress or cognitive disabilities, for whom "staying in the institution aggravates disease rather than helping it" (S. Newman 273), Pomp suggests that the institution of the jail and the companionship and ministry he received there had the opposite effect. He explains,

> I approve of [illegible] advice, and spend great part of my time in [illegible]ayer, even ten or twenty times in a day I p[illegible] though I find it hard work, I do not how[illegible] find fault with the hardness of the task, for [illegible]ieve it has been attended with great success. I have good hopes that I have got a new hear[illegible] the one that I used to have, used to ache [illegible]d, but the one I now have feels easy. I never [illegible] so well and hearty in my life as I now am, [illegible] fits and lunacy have left me entirely [illegible] hope to behave cleverly and graciously in this world.[20]

In keeping with the dying words genre's conventional conclusion, Pomp and his community are restored to order. For Pomp in particular, this return to orderliness manifests in his physical body as well, for his "fits and lunacy" leave him. The rehabilitative aspect of the criminal confession in general suggests the corrective influence of the social body on the disorderly and disruptive individual, but I'll reiterate that DeLombard points out how Black people's printed confessions also mark the author's expression of civic authority (*Shadow*). The fact of this expression resists the idea of a completely rehabilitated society, even as the genre promotes it. Though the person in prison is locked away and eventually executed, the crime and the confession signal their inclusion into the social order with the acquisition of legal standing as a person, if only temporarily.

For Pomp, his disability adds another layer of disorderliness to his already disruptive character. He reveals that the Black person with a disability convicted of murder is an even more frightening threat than non-Black or nondisabled killers to an already anxious social order. Referring to the work of influential Philadelphia physician Benjamin Rush, who was noted for "phrenzied" behavior of his own when studying the 1793 yellow fever outbreak, and who attributed mental distress to disruptions of the vascular system, Tannenbaum explains how "in the larger culture, fears of social disorder were growing, and the mentally ill were terrifying symbols of what could happen when a person (or a nation) lost self-restraint" (148). Furthermore, as critical disability scholars Nirmala Erevelles and Andrea Minear argue, "Colonial ideologies conceiving of the colonized races as intrinsically degenerate sought to bring these 'bodies' under control via segregation and/or destruction. . . . The association of degeneracy and disease with racial difference also translated into an attribution of diminished cognitive and rational capacities of non-white populations. Disability related labels such as feeble-mindedness and mental illness were often seen as synonymous with bodies marked oppressively by race" (133). Though Pomp's fits leave him, the reader might well wonder whether they will return, especially if, as he suggests, knowledge of his enslavement combined with his suffering of physical abuse caused the convulsions and voices and ultimately prompted the murder. He is for his readers an image of individual and social disorder. As we will see later in this chapter in a sermon from John Free, published in London in 1768 and reprinted in Boston in 1773, fear of social chaos and the symbolic value of murder and the unrestrained murderer in this regard were concerns on both sides of the Atlantic. Pomp's narrative implicitly questions whether physical individual and symbolic social rehabilitation through imprisonment and confession may be only temporary, especially if slavery and corporeal abuse continue. Pomp suggests that Furbush's lack of self-restraint produced the same lack in himself. In this respect, we can read both Furbush's killing and Pomp's imprisonment as symbolic of the sort of social disorder a loss of self-restraint causes and of the corrective impulses that initiate the restoration of order.

Either way, the confession's liberation narrative disrupts the genre's rehabilitative narrative at least somewhat. That Pomp's disability is not wholly detrimental but rather liberates him from Furbush's tyranny and leads him to comfort and ease partially unsettles the genre's corrective agenda. The narrative argues that jail is not only a state preferable to enslavement—and, of course, Pomp still is legally enslaved—but is an intellectually generative place as well. Furthermore, as this aspect of the confession situates Pomp at the forefront of the much broader tradition of the Black prison writer/intellectual, we are reminded of the nation's perpetual desire to contain and in some cases eradicate its Black presence, particularly when this presence is perceived to threaten a white supremacist status quo. Pomp's disability, with its violent unpredictability, is a further threat to social order and by extension national security—a point that Johnstone and other later Black prison intellectuals dispute. As do the other figures studied in this book, Pomp thus prompts us to question the implications of the state's definition of criminal and enemy.

Murderer as Public Enemy

Two decades prior to the publication of Pomp's confession, a Boston reprint of an English execution sermon defined the murderer as a public enemy. Doctor of divinity John Free, preaching on the anniversary of the murder of William Allen the Younger in 1768, indicates anxiety about the erosion of social order. Beyond the context of the murder to which Free directly refers, his sermon also appeared amid the anxious aftermath of the Seven Years' War, a time of revolutionary fervor in the colonies as well as industrial growth. The sermon's reprint in Boston in 1773 speaks to similar fears of social chaos in Massachusetts and the symbolic value of murder in the wake of the Boston Massacre, not to mention the irony of commensurable violence in empire and colony. Alluding to the biblical story of Cain, Free argues, "From the regulations of some of these well ordered societies, who by reason of the growing barbarity, and insecurity of the times, might be very vigilant against a fugitive, *Cain* seems to have had the greatest apprehension of danger—*I shall be a fugitive*, says he *and a vagabond in the earth, and it shall come to pass that every one, that findeth me, shall slay me*" (8). Analogous to Free's own geopolitical context and (by extension through the reprint) that of Massachusetts, Cain's example emphasizes a growing fear of the disruption of "well ordered societies" and the socially symbolic value of individual murders and vigilantism. Free continues:

This forlorn and restless condition of a fugitive, driven from place to place like a wild beast from the desert, and constantly denied reception, is no more than the natural consequence of committing murder. The whole species are alarmed at the approach of such a monster, they shun him as a lion, that spares no man in his rage, arm themselves against him as a *public enemy*, that can neither be trusted nor reclaimed; and if they slay him, think that they are doing God service, by removing the common disturber of the peace of mankind. (8–9, emphasis mine)

Free's analogy, appearing in late eighteenth-century Massachusetts, assigns the murderer the status of public enemy and affirms the state's application of capital punishment in such cases. Furthermore, the medical historical relation between disability and monstrosity adds another layer to Pomp's particular enmity as murderer. Free argues that the murderer "can neither be trusted nor reclaimed," indicating that the only means to protect the social order is to eradicate the disruptive figures lurking within it. In Free's estimation, there is no justification for murder, restoration comes through execution, and, furthermore, the process is a service to God.

The contradiction that the country's founders saw—and that Johnstone's narrative highlights—between the practice of capital punishment and republican ideology may have been one reason for the reprinting of Free's pamphlet in Massachusetts. And though it is impossible (as yet) to know whether Johnstone was familiar with this pamphlet (and it's really neither here nor there), Johnstone, writing twenty years after its reprint, counters Free's claim quite directly to argue that it is *not* the murderer who should be treated as a public enemy, but the false oath taker; it is the liar who cannot be trusted. In Johnstone's theorization of enmity, he explicitly examines racialized injustices. Free's and Johnstone's pamphlets, taken together, suggest an agenda of racial control behind the former pamphlet's reprinting in Massachusetts at a time when "the vast majority of [the 5.2 percent of Boston's population who were Black] were enslaved" and "colonial governments created legal codes specific to slaves that resulted in corporal punishment in the name of promoting order" (Ryan 89).[21] Free's rhetoric of monstrosity and wild animals, particularly the reference to a "wild beast," perhaps an allusion to the very law meant to protect those who don't understand the consequences of their actions, resonates more vehemently when we read Pomp's confession in this context. Historically, "The desire to maintain racial order also meant the [colonial] government created laws for African

Americans that did not apply to whites. . . . The routine use of public and physical punishments against African Americans, who faced a higher conviction rate, reinforced the acceptance of more brutal treatment of slaves and the social economy of violence" (Ryan 89–90). Recalling long-standing white/colonial equations of Black people with savagery and animal appetites, and disabled people with monstrosity, Free provides an almost tailor-made justification for Pomp's condemnation.

In light of the popular interest in street literature, particularly the criminal confession genre, with its disproportional attribution to Black people, Massachusetts readers could find affirmation for the idea that the spectacle of the scaffold functioned in the service of God and the health of the social body, the Black male cognitively disabled convicted person its most serious threat. In the mid-eighteenth century, addressing the perceived danger of mental illness, the Pennsylvania Hospital opened a ward for the mentally ill, one of the first in the colonies. Tannenbaum explains that "the original legislative declaration authorizing funds for the hospital stated that the purpose of the mental ward was to protect the 'Neighbors' of the mentally ill, who 'are daily apprehensive of the Violence they may commit'" (149). In this example, we begin to see the institutional affiliation of the hospital and prison that Michel Foucault and others have demonstrated as disciplining and separating unfit from fit in the project of preserving social order. Through this logic of public threat, Free's analogy to Cain leads him to declare in the second of his three articles of proof, "That murderers being guilty of opposing and defeating these ends of society, ['mutual assistance, and friendship, a greater degree of comfort, security, and peace'] declare themselves *ipso facto* to be public enemies; and consequently, that *every one, who findeth* them has a *right to slay them*" (10). In this context, the perceived murderous mentally distressed Black person reads as a triple threat to social stability. Through the register of the public enemy, the state justifies the execution of the Black person convicted of murder, all the while still classifying, officially, this person as a criminal. The fact of the killing, regardless of the history leading up to it, permits justification for condemnation. As a Black bondsman or woman commits a crime and simultaneously acquires legal personhood, that person also garners, or should, according to Free, official status as an enemy of the state. Admission into the social body starts the clock that counts down to eradication from it.

The execution of the Black person convicted of a crime is also an act of national self-making, facilitating the creation of state sovereignty. As I've acknowledged in the previous chapter with regard to Johnstone's *Ad-*

dress, legal scholar Paul Kahn explains how "punishment was once a display of sovereign power—the spectacle of the scaffold. That display cast the criminal as the enemy" (148). He continues, "The coming into being of the sovereign is the violent act at the foundation of the state. That violent act establishes the boundary between self and other—in [Carl] Schmitt's terms between friend and enemy. Without enemies, no sacrifice; without sacrifice, no sovereign; and without sovereign, no identity" (154). For Free, the murderer is the enemy of the state. For Johnstone, it is the perjurer; more so, enslavers and slavery supporters are enemies of the state as they are "enemies of freedom" (14). The unjustified violence of the scaffold and the vulnerability of the state to liars highlight the difference between capital punishment for white people and Black people. According to Johnstone's logic, white people are not made enemy by the spectacle of the scaffold in the way Black people are, and national self-making determined through that spectacle is a sham. And, in what is perhaps the foremost distinction, we imagine the Revolutionary War as the violent act Kahn describes (establishing state sovereignty and demarcating otherness), yet the condemnation of the Black person convicted of a crime (which recasts "the criminal as the enemy") reasserts the "white and free" ideal national self that had dominated since colonial times and that found formal and explicit articulation in the Naturalization Act of 1790.[22] Five years after this act, Pomp's execution upheld the racial dimensions of the state's linkage of criminal and enemy, a flaw that (dangerously for the state) implies the essential political or revolutionary meaning of the violent act. Pomp's narrative demonstrates that his killing of Furbush is such an act, even in a context in which white citizens make up the national self that requires the Black noncitizen on the gallows for their self-definition, their sovereign identity. Pomp's *Dying Confession* exposes the fragility of this configuration.

One irony here is that the little information available about Pomp reveals that he was a soldier in the Revolutionary War, that larger violent act of sovereignty, which Pomp's execution helped maintain. Overlooked details about Pomp appear in John J. Currier's *History of Newburyport, Mass., 1764–1905*, which came to light through historian Joanne Danaher Chaison's 1985 typescript "Early American Street Literature: The Broadsides of Jonathan Plummer," held at the American Antiquarian Society. Currier's history includes information about "Jonathan Jackson, a wealthy and influential citizen of Newburyport, who built in 1771, or in 1772, the Dexter house on High street" (71). The Dexter to whom Currier refers is Timothy Dexter, a wealthy eccentric who fashioned himself "Lord Dexter" and

Antislavery Argument in the *Dying Confession of Pomp* (1795) · 67

Figure 2.2. "Lord" Timothy Dexter. Engraving by James Akin, 1805. Courtesy of the American Antiquarian Society.

Figure 2.3. Jonathan Plummer, Pomp's amanuensis. Engraving. Courtesy of the American Antiquarian Society.

appointed Pomp's amanuensis, Jonathan Plummer, his poet laureate (see figures 2.2 and 2.3). A potential glimpse into the connection between Plummer and Pomp appears when Currier explains, "Before the declaration of independence was signed [Jackson] gave 'to his negro man Pomp,' who afterwards served in the Continental army, the following certificate or bill of sale" (71). The manumission letter appears in full and is dated June 19, 1776. In it, Jackson tells of the "Impropriety I feel & have long felt, in holding any Person in Constant Bondage more especially at a time when my Country is so warmly contending for the liberty every man ought to enjoy, and having some time since promised my negro man Pomp that I would give him his Freedom, and in further consideration of five shillings paid me by said Pomp, do hereby liberate, manumit, & set him free, and I do hereby from the date of these Presents remise & release unto the said Pomp all Demands of whatever nature I have against the said Pomp" (71). Jackson's letter, though bearing the formal conventions of the manumission letter, provides a sense of the conflict he saw between slaveholding and his political ideals, and indicates a harsh contrast between himself as an enslaver and the impression we get of Pomp's later enslaver, Captain Furbush.

It is rare to have much or any information about the history of a condemned eighteenth-century Black person. And indeed, DeLombard rightfully emphasizes the value of reading the Black print persona that the condemned performs in its own right, which I have mostly done up to this point (*Shadow*). Nevertheless, in Pomp's instance, supplementary information is useful not so much in service to any project of authentication, but rather for the purposes of contextualizing and emphasizing the ironies and ambiguities of his situation, his crafting of a print persona, and the publication of his confession.

Beyond the few details available about Pomp (his service in the Revolutionary War and manumission by a self-described morally conflicted Jonathan Jackson), much more information is available about his amanuensis, Jonathan Plummer, and Plummer's publishing enterprises. Pomp's confession is one of many of Plummer's broadside publications about current news and events. Chaison explains, "Plummer's sheets were quickly printed and they exhibit no elegance in typography or design. But he was not concerned with the elements of fine printing. He wrote about events and wanted his news on the streets as quickly as possible. A contemporary of Plummer's wrote that 'he knew the signs of the times, and the tastes and habits of the public . . . his works were read by the thousands'" (9). Plummer's oeuvre includes ballads, religious interpretations of disasters and diseases, and philosophies about war and morality. His readership of "clerks, apprentices, mechanics, tavern keepers, sailors and indentured servants" purchased his broadsides for a penny or two (Chaison 7). Chaison's and Currier's portrayals of Plummer give an impression of a flamboyantly dressed, mercantile, and popular journalist—not to mention self-fashioned poet of questionable talent—who eventually also suffered "strange hallucinations [which] led him to self-mutilation" (Currier 437).

Marcus Wood sees Plummer as "blind" to the possibility of a "moral or liberationist motive for [Pomp's] attack [on Furbush]," arguing that he rather puts it down to "only religious fanaticism" (161). We'll see a similar reading of Black revolutionary violence as "fanaticism" from Thomas Gray, the amanuensis of Nathaniel Turner's *Confessions*, in the next chapter, signaling a white inability or refusal to read Black-on-white violence as politically motivated. Nevertheless, though there certainly is a moral and liberationist motive for the murder, Plummer's response seems more complicated and sympathetic than Wood's reading portrays (and certainly more than Gray's regarding Turner). Indeed, Plummer's reading of Pomp's actions is perhaps even empathetic, depending on the timing of the onset of his own hallucinations, which may have coincided with the publication of Pomp's *Dying Confession*. Against these impressions of the commercially minded, judgmental, heavy-handed editor, Plummer's letter (appended to Pomp's confession) reveals not only greater insight into his subject's condition and situation as potentially contributing to the murder, but a considerable amount of sympathy for his situation as well. Now, before I potentially unduly sanctify the amanuensis who profited from publication of the confession, and whom some critics credit with shaping Pomp's confession entirely, I'll note that his sympathy is in keeping with broader literary trends that "from the mid-eighteenth century onwards, were beginning to represent disability in ways that were deliberately aimed at producing compassion or admiration from readers" (D. Turner 73). And, as noted earlier, Plummer was no stranger to the tastes of his time. Indeed, taken together, Pomp's dying words and Plummer's letter present a figure who blurs the line between "'innocent' disabled characters deemed worthy of compassion" and "'guilty' figures that were deserving of derision, fear, or contempt" (D. Turner 73).

Plummer's commentary, appearing immediately after the confession, functions paratextually, guiding the reader's interpretation of Pomp's situation. Plummer's letter opens with a comely physical description of Pomp, "a well made, considerable large, likely looking Negro," and argues that with his strength, industry, and knowledge of and capacity for the business of farming, "besides the [illegible] which he received for his labour, Capt. Furbush could very well have afforded him 50 dollars per year." Plummer argues that "with such wages, or even with half that salary he might soon have acquired money enough to purchase 50 acres of excellent [illegible] land, and to have enabled him to clear and improve the same—In that situation some unfortunate white woman might possibly have sought [illegible] assylum in his arms, or at least he likelie [illegible] to girl that fell within the line of his ac[illegible]nce would have sprung like a nimble doe[illegible] his marriage bed—The animating sweets of freedom, and of domestic life, had then been all his own." Plummer reiterates Pomp's desire for freedom, a wife, and the property he easily could have attained had Furbush paid him his due and released him from slavery. Dramatically contrasting this image of agrarian domesticity with the violent desire for liberation, the amanuensis continues, "He would neither have sullied his hands with innocent blood, nor have been forced with unutterable woe, to breathe his last in a h[illegible]. But alas! instead of running this happy course, for want of understanding, and skill [illegible] him, to wife and laudable pursuits, we have seen him experience the sad reverse." Even as Plummer refers to "innocent blood," his opening emphasizes how the murder could have been prevented and suggests that injustice prompted the unlawful act.

In Plummer's rendering, Pomp demonstrates the Deleuzian-Guattarian "concept of desire . . . not just as a component of specifically sexual being, but as an element of *self-becoming* that permeates all aspects of what it means to live in the world . . . enabl[ing] a productive positivity that leaves behind the normal/abnormal binary to mobilize instead the ungovernable energies and intensities that emanate from a series of unrestrained and often unpredictable conjunctions" (Shildrick, "Critical" 39). Pomp's narrative and Plummer's reading of it resonate somewhat with Johnstone's *Letter to His Wife*, in that they recognize the importance of intimate, romantic, sexual desire, and the political power of love. Beyond delineating a socially produced set of causal circumstances that culminate in murder, Plummer's letter points to Pomp's desire in sexual being and self-becoming.

Contra the conventions of the earlier execution sermon, which preceded the condemned's dying words, Plummer's appended letter functions less as a warning to the readers about their own sinfulness and admonishment for Pomp to repent, and more as a lament for—or even critique of—the social circumstances contributing to the crime and, implicitly, the failure of entwined late eighteenth-century medical and national discourses valorizing self-control (see Tannenbaum; D. Turner). Though Plummer believes that Pomp contrived the voices he heard urging him to kill Furbush in order "to excuse his conduct," he allows that "[Pomp's] understanding was undoubtedly considerably injured by convulsion fits, though his parts were vastly superior to those of an ideot." Again, Plummer's main concern is to account for Pomp's social condition and the dire effects of his alienation and oppression, both despite and because of his Blackness and disability. He contends,

> for a rational being his mental improvements were extremely small; though when we consider the situation that he has lived in, this is not so very strange as we at first should think it. He lived either alone in the field, in bed, or in the kitchen of some people, who were too much above him to be his associates: and probably was never learned to read—There were few Negroes in Andover or any where near him, and all there was were unlearned people. From whom then or in what manner was it in his power to gain knowledge?

The contextualizing function of Plummer's letter doesn't so much authenticate Pomp's confession—indeed, the amanuensis states that he does "not attest to the truth of Pomp's dying speech"—as provide insight into the complex conjunctions that designated him in order to disappear him.[23] Plummer's addendum doesn't outright condemn his subject's treatment in slavery, as would later white abolitionist slave narrative addenda. The decidedly nonpropagandistic and (at most) implicitly critical approach Plummer takes with Pomp's dying words offers his readers context for Furbush's killing, from which they may make their own conclusions about Pomp's, Furbush's, and the greater society's individual and combined culpability for the actions for which Pomp hanged. For us, more than two hundred years later, the dying words and letter demonstrate the tangled and dire interrelations of notions of self-consciousness, disability, desire, Blackness, criminality, and enmity particular to the early national period, but resonating into our own time.

On the surface, the broadside of the *Dying Confession of Pomp*, with its crude, stock woodcut of a body hanging from the gallows before a crowd of "solemn onlookers [who] affirm the civic function of the juridically mandated ritual" (DeLombard, *Shadow* 295), combined with its enlarged font and uppercase emphasis in announcing that Pomp is a "NEGRO MAN, who was executed," suggests the sensational account of a violent act, much as readers could expect. Pomp's confession and Plummer's supplement also depart from convention, however, by critiquing the social circumstances of enslavement, alienation, and physical and mental abuse that combined to influence Pomp's overlapping designations as official criminal and undeclared enemy, thus requiring his eradication from the national body. In this way, we can read Pomp through a broader narrative trajectory of Black prison writing that critiques the dominant institutions, which preserve and protect their power through ever-changing but consistent mechanisms and strategies of subjugation.

Pomp disrupts ableist discourse. He embodies and demonstrates the multiple registers through which the period understood and attempted to contain or eradicate what it considered degenerate. His articulations of cognitive disability critique the workings of power in late eighteenth-century New England and demonstrate the transgressive and liberatory, if temporary, potential of such differential mental states. Ultimately Pomp hangs for his transgressions. Though his liberation is temporary, he explains that he prefers jail to enslavement, and finds there an intellectually generative and communally fulfilling environment. Pomp's (and Plummer's) critiques of the culture that produces criminality, maps it into a status of enmity, and then eliminates from the social body the legal person newly minted through the commission of crime articulate the triple threat that the early national Black disabled person convicted of a crime posed and highlight the flawed and ironic logic that structured such a society. His narrative and, indeed (perhaps ironically), his death, complicate the categories of the early national enslaved, disabled, and Black man deemed criminal. His confession questions the sociopolitical relations that imagine such individual categories as discretely dangerous and sees them together as representing a compounding threat to public safety. Pomp calls into question the efficacy of modeling the social body on a healthy ideal. His disruption of that very body crips the processes that attempt to produce it. We'll see in the next chapter, by extension, how a Black prison intellectual's work of a prophesied organized violent attack and subsequent confession of it produces and refutes theories of criminal insanity and Black enmity to rationalize and justify Black revolutionary violence.

3

Nineteenth-Century Counter/Terrorism

Black Prison Intellectual Nathaniel Turner's *Confessions*
and the Southampton Revolt (1831)

So far, this book has read the dying words of Abraham Johnstone, who was framed, convicted, and executed for murder in New Jersey in 1797; and Pomp, who killed his abusive enslaver and was executed in Massachusetts in 1795. These works were published in the wake of revolutions both at home and abroad: in Europe, where, particularly in France, imprisoned people were released as a result; and in Haiti, the site of the most successful Black revolution in history. These events contextualize the men's actions and words—and may have even partially inspired them. Both Johnstone and Pomp were and are relatively unknown figures, and yet they extend the deep history of the Black prison intellectual tradition through words that are still enduringly relevant. Paying close attention to these mostly overlooked figures, we see how they theorize Blackness, slavery, jail, criminality, and enmity—and, in Pomp's instance, prophetic communication and mental distress as well—threads that run through the prison intellectual tradition even today, two hundred years later. This chapter turns to *The Confessions of Nat Turner*, which was written more than three decades after the work of Pomp and Johnstone, but which theorizes all these same subjects, including prophetic communication. Turner, far from being unknown in his time or in ours, garnered national attention through his and his army's actions and his public account of them. In contrast to Johnstone and Pomp, Turner has been the subject of much scholarly attention and debate. This chapter's objective is to contextualize his work and reactions to it within the criminal/enemy rubric that is a central register of this book. Turner is an important ancestor in the Black prison intellectual tradition, revealing the roots of collective Black activism and the enduring injustices that result from the flawed logic not only of enslavement but of the enmification of Black people deemed criminal in the United States.

The Southampton revolt is part of a much longer tradition of Black violent resistance. Turner's predecessors include insurrectionary leaders such as Gabriel Prosser (Virginia, 1800) and Denmark Vesey (South Carolina, 1822), as well as David Walker, who did not take part in armed resistance, but whose influential *Appeal to the Coloured Citizens of the World* (1829, rev. 1830) urged, "If we *are* men, and see [white people] treating us in the manner they do, [then] there can be nothing in our hearts but death alone, for them. . . . They themselves, (and not us) render themselves our natural enemies, by treating us so cruel" (63–64). Walker's identification of the enemy picks up on that of figures such as Pomp and Johnstone and precedes that of others, continuing into the twentieth and twenty-first centuries, long after emancipation in the United States. As historian Christopher Cameron notes, "While advocates of pacifism and nonviolence often based their positions on their Christian faith, it was [David] Walker's Christianity which lent support to his calls for revolutionary violence. . . . Walker firmly believed that God would have his vengeance on blacks' oppressors and that the vehicles for that vengeance might very well be the slaves themselves" (1190). He continues, "While revolutionary leaders balked at the idea of slaves following their lead, African Americans nonetheless used the history of the American Revolution in their own struggle against slavery. But even more important to black abolitionist leaders was the success of the Haitian Revolution [1791–1804] and the creation of the first independent black republic in the western hemisphere. The Haitian Revolution demonstrated to African Americans that slavery could be overthrown by violent means" (1192). Certainly, nearly three decades after this revolution (and in the lead-up to the passage of the Fugitive Slave Act of 1850, during which time Frederick Douglass would publicly justify violent resistance), Turner and his army drew on revolutionary history at home and abroad in their attempt at just such a violent overthrow.[1]

Historian Brandon R. Byrd elaborates on the significance of the Haitian Revolution for the United States, arguing that "for free and enslaved black people, Haiti became a singular beacon of liberty. Enslaved revolutionaries including Gabriel [Prosser], Denmark Vesey, and Nat Turner tried to emulate the Haitian Revolution, the lone successful slave rebellion in modern global history" (3). He continues:

> Haiti was what Frederick Douglass called it: "the only self-made Black Republic in the world"; a black "city set on a hill." That analogy suggests the complexities of the association of Haiti with black freedom

and self-determination. Douglass and other black intellectuals in the United States often imagined Haiti much as John Winthrop and the Puritans had thought of Massachusetts. From their perspective, Haiti was unique albeit imitable, exemplary but imperfect, symbolic though real. It was an experiment in black self-government, distinct yet inseparable from the flawed world that its singular example had the power to change. (5)

The desire not only for freedom but for self-governance as well, a desire embodied in US and Haitian revolutionary history, resonated with enslaved and free Black people as Turner and his army prepared their revolt.

Of course, this revolutionary history had a different meaning for white people, particularly proslavery advocates, and fear of Black revolt swept the slaveholding states of the United States. Historian Ashli White notes the common rhetoric undergirding this fear:

> Among slaveholders in the Atlantic world, one of the common tropes used in describing slave revolts was "contagion." The term likened an insurrection of the enslaved to an unpredictable and voracious malady, spreading quickly and striking the innocent without warning.... The figurative equation of contagious diseases with slave rebellions, including the Haitian Revolution, has many implications. On the one hand, it served as yet another means to delay the ideological motivations of the enslaved: disease did not have a political agenda, nor did it control its own actions. As in the portrayal of the Haitian Revolution as a "volcano," insurrection was seen as a malevolent force of nature—a reading that played into the hands of the master class. On the other hand, the metaphor of contagion provides an interesting point of entry for considering how populations reacted to slave rebellion.... Extending the metaphor of contagion produces a more nuanced interpretation of fear in action, one that includes not only terror and flight but also efforts to control or mitigate the potential dangers of exposure to rebellion. (124–25)

Analogies of Black revolt and contagion in the white imagination call to mind the 1793 yellow fever epidemic in Philadelphia and the prevalent and mistaken white belief in Black immunity, a history that provided some context for the publication of Johnstone's pamphlet in the city. Metaphors of contagion to describe Black violent resistance also remind us of Johnstone's own use of *pestilence* in his analysis of perjury, the crime he identifies as the worst of all. Contagion thus offers a multiply complex rhetorical evocation of fear for enslavers and Black prison intellectuals.

The influx of immigrants from Saint-Domingue to Philadelphia during the Haitian Revolution provides an intricate backdrop for conceptions, Black and white, of Black violent resistance in pursuit of self-rule. White continues, "As white Americans worried it might, the example of the Haitian Revolution did spread ideas among African Americans. From their perspective, the Haitian Revolution represented not a deadly disease but, a possible cure for the ills of enslavement and racism" (125–26). The twofold notion of disease and antidote also provides a context for white suspicions of unsanctioned Black religiosity, fanaticism in particular. "Slavery's defenders ascribed rebellious activity among antebellum slaves to the rash interference of outsiders. Southern historians maintained that Gabriel's Rebellion was motivated by 'religious fanaticism, that frequent instrument used by designing men,' by the French Revolution, and by 'the success of the efforts of the same race in Hispaniola in overcoming and slaughtering the whites.' White southerners trotted out similar excuses in accounting for Denmark Vesey's conspiracy in Charleston in 1822 and for Nat Turner's rebellion in Southampton, Virginia, in 1831" (White 207, quoting "History of Richmond"). Such assumptions speak to the white fear of Black violence motivated by enslaved resistance to abuse and oppression. A religious explanation—or notions of madness, as we'll see in Turner's example—provided enslavers with a continuing rationale for slavery, as something meant to prohibit or at least inhibit the underlying causes of the uprisings. Such conceptual stretches underscore the potential for Black violent resistance as a possible cure for the ills of enslavement and racism. All these interconnected revolutionary contexts and rhetorics of contagion and fanaticism provide the backdrop for Turner and his army's revolt and the response to it. His *Confessions* highlights the internal enemy status that Black people occupied, particularly in instances of violent resistance. His actions and words reveal the role of the Black prison intellectual in the years leading up to the Fugitive Slave Act, a significant factor precipitating the Civil War (see White; Byrd; Cameron).

Furthermore, the 1831 revolt that Turner, an enslaved Black man, led in Southampton, Virginia, would have far-reaching repercussions, both locally and nationally. Within a mere forty-eight hours, the revolt had left between 57 and 60 white people dead. It would ultimately result in the deaths of some 200 people, including approximately two dozen Black people hanged after trial or executed as suspected rebels, and as many as 120 Black people killed within twenty-four hours by volunteer patrols that also tortured, burned, and maimed individuals.[2] Reports indicate the indiscriminate nature of these attacks on the Southampton Black population. This chapter details the powerful critique of slavery and national enmity that Turner's *Confessions* provides, and analyzes what Virginia's white population's desperate response to the revolt reveals about early nineteenth-century notions of Black revolutionary violence. The emphasis on Turner's mental state in his published *Confessions*, the document's paratext, and newspaper reports read in conjunction with Turner's words illuminate much about his role as an early Black prison intellectual, and his impact on this tradition both in his own time and beyond.

Local lawyer Thomas Gray, who was not Turner's legal representative, transcribed and published in Baltimore what he referred to as the man's *Confessions* in the same year as the revolt. The print run of fifty thousand copies underscores the force of Turner's narrative, taken down while he was in jail, as well as the contemporary popular desire to read about what was at the time the largest Black revolt in US history (Bernier 102). There are many ways to read the general hunger for Turner's story, but here the focus will be on what it reveals about notions of criminality, enmity, and Blackness in early Virginia that resonates throughout the rest of US history and into our current time. Whereas Pomp's *Dying Confession* highlighted the relation between enslavement, mental distress, and individual retributive Black violence, Turner's printed account and the Southampton revolt more broadly reveal how socially dangerous organized, collective Black armed action aimed at the institution of slavery and its supporters was to the white population of Virginia. An important forerunner in the Black prison intellectual tradition, Turner has inspired Black leaders for centuries. His case reveals how white fear of the power of Black-authored and Black-led critique inspired some to label him mad in order to contain the force of the narrative of his and his army's deeds—madness is another trope of Black-on-white violence that continues to endure.

Rather than fulfill the conventions of the dying words genre by demonstrating remorse for his actions or acknowledging any wrongdoing, Turner casts his and his compatriots' efforts as laudable work. He begins by acknowledging that Gray has asked him "to give a history of the motives which induced me to undertake the late insurrection, as you call it," a rhetorical move that suggests two important concerns (44). First, atypical of earlier confessions, motive is what Gray sought to discover through Turner's account. I find this curious as it opens a space for Turner to declare slavery and its supporters as the rationale behind and the focus of the attacks. Whereas Jonathan Plummer surmises Pomp's motives, Gray seems to invite Turner to explain them himself. Second, Turner suggests the inaccuracy of Gray's term to describe his work. *Insurrection* denotes an uprising "against established authority"; Turner's implied rejection of the term suggests that he does not accept the "established authority" of the institution of slavery, enslavers, slavery supporters, or the Commonwealth of Virginia more broadly (*OED*). Turner suggests that he understands Black people, enslaved people in Virginia, as having their own authority (if unrecognized), and his and his army's work as an assertion of this authority. As this chapter will demonstrate, participants in the revolt perceived their enemies as just that and attacked in warlike fashion, with the civilians they killed—even children—seen as part of an army representing the institution of slavery. What many of us refer to as *revolt* was, in Turner's and his army's estimation, actually a waging of war. His suggestion that *insurrection* is an insufficient or misleading term asserts an authority that simultaneously undermines that of the lawyer/transcriber's.

From the very outset of *The Confessions*, Turner defies convention and subverts authority. In fact he doesn't use the word *confession* until his trial. When asked, "Have you any thing to say why sentence of death should not be pronounced against you?" Turner responds, "I have not. I have made a full confession to Mr. Gray, and I have nothing more to say" (56). He may have admitted to his deeds, chronicling them in fair detail, but it seems that he doesn't understand them as crimes. As the law stands, he has no grounds to refute his death sentence. Perhaps in his mind, he is a captive enemy combatant.

Turner, by framing the terms of the "history" of motives Gray has asked him to provide, uses his account as a platform to portray himself as a leader, detail events of the revolt, and theorize his actions on his own terms. Even in the interview section with Gray, Turner asserts his intellectual authority. From the start, rather than do as asked and give a history of motives or follow a conventional confessional model and offer a direct admission of his involvement in the revolt, Turner authors an autobiography beginning with his childhood. Through this, he indicates his desire that people will know and understand him and his ideas. Turner creates a hybrid of the dying words and slave narrative genres as he begins: "I must go back to the days of my infancy, and even before I was born . . . the property of Benj. Turner, of this county," this opening resonant with the "I was born," so common to the latter genre (44).[3] In his following discourse he uses what he knows will become the printed "confession" to provide his own intellectual history. That he delivers this history in jail instead of in fugitivity or after manumission positions him as an early Black prison intellectual who would become famous and whose actions and ideas would shape generations to come.

Turner's self-fashioning as exceptional provides a rationale for his role not just as leader of the revolt, but as a model, a prophet for a Black antislavery movement rooted in religious belief and carried out through physical action. He describes how at the age of "three or four" he was able to recount during "play with other children . . . things that had happened before [his] birth," things the Lord showed him (44). This ability at such a young age to know a past that predates him, he says, confirmed to his parents that he "was intended for some great purpose" (44). Historian of religion and law Christopher Tomlins notes not only that it is also unusual as we have seen for enslaved people to know their exact ages, but also that Turner's age corresponds with Jesus's age when he was crucified. They were both thirty at the time of crucifixion, which is how Turner rhetorically would refer to his impending execution. This connection between Christ and Turner as prophets sets up the description of the work of the revolt and the enthusiasm that inspired it, but, as Tomlins also argues, his "account of himself in the first part of *The Confessions* is not simply an account of a figure that is Christ*like*. Considered typologically, Turner creates himself as the antitype of the Christ whose return in a postmillennial eschatology coincides with the Last Judgment" (76). Referring to eighteenth-century revivalist preacher Jonathan Edwards, Tomlins argues that "just as Christ crucified had been brought 'under the power of death' to complete the purchase of human redemption, as Edwards repeatedly noted, so Christ's enemies had themselves finally to be brought under the power of death to complete the work of redemption itself. 'Those mine enemies, which would not I should reign over them, bring hither, and slay them before me'" (81, and see 76–77). In *The Confessions*, the criminal/enemy distinctions appear in relief along religious and legal lines. To Turner's way of thinking, judgment will fall heavily on his enemies, who are also the enemies of those he serves and whom he and his army have fought and slain. The last shall be first.

In keeping with Turner's description of himself as exceptional, he mentions physical signs that indicated his uniqueness when he was a child. "Certain marks on my head and breast," he says, confirmed for his parents that he would be great (44). Gray parenthetically interrupts Turner's narrative and dismisses these marks as "excrescences," which, he claims, are not uncommon to Black people. *Excrescence* evokes excess, abnormality, exuberance, and so forth, and represents Gray's attempt to undercut the validity of Turner's exceptionalness and of his and his parents' reading of his body (*OED*). Gray's language relies heavily on stereotypes about Black people that readers would recognize, if not as such. Turner's description of physical marks and reading of signs along with Gray's dismissal of Turner's and his parents' interpretation signal also to the reader a double standard regarding typology. Whereas white religious people routinely read physical signs as providential, they also disregarded the idea that divine providence would work in the service of Black people, doubting that even if it did, Black people would have the capacity to read the signs accurately. That Turner follows up with a description of his "uncommon intelligence" contradicts Gray's argument—regardless of whether Turner was aware of his amanuensis's parenthetical comment. Turner makes explicit reference to his understanding of his own intelligence. He refers to his mind specifically, but he does not separate mind from physical action; nor do I believe he understands the mind and body in a hierarchical or discrete manner per se.[4] His visions are as abstract as they are concrete. Take for instance this description: "I had a vision—and I saw white spirits and black spirits engaged in battle, and the sun was darkened—the thunder rolled in the Heavens, and blood flowed in streams—and I heard a voice saying, 'Such is your luck, such are you called to see, and let it come rough or smooth, you must surely bare it'" (46). This serves as just one example of Turner seeing and hearing something that seems commensurably otherworldly and earthly, signaling the communion of and his capacity to access and interpret both.

Perhaps anticipating or understanding how people will try to interpret his *Confessions*, Turner takes the time to portray himself as a gifted, foresighted leader. Through his self-characterization, he perhaps seeks to preempt further attempts to classify him as mad, and even invites readers to reconsider their notions of madness, particularly in light of state-sanctioned slavery in early nineteenth-century Virginia. Describing his childhood, he refers to his grandmother's role in his education. Grandmothers also often feature in slave narratives, and though he doesn't mention very much directly about her, her influence on Turner's formative years is palpable in his description of his upbringing, again validating claims about how extraordinary he was as a youth and how his childhood signaled greatness and prepared him to be the leader he was to become. Her maternal effect at a respectively older age, her religious teaching, and presumably her love all come across as central to Turner's development. He explains:

> My grandmother, who was very religious, and to whom I was much attached—my master, who belonged to the church, and other religious persons who visited the house, and whom I often saw at prayers, noticing the singularity of my prayers, I suppose, and my uncommon intelligence for a child, remarked I had too much sense to be raised, and if I was, I would never be of any service to any one as a slave—To a mind like mine, restless, inquisitive and observant of every thing that was passing, it is easy to suppose that religion was the subject to which it would be directed. (44–45)

Turner's emphasis on the "singularity of [his] prayers," his "uncommon intelligence," his "too much sense to be raised . . . [to] be of any service to any one as a slave," and his "restless, inquisitive and observant" mind unsurprisingly "directed" toward religion accounts swiftly for how he assumed the role of leader. But it also implies the dire need for such a commander and for a show of violence to counter slavery in Virginia, so as to render evident the injustices and terror enslaved Black people there endure. A combination of his selection for this role, his familial support, and his interpretation of the time of judgment provides the reader with a blueprint for reading *The Confessions*, no matter Gray's and others' interventions in and attempts to control it.

Turner, by emphasizing his literacy, joins the company of nineteenth-century Black intellectuals such as Frederick Douglass (also enslaved and imprisoned), Mary Ann Shadd Cary, Martin R. Delany, and many others who stressed the importance of reading and writing in their own written texts, newspaper articles, and lectures. Turner explains how at a young age, when shown a book, he "began spelling the names of different objects" to the astonishment of many, particularly Black people, again stressing his exceptional character among his peers (45).[5] He seeks time for study and reflection, in this way prefiguring many other Black intellectuals as well as those in prison who look to solitude for study. Though he was still on the "outside" at the time, Turner notes, "having soon discovered to be great, I must appear so, and therefore studiously avoided mixing in society, and wrapped myself in mystery, devoting my time to fasting and prayer" (45). In 1831, Turner is the prototypical radical Black prison intellectual, a figure that we would see become so influential in the years surrounding the long US civil rights movement.[6]

As many scholars have noted, one cannot overstate the influence of religion on Turner. Through direct reference or allusion to scripture as well as use of religious rhetoric, he provides a faith-based justification for his actions. Similar to what happened with Pomp, Turner's learning of his enslaved status is catalytic. He explains, "Now finding I had arrived to man's estate, and was a slave, and these revelations being made known to me, I began to direct my attention to this great object, to fulfil the purpose for which, by this time, I felt assured I was intended" (46). His reference to *revelations* to detail his coming into the knowledge of his legally dependent status foreshadows the tale of reckoning to come in his *Confessions*, which draws heavily on Revelation, the final, apocalyptic, and prophetic book of the Bible.

Interpreting more signs, Turner details working in a field and finding "drops of blood on the corn as though it were dew from heaven," "hieroglyphic characters" on "leaves in the woods," and "numbers, with the forms of men in different attitudes, portrayed in blood, and representing the figures I had seen before in the heavens" (47). He reads these signs as proof that "the Saviour was about to lay down the yoke he had borne for the sins of men, and the great day of judgment was at hand" (47). Inspired by these signs, Turner explains how he began his work of reckoning, the allusion to Revelation and judgment situating him as the one who would bring about God's ruling on the institution of slavery and its proponents.[7] He aligns himself with Christ the prophet. Also, by extension, he places his readership in a similar position to slave narrative readers, who serve as the "jury" in slavery's trial. Turner extends the metaphor of the juridical trial of slavery to the day of judgment of the Bible, inviting readers to imagine themselves at the time when "the dead were judged according to what they had done" (*New American*, Rev. 20.11–15). Perhaps the terror that Turner's allusions produced in his slaveholding/white supremacist readership approximated the terror that his and his army's actions produced in the white population of Southampton and beyond. His references create in his *Confessions* similar prophetic and apocalyptic interpretative possibilities to those in the Book of Revelation, his in the service of teaching those who justify and practice enslavement about the fate awaiting them, the terror they will meet in both their earthly lives and their afterlives.

By alluding to the reversal of fortune Revelation prophesizes, Turner typologically interprets the enslavers' sins and the judgment day they will face. He emphasizes his personal role in fulfilling the book's prophecy. Of the day of judgment, he states, "on the 12th of May, 1828, I heard a loud noise in the heavens, and the Spirit instantly appeared to me and said the Serpent was loosed, and Christ had laid down the yoke he had borne for the sins of men, and that I should take it on and fight against the Serpent, for the time was fast approaching when the first should be last and the last should be first" (47). We can understand his reading of a coming time when the first and last should trade places, of course, as implying that it was his job to fight the serpent of slavery, enslavers, proslavery people, and even white people in general, so that he and his fellow enslaved people should be first—in other words, not only freed from slavery, but made first in the eyes of God as well.

Tomlins believes that Turner's greatest scriptural influence was Luke, citing among other reasons his possible christological reading of his residence in St. Luke's Parish. Referring to Luke's Gospel, "a narrative of Christ's life and works," Tomlins states that "like Luke's life of Christ, Turner's account of himself begins with events prior to his own birth, describes an emerging awareness of 'some great purpose,' and culminates in a climactic sacrificial act of atonement. Throughout, Turner employs typological reasoning for the messianic purpose of re-creating himself as the Redeemer returned" (52–53). Tomlins also references New Testament scholar I. Howard Marshall, who distinguishes Luke from Matthew in the way that both include a variation on the passage "Seek ye the kingdom of Heaven." While this passage in Matthew appears in the Sermon on the Mount, "teaching . . . that spiritual virtue will be rewarded, in Luke the meaning of 12:31 and associated passages is 'that there will be a reversal of places in the kingdom of God'" (Tomlins 55). Turner's exegesis of Luke and his emphasis on the reversal of last and first not only reveal his faith in the work he has carried out on God's behalf, but also provide a rationale for that faith and that work. He draws together the legal and the religious, commencing with his expert scriptural interpretation and thereby undermining the authority of the legal rule under which he lives. *The Confessions* typologically as well as directly confronts the power structures governing him and other enslaved people in Southampton. In the tradition of those who came before him and those who later would find inspiration in his work, his challenge to power in *Confessions* comes from within the confines of incarceration—and for him as for many others, as he awaits his execution.

Turner's allusions to scripture and his self-alignment with Christ emphasize the sacrifice that he, like Christ, was prepared to make, demonstrating his commitment to his faith and his work in the face of abusive and exploitative individual and institutional power (see Tomlins, ch. 2). Following

Turner's exegetical reading of Luke's reference to the judgment day reversal, Gray, referring to Turner's imminent hanging, asks him, "Do you not find yourself mistaken now?" Turner's reply is, "Was not Christ crucified" (48). Going beyond the trope of the sacrifice of the political outsider and implied association with the Son of God that we saw in Johnstone's *Letter to His Wife* in chapter 1, Turner's messianic mission is much more explicitly drawn, and yet the biblical chapters and verses Johnstone recommends to his wife are also from Luke. Johnstone, recall, speaks through allusions to Luke as he critiques institutional legal and political power in New Jersey, and by extension Philadelphia, his pamphlet's place of publication and the federal capital at the time. He leaves it to the reader to remember or track down the references, but when we do, we see how in his self-presentation he clearly analogizes himself to Christ. The parallels between Christ's life and his own forgiveness of his enemies, betrayal, subjection to a corrupt and tyrannous government, and execution form a stark political critique and reinforce his theories of Blackness, crime, and enmity. The question of why Luke informs both men's critiques begs an answer.

In general, Luke's Gospel and the Acts of the Apostles (also credited to Luke) characterize Christ in ways that potentially would appeal to both Johnstone's and Turner's communities of enslaved Black people, facilitating an exacting critique of the local white slaveholding and slavery-supporting populations.[8] Taken together, Luke's writings exhibit a few key characteristics. First, his address is mainly directed toward gentiles—the people at the time of his writing charged with proclaiming and safeguarding the mission of Christ—and his emphasis with this audience is on wealth and its effect on salvation. Given Turner's and Johnstone's readerships (largely Christian and located in a slaveholding state with a disproportional distribution of wealth, particularly disadvantaging Black people, even for those not enslaved), it's fair to imagine that Luke's portrayal of Christ in this respect might make their contemporary white audiences think twice about wealth and salvation. Their references would also possibly resonate with enslaved Black people, even inspiring them to resist. Certainly, the reversal of earthly material wealth in the kingdom of God is central to Turner's *Confessions*.

Second, Luke's emphasis on the compassion of Christ would, for readers, underscore the cruelty of slavery and imprisonment. Among other professions Luke occupied, he was a physician, and he spoke of Christ's healing of others—providing a stark contrast to the abuses enslavers, mistresses, overseers, slavery supporters, and the penal system meted out on enslaved peoples and Black people. Luke further discusses Jesus's release of enslaved and imprisoned people. Describing Luke's miraculous account of the imprisoned Paul and Silas, who sang hymns while their fellow imprisoned people listened when an earthquake erupted and crumbled the "foundations . . . and immediately all the doors were opened, and everyone's chains were unfastened" (*New American*, Acts 16.25–26), biblical scholar Lee Griffith argues, "On both of these levels [informational and symbolic], the accounts of release from prison serve to echo the message of liberty and renounce the power of the prison" (13). Johnstone and Turner may well have found inspiration in Luke's attention to prison as well as enslavement.

A third possible connection is that Luke uses the epistolary mode to characterize Christ. Certainly, Luke was not the New Testament's only letter writer, but that Johnstone and Turner find inspiration in Luke and channel his letters through their "confessions" suggests that generically there might be something about this literary form, the ostensibly direct address of epistolary biblical writing, that also appealed to them. In Johnstone's *Letter to His Wife* references to Luke function almost as a kind of allegorical code, whereas in Turner's *Confessions* the parallels are more explicit. And yet, both texts address one person—Sally Johnstone and Thomas Gray, respectively—even though the authors' knowledge that their texts would be published means that they knew their "confessions" would reach a much broader audience. Recall Johnstone's hope at the end of his letter that his words would live on forever: "for as the water by continual and incessant dropping makes an impression on the stone, so will these my admonitions make an impression on your minds by frequent readings and recourse to them" (31). Further to the point, another feature of Luke's biblical writings is their attention to the spread of the gospel through the form of letters. It seems that Johnstone and Turner use their deathbed authorship to follow Luke in this project and spread the Word and their own words well beyond the ostensible addressee, but also to emphasize to a wide audience Luke's relevance to a critique of slavery and prison, both products of the individual and institutional abuses of power and the hypocrisy of white oppressors.

The biblical connection between enslavement and imprisonment adds another dimension to this comparison between Turner and Johnstone as they channel Luke from their places of incarceration. As they explain their actions and theorize about criminality and enmity, they reiterate the prophets' notion of the inherent failure of slavery and prisons. Griffith argues:

> It was from the experience of exile that Israel learned of the fundamental kinship between enslavement and imprisonment. The experi-

> ence of the exile prepared the covenantal community to understand the truth of the prophets' words: the same God who frees the slaves frees the prisoners too. In the calm reflections of the wisdom literature, the community even proclaimed the possibility that a freed prisoner would lead the people: "For he has come out of prison to become king, even though he was born poor in his kingdom" (Eccles. 4:14). And in moments of anguished hope, the community even proclaimed the messianic expectation that one would appear to say, "I have set your prisoners free" (Zech. 9:9–12). (102)

The parallels between enslavement and imprisonment here and elsewhere in the Bible, for Griffith, demonstrate the Bible's condemnation of both. Furthermore, he argues that "the imagery attributed to Jesus in Luke 12:57–59 makes the point clear that the courts can offer only prison, not reconciliation" (117). In other words, it is useless to rely on the court system to maintain community. Johnstone's characterization of enslavers and slavery supporters as "enemies of freedom," combined with his critique of perjury and the undue political and legal reliance on oath taking, argues for the fallibility of the institutions of slavery and the penal system in New Jersey, and potentially in Pennsylvania as well. Turner's revolt and his unrepentant stance about it—his response of "Was not Christ crucified" even while awaiting the gallows—demonstrate his condemnation of both institutions as well (48).

The formerly enslaved Johnstone and the currently enslaved Turner, each imprisoned and writing from his respective jail, both drew parallels between themselves and Christ regarding their subjugation. These parallels underscore the hypocrisies of their Christian oppressors. Biblical knowledge informed their behavior and their authorship, and both imagine they will reach a wider audience through publication of their "confessions." In keeping with Ecclesiastes, both recognize the potential for a freedperson to ascend to a leadership role. Johnstone in his *Address* is clear that he means to educate and exhort his audience—as chapter 1 argues, both Black and white. Turner frees himself (even if he's not legally free) and becomes the messianic leader of the Southampton revolt, aiming by force to free his fellow enslaved people. To a certain extent, we see this impulse in Pomp as well: he imagines he could be a good leader after spending time in jail studying the Bible and preaching. Celia, whom chapter 4 addresses, becomes a leader of sorts when she escapes jail. And we will see a similar argument to Johnstone's, Pomp's, and Turner's in chapter 5, in James Foster's parole request letters, which also make use of biblical allusions to assert his potential for leadership upon release from prison. The authors situate themselves to varying extents as people of promise, intellectuals whose ideas can counter the racist corruption and exploitation that lead to the enslavement and imprisonment of Black people. They expose and reject the mode of thinking that imagines a Black person deemed criminal an internal enemy.

Turner and his army situate those whom they fight and kill as their enemies. Editor Kenneth S. Greenberg estimates that "[Turner] did not undertake his revolt as an act of revenge against a particular person. Nat Turner's enemy was slavery rather than his master" (N. Turner 2). Unlike Pomp or Celia, who kill their individual enslavers, Turner's "work"—and he uses the word *work* twelve times in thirteen pages to describe the massacre, the "work of death"—is targeted against a much greater enemy than an individual enslaver. Turner explicitly identifies those he and his army have killed as their enemies. His militaristic language throughout the account emphasizes strategy, valor, and rank. He salutes his men, he himself "spill[s] the first blood," and he forms his company "in a line as soldiers . . . and march[es] them off" (47–48). Addressing *The Confessions*' use of military language, Jeannine Marie DeLombard argues, "Standing outside the social compact and doing their duty, Turner's 'soldiers' conduct acts of war rather than perpetuate crimes" (*Shadow* 181). Turner's rhetoric of labor and war supports his distinction between criminality and enmity and asks readers to question the definition of terrorism and its role in perpetuating US slavery. Referring to historian and political theorist Jacques Sémelin's notion that massacres are not indiscriminate, Tomlins explains, "Before massacre can take place, a 'prophet[ic]' intellectual construction of the other as enemy must occur" (106). He posits that "Turner's rebellion was an instance of countersovereignty, 'insurrectory' force deployed by members of a despised population who had discovered their own capacity for willful action and were intent on expressing it through the destruction of a regime that oppressed them" (119). I agree with the definition of countersovereignty here as it applies to Turner and his army, but in the context of the United States more broadly, I find *counterterrorism* to be a more productive term for the work of the revolt.

The status of the United States as a sovereign nation faces critical challenges that complicate the argument that the Southampton revolt is an example of countersovereignty. Historian Manu Vimalassery argues, "United States sovereignty claims are actually claims of counter-sovereignty. That is, US claims to territorial authority are generated, in the first instance, in claims of discovery and the preemption of other non-Native claimants to Native lands and waters. . . . As counter-sovereignty, US sovereignty is in perpetual reaction to the prior and primary claims of Native peoples on the territories that the United States claims as its own" (142). In this light, countersovereignty appears to apply less to Turner's actions or the Southampton revolt, which rather functioned counter to the terror of enslavement. That said, Tomlins's definition of countersovereignty, which I'll repeat here, certainly applies to the revolt: an "'insurrectory' force deployed by members of a despised population who had discovered their own capacity for willful action and were intent on expressing it through the destruction of a regime that oppressed them."

Turner identifies the revolt's objective as being to "carry terror and devastation wherever we went" and to "strike terror to the inhabitants" (49–50). Historian David F. Allmendinger Jr. argues, "The word *terror* appeared twice in the narrative, both times in the account of the assault on the Waller farm. In the first reference, Turner described the approach at full speed (*'and as it 'twas my object to carry terror and devastation wherever we went, I placed fifteen or twenty of the best armed . . . in front, who generally approached the houses as fast as their horses could run'*). In the second, he explained his purposes (*'to prevent their escape and strike terror to the inhabitants'*). In each case, he used the word in its oldest meaning—the state of being greatly frightened, or paralyzed with sudden fear" (251). Allmendinger goes on to hypothesize that "at least two of the insurgents had understood *terror* in a new way: Henry Porter and Will Francis, through the deed, had meant to instill a fear deeper than one that merely paralyzed immediate victims. They had intended to create an enduring dread in an entire population, an intention that reappeared in the seven infanticides that followed and in the killing of Rebecca Williams" (251). I won't focus on the rhetoric of disability in this analysis, and indeed I've written about this metaphorical approach before (see "Black Atlantic"). Rather, my attention here is on the production of terror.

What Allmendinger notes as the oldest meaning of the word *terror* aligns with the *OED*'s first listed meaning of the term. This, along with Allmendinger's extension of the term to refer to the creation of "an enduring dread in an entire population," makes sense, but further analysis of *terror* and related terms as they intersect with *The Confessions* can help us not only better uncover Turner's and the other participants' motivations and desired outcomes, but also reveal their relation to the state as its enemy, as well as the state's perpetration of terror against the entire enslaved population.

Turner's usage of the word *terror* is more in line with what the *OED* identifies as *terrorism*: "The unofficial or unauthorized use of violence and intimidation in the pursuit of political aims; (originally) such practices used by a government or ruling group (frequently through paramilitary or informal armed groups) in order to maintain its control over a population; (now usually) such practices used by a clandestine or expatriate organization as a means of furthering its aims" (*OED*, sense 2.a). What this definition illuminates in the context of Turner's revolt is that terror/terrorism as "unofficial or unauthorized use of violence . . . in the pursuit of political aims" seems to have been Turner's objective, but the second part of the definition underscores that the revolt is a response to the form of government terrorism that is slavery: violent "practices used by a government or ruling group . . . in order to maintain its control over a population." Furthermore, in the European revolutionary context preceding Turner's time, *terror* defined the "period of remorseless repression or bloodshed during which the general community live[d] in constant fear of death or violence," a definition that also describes enslavement in the United States (*OED*, s.v. "reign of terror").

Whereas Abraham Johnstone protests his innocence throughout his *Dying Confession*, and Pomp confesses to his crime and ultimately seeks forgiveness in his *Dying Confession*, Turner narrates his acts rather than confess to any crime that he understands as such. Turner describes his "revelation, which fully affirmed in me the impression that I was ordained for some great purpose in the hands of the Almighty," and understands his great purpose as the "work of death" (46, 50; see Tomlins, ch. 4). His impression of the revolt as work supports the notion that he and his army were conducting acts of war against enemies rather than committing crimes against civilians.

White proslavery and antislavery people alike perceived Black people as a threat to the eighteenth- and nineteenth-century US ruling classes and US imperialism more broadly (see Hunt-Kennedy 149). For example, perceptions of Pomp's and Turner's mental states as distressed or mad, combined with their physical ability to kill and maim, demonstrate the fear the slaveocracy held of such Black embodiments. In *The Confessions*, Turner heralds himself a prophet, called to fulfill God's work and to "arise and prepare [himself], and slay [his] enemies with their own weapons" (48). At the time, people assumed that he was a madman. In fact, Turner demonstrates how madness became a socially convenient, perhaps even necessary explanation for Black organized violence. Gray characterizes his subject as a "gloomy fanatic" and expresses his wish that "[Turner's] own account of the conspiracy ... submitted to the public ... reads an awful, and it is hoped, a useful lesson, as to the operations of a mind like his, endeavoring to grapple with things beyond its reach. How it first became bewildered and confounded, and finally corrupted and led to the conception and perpetration of the most atrocious and heart-rending deeds" (41). Beyond Gray's assessment of Turner, a good deal of newspaper coverage of the revolt also read antislavery critique as madness and highlighted notions of Black enmity.

Turner's work underscores the enmification of Black people convicted of crimes, but it also (when viewed alongside society's response) exposes the myriad ways in which law, custom, and white supremacy (responding to the long-standing fear of slave revolt) coalesced to produce the very enmification that Turner and his army faced. Literary critic Eric J. Sundquist's influential work on *The Confessions* reminds us, "In the wake of Vesey's near revolt, Charleston editor Edwin C. Holland called for vigorous suppression and warned his readers not to forget that 'our Negroes are truely [sic] the *Jacobins* of the country; that they are the *anarchists* and the *domestic enemy;* the *common enemy of civilized society,* and the barbarians who would, if they could, become the destroyers *of our race*'" (33). As we have seen in the introduction and the first two chapters of this book, the perception of Black enmity has a history older than the United States itself, and particular to the Southampton revolt, the concept of that enmity reached its logical conclusion in the wake of the American Revolutionary War and the Haitian Revolution. The Southampton revolt and *The Confessions* demonstrate the arbitrary and racially directed nineteenth-century concepts of Blackness, criminality, enmity, and terrorism.

Writing in the *Liberator* soon after the revolt, William Lloyd Garrison placed the events of 1831 Southampton in the context of European revolutions and the United States' own struggle for independence: "excesses of the slaves ... deserve no more censure than the Greeks in destroying the Turks, or the Poles in exterminating the Russians, or our fathers in slaughtering the British" (quoted by Greenberg in N. Turner 71). The *Liberator*'s reading moves the revolt out of the context of a random massacre perpetrated largely by one madman and situates it in a legitimate tradition of struggle against tyranny. In a much more recent reading, literary critic Paul Downes argues that the terrorism in 1831 Virginia exposes the legal exploitation of violence lacking a relationship to justice. "The 'terror' associated with Turner's rebellion ... is the terror of a Hobbesian state of nature [in which law and justice are meaningless], but it is also the terror that had been nurtured, sustained, and exploited by a slaveowning culture determined to profit from the maintenance and control of that very terror. . . . Nat Turner was not revolting against a form of Hobbesian sovereignty: his was the revolt of a Hobbesian model of sovereignty against at least two hundred years of counter-Hobbesian terror" (223). Rather than seeing the Southampton revolt's slaughter of innocents as a decline into the Hobbesian state of nature, Downes "reminds us that sovereignty had *already* dissolved in the slaveholding United States" (222). Turner's terrorism is thus more accurately counterterrorism.

Turner's *Confessions* asks us to read slavery as both terrorism and a state of war. A Lockean approach views "slavery as the perpetuation of a state of war inimical to justice and democratic society in a successful republic" (Michael 141). But this is an unofficial state of war between the enslavers and the enslaved; the official narrative must not declare it as such. Doing so would put the state and the nation more broadly at risk of recognizing Black violence as revolutionary and therefore political rather than criminal. "For Gray, and for his readers, Turner and his rebellion cannot signify violence met by violence, the resistance of identifiable human subjects to an inhuman situation, a state of war provoking warlike acts that will continue to threaten white society until the injustices motivating them are rectified" (Michael 155). The intellectual work of the revolt is to lay bare, through its own targeted violence, the targeted violence of the system, the institution against which Turner and the other participants were revolting.

With particular attention to Virginia law, civil rights defender and federal appeals court judge A. Leon Higginbotham Jr. and research associate Anne F. Jacobs take up the more general lament of abolitionist William Goodell, who "wrote that the slave 'can know *law only as an enemy, and not as a friend*'" (971). Higginbotham and Jacobs demonstrate "how the Virginia legislature and courts most often made the law 'only an enemy' for blacks—and never a friend" (971). If the law was the enemy of enslaved Black people, then at least implicitly the law also understood enslaved Black people believed to have broken the law as the enemy of the state, thereby producing, if unofficially, a state of mutual enmity between the state and its enslaved population. Even the fear that Black people might break laws seemed to create a sense of enmity. The Southampton revolt makes real these hypothetically drawn legal battle lines and bears out this book's more general thesis about the enmification of Black people deemed criminal in the United States.

One consistent feature of antebellum Virginia law both before and after 1831 is that Black offenders (but not white offenders) were expelled beyond state and sometimes national boundaries, with free Black people sold into slavery. As we see in Turner's *Confessions* and the aftermath of the uprising, deportation, torture, and execution were all methods of punishment applied to varying extents to Black participants, even those only suspected of involvement. Legal terms like *alien enemy* and *petit treason* both linguistically substantiate and complicate the enmity between Virginia law and the state's enslaved population, demonstrating how far the law had to go to enmify a domestic enslaved population, one on which, paradoxically, the state's economy depended.

Beyond simply expelling enslaved Black people convicted of crimes from the state body, Virginia law also used crime as a pretext to displace free Black people from the general population into the enslaved population. Several criminal statutes existed to remove the state's de facto enemies to the margins. "Perhaps the most profound example of free blacks' precarious and unique status was the fact that as punishment for committing what was for whites a noncapital crime, free Blacks could be sold into slavery" (Higginbotham and Jacobs 978). Not only was the law an enemy to the enslaved, as Goodell argues, but the law also made free Black people into enemies by selling them into slavery as punishment for being convicted of a crime. Once enslaved, they were then liable to deportation. The 1824 ruling in *Aldridge v. Commonwealth* determined that free Black men in Virginia could not only be sold into slavery but also effectively deported from the United States: "Aldridge, a free black man convicted of grand larceny, was sentenced under an 1823 statute to receive thirty-nine lashes and to be sold as a slave and transported and banished beyond the limits of the United States" (Higginbotham and Jacobs 1023). Grand larceny as grounds for deportation underscores the extent to which the state would test the limits of Virginia's Constitution and Bill of Rights when the defendant was Black, as "Aldridge . . . assert[ed] that his sentence constituted cruel and unusual punishment" (Higginbotham and Jacobs 1023). When we turn more specifically to the law's enmification of enslaved Black people suspected of what it deemed criminal activity, the punishments demonstrate even fancier racist legal footwork and are even more contradictory and bleak.

Just like in New Jersey and Massachusetts, when it came to the issue of slavery, Virginia adopted contradictory logic, passing legislation that underscored the racial limits of the concept of revolutionary freedom. The contradictions in postrevolutionary Virginia around free speech and freedom of the press exposed anxieties about abolitionist free speech and the service of antislavery jurors. The prided US concept of freedom had severely biased social, racial, and ideological limits. Virginians drafted the First Amendment of the US Bill of Rights, but they also passed statutes denying "on the issue of abolition . . . totally all freedom of speech, freedom of the press, freedom to assemble, and freedom to petition the government for a redress of grievances" (Higginbotham and Jacobs 1018). Furthermore, even prior to the revolution, any acts resembling the advocacy of Black liberty or abolition were crimes punishable by fine and imprisonment. Later, in 1798, a statute declared that "in all cases, wherein the property of a person held as a slave demanding freedom shall come before a court for trial, no person who shall be proved to be a member of any society instituted for the purpose of emancipating negroes from the possession of their masters, shall be admitted to serve as a juror in the trial of said cause" (quoted in Higginbotham and Jacobs 1020–21). As we'll see, even when the law acknowledged inconsistencies in logic, those inconsistencies become another method of limiting the rights of the enslaved.

Citizenship was then as now far from a right to which everyone was entitled. Judge Dade's opinion in the *Aldridge* case reasoned that the Commonwealth's Bill of Rights

> not only was not intended to apply to our slave populations, but that free blacks and mulattoes were also not comprehended in it. . . . And yet, nobody has ever questioned the power of the Legislature, to deny to free blacks and mulattoes, one of the first privileges of a citizen, that of voting at elections, although they might in every particular, except color, be in precisely the same condition as those qualified to vote. The numerous restrictions imposed on this class of people in our Statute Book, many of which are inconsistent with the letter and spirit of the Constitution, both of this State and of the United States, as respects the free whites, demonstrate, that, here, those instruments have not been considered to extend equally to both classes of our population. (quoted in Higginbotham and Jacobs 1024)

Even when Judge Dade acknowledged the law's racial inconsistencies in ideology, he used them to justify the denial of free Black civil rights. As historian Robert G. Parkinson argues, "In short, citizenship is a club. Members can choose whom they let in and whom they exclude. The patriots based inclusion on what one scholar [James H. Kettner] termed 'volitional allegiance': 'Every man had to have the right to decide whether to be a citizen or an alien.' It would be naïve to think this choice would ever be free or universal" (23). This logic is similar to a critique of French citizenship voiced by Anatole France in his 1894 novel *Le Lys Rouge* (*The Red Lily*): "For the poor it consists in supporting and maintaining the rich in their power and their idleness. At this task they must labour in the face of the majestic equality of the laws, which forbid rich and poor alike to sleep under the bridges, to beg in the streets, and to steal their bread. This equality is one of the benefits of the Revolution" (95). Revolution in these examples produced not equality but an imbalance of wealth and power; in the United States, Blackness was a persistent defining factor.[9]

Besides the naivety of assuming that anyone could really "decide whether to be a citizen or an alien" (Parkinson 23), enslaved Black people in antebellum Virginia occupied a "lower status even than alien enemies loyal to a foreign government," in that the alien enemy was not subject to expulsion from the United States in the way that an enslaved person who, for example, stole from or assaulted a white person under an 1823 law would be subject to whipping and *permanent* removal (Higginbotham and Jacobs 1054). Even worse than what awaited the alien enemy, the bondsperson's enmity could entail banishment from their home country. If they were to return, the result would be execution "without the benefit of clergy" (quoted in Higginbotham and Jacobs 1055). "In the aftermath of the August 1831 Nat Turner rebellion, the punishment [for offenses against white people] was changed to death." By contrast, "Whites who assaulted free blacks or other whites with intent to kill were subject merely to imprisonment for one to ten years" (Higginbotham and Jacobs 1055). Whether by deportation or by execution, the Black person deemed offender was, under Virginia law, subject to permanent removal from the state. Such penalty speaks to the level of enmity that enslaved Black people convicted of crimes occupied in antebellum Virginia, a deeper level of enmity than even alien enemies with allegiances to foreign governments held. By extension, it's possible to imagine how enslaved Black people could understand themselves as having their own government/system of governance within the United States.

Turner's work tested the state's commitment to making its own enslaved Black population convicted of criminal offenses an undeclared enemy. If an enslaved person or servant murdered an enslaver, the term for the offense was *petit treason*, and it carried the same punishment in Virginia—beheading, quartering, and displaying the head publicly—as the offense of high treason, "a crime that presumes the defendant is a citizen who owes fidelity to his government. Slaves were deemed to owe allegiance not to the country, but only to their white masters" (Higginbotham and Jacobs 86).[10] The enslaved person's noncitizen status meant that their loyalty legally lay with their enslaver, not the state, but betrayal of one's enslaver or one's state seems to have been weighted the same, at least in terms of the punishment. This was the case even though, "according to Virginia law, only free subjects of the Commonwealth, not slaves, could be prosecuted for that high crime [treason]. In other cases, lower courts declined to try free persons of color because their jurisdiction in capital cases extended only to the enslaved" (C. Smith, *Oracle* 158). In antebellum Virginia, enslaved people occupied a separate brand of state enmity that provided them with punishment fit for a high crime that the law deemed it impossible for them to commit. It seems that regardless of enslaved people's de jure noncitizen status the state needed to regard and punish them as enemies, no matter what legal contradictions that entailed. Black resistance in Virginia, even on an individual scale, could legally meet with the punishment of a high crime.

Before publication of *The Confessions*, newspapers seemed to anticipate and therefore deflect attention away from the political aims that Turner would eventually express in print. Proslavery papers focused on defining Turner as an individual madman. Their race to eliminate any provocation or motive for the revolt demonstrates the success of Turner's and the other participants' motive "to strike terror into the inhabitants" (50). The *Richmond Enquirer* on August 30, 1831, argued, "A fanatic preacher by the name of Nat Turner (Gen. Nat Turner) . . . was artful, impudent and vindicative [sic] without any cause or provocation [this imitating the language of ads for capture of runaways] that could be assigned" (quoted by Greenberg in N. Turner 67–68). Here Turner's perceived fanaticism is the cause of what the press wanted to characterize as random attacks, not a high crime but merely revenge. Even the *Constitutional Whig* (September 3, 1831), critical of exaggerated accounts of the massacre and the slaughter of Black people without trial, referred to Turner as a "fanatic" who "acted upon no higher principle than the impulse of revenge against the whites, as the enslavers of himself and his race." The *Whig* cautioned its readers, "Let the fact not be doubted by those whom it most concerns, that another such insurrection will be the signal for the extirmination [sic] of the whole Black population in the quarter of the state where it occurs" (quoted by Greenberg in N. Turner 75–76). Even as the paper's editor and author of the account John Hampden Pleasants acknowledged a potential motive for the attacks (revenge), he discounted its validity by undercutting the value of the principle of revenge for enslaved people. Furthermore, his use of *revenge*—rather than, for example, *revolt*—somewhat removes the political from the motivation. The proslavery refusal to see the intellectual work behind the attacks, and the corresponding insistence on Turner's madness, signals white people's fear of Black violence, and of public acknowledgment of their own implicativeness in it.

By contrast, but still with the anticipation of extermination in mind, the antislavery *Liberator* on September 3, 1831, rather than concentrate on Turner's mental state, read the revolt as the fulfillment of something the paper had long predicted and that it justified by likening the work of the rebels to that of the Greeks, Poles, and even Americans in their revolutions. The *Liberator*'s report took the opportunity to chastise the nation as a whole and warn readers of an unavoidable escalation of war if slavery continued:

> You have seen, it is to be feared, but the beginning of sorrows. All the blood which has been shed will be required at your hands. At your hands alone? No—but at the hands of the people of New-England and of all the free states. The crime of oppression is national. The south is only the agent in this guilty traffic. But, remember! the same causes are at work which must inevitably produce the same effects; and when the contest shall have again begun, it must be again a war of extermination. . . . But we have killed and routed them now—we can do it again and again—we are invincible! A dastardly triumph, well becoming a nation of oppressors. (quoted by Greenberg in N. Turner 70)

Whether pro- or antislavery, the newspapers reveal the severity of the white people's perceived threat of Black revolutionary violence (sometimes understood as fanaticism). The revolt, the violent fallout, and the newspaper coverage all highlight the lengths proslavery advocates thought they had to go to in order to remove political motive from the attacks. If they did not, the intuitive logic would bear out Sundquist's contention that "to watch the spread of Black rebellion in the New World, or to observe its potential in the United States, was to witness not necessarily the erosion of the ideology of the American Revolution, but rather its transfer across the color line" (36). Whereas white revolution became central to US identity, Black revolution became, to proslavery advocates, a signal of madness. If Turner himself in his *Confessions* didn't make this explicit, his amanuensis made sure to provide a documentary apparatus that would (see Tomlins, ch. 1).

Gray's introduction to the *Confessions*, "To the Public," which provides the paratext or guidelines for reading Turner's words, sets up a scene of unmotivated Black mad behavior and then proceeds to argue the need for a far more rigid, stricter enforcement of existing laws. Gray's address serves as a short essay against leniency. Just as the rubric of madness bolstered arguments for increased policing of southern Black populations, DeLombard explains, "print coverage of the Southampton uprising left little doubt that the problem with the slaveholding South was not that it lagged behind the industrialized North, but that it produced the wrong thing. Rather than virtuous Christian citizens that disciplined free labor was supposed to yield, the peculiar institution appeared to be in the business of speedily and efficiently churning out criminals and victims" (*Shadows* 183). Of even greater significance along the lines of DeLombard's argument is that Turner's *Confessions*, related documents, and the laws of Virginia reveal that not only did the peculiar institution churn out criminals and victims, but enslaved Black people convicted of crimes became de facto enemies of the state. By implying that the rebels' attacks were random, Gray attempted to demonstrate proof of the possibility that similar massacres would occur in the future, a sentiment echoing the newspapers. For Gray and the newspapers, the promotion of fear was a way to justify even more increased surveillance and decreased freedoms for Black people. This sounds familiar to us in our current time, but as historian Isaac Land has shown, the relation between fear and the power to police oppressively extends to the beginnings of US history.[11]

The racialization of fear is particular to this project. Land, referring to fellow historian Bryan Rommel-Ruiz's work on the Turner revolt, reminds us that "[Gray's] invocation of mental illness as a way to isolate terrorist attacks from their political context was a classic maneuver," one that played a role in the Virginia legislature's acceptance of the "argument that the root cause of the revolts was not slavery but 'leniency'" (10). Land argues, "equat[ing] the enemy with a public health menace ... implied that the war on terrorism was against an entire (subhuman) population" (6). The notion of the enemy as a sort of disease affecting the health of the state runs through proslavery arguments (medical, religious, and political alike), but it may not mean that the proslavery writers perceived this "public health menace" as "subhuman."

Many scholars have discussed the dehumanizing forces of slavery, and yet critical disability studies scholar Stefanie Hunt-Kennedy argues that "slavery disabled (discursively and materially) the human, rather than created a dehumanized object ... [and] that in order to justify the systematic exploitation, persecution, and murder of an entire group of people (blacks in this instance), the perpetrators of systematized racist violence constructed a danger based on anthropological uncertainty" (6). DeLombard distinguishes the concepts of human and person legally and culturally to argue that "detaching 'human' from 'person' requires us to think far more deeply about not just slavery but the complex interrelationship of nineteenth-century American law and culture. For if Americans did not define 'slave' by simply opposing that concept to 'human,' they *did* tend to understand 'citizen' and even 'person' in definitive opposition to 'slave'" ("Very Idea" 31). In this light, the context of rights and the enslaved Black person charged with or convicted of a crime as the de facto public enemy is more complicated than a white perception of Black people as subhuman. This might explain the philosophical footwork white supremacists felt was required to justify their exploitative actions and their notions of Black enmity, madness being a feature of that rubric (on Black perception/enactment of citizenship in the antebellum era, see Jones; Spires).

Even into the century following the publication of *The Confessions*, the desire to find something peculiar about Turner's state of mind found its way into discussions about his skull. Historian Daina Ramey Berry considers Turner's postmortem and the preservation of his cranium, hypothesizing that "Turner's skull was likely trafficked through a domestic trade that similarly brought his remains through multiple states and facilities, where it was either displayed or examined" (106). Quoting from William Sidney Drewry's *The Southampton Insurrection* (1900), Berry continues: "Nearly seventy years after his execution, at the turn of the twentieth century, many people claimed they had seen Turner's skull. They noted that it 'was very peculiarly shaped, resembling the head of a sheep and at least three-quarters of an inch thick.' They seemed to want to find something different about Turner, something that would explain his behavior and justify their view of him as a monster" (106). The seeming desperation with which people endeavored to prove Turner's madness extended to an examination of his physical body, revealing the danger his narrative posed to proslavery and white supremacist ideology in his own time and beyond. Virginia law of Turner's time signals the state's deep-seated efforts to secure and maintain white supremacist interests in the face of obviously contradictory logic.

Turner's mental state remains of great scholarly interest; however, some have argued that despite the "ravings" contained in the published *Confessions*, he is part of a much longer trajectory of US political movements ostensibly prompted by divine inspiration (see Kilgore). Similar to Jonathan Plummer, who attributes Pomp's actions to "religious fanaticism" (Wood 161; see ch. 2), Turner's amanuensis, Gray, also attributes the violence to the leader's "fanaticism" (41). The failure of their contemporary white amanuenses and perhaps readership to see the intellectual work behind the actions and transcribed accounts of Pomp and Turner implies a reluctance to acknowledge the critique these men's works and words pronounce. Both men referred to their own communications with forces beyond their immediate physical world; readers implicated in these critiques, however, rejected the validity of these experiences as anything other than violent manifestations of mental distress, refusing to see them as responses to the systemic and individual violence of slaveholding—even as early white inhabitants of the United States had long sought and believed in violent providential guidance. Furthermore, cultural demarcations of sanity and madness reflect cultural biases, particularly regarding Blackness.

American studies scholar La Marr Jurelle Bruce theorizes "psychosocial madness." He explains: "acts and attributes such as insurgent blackness, slave rebellion, willful womanhood, anticolonial resistance, same-sex desire, and gender subversion have all been ostracized as *crazy* by sane majorities who adhere to Reasonable common sense... psychosocial madness is sometimes an *unruliness of will* that resists and unsettles reigning regimes of the normal" (8).[12] This reorientation of the divide between Reason and unreason helps contextualize Turner's work in the revolt and his characterization as inhabiting what Bruce refers to as "epistemic alterity.... As portrayed in 'Confessions,' Turner traverses a genius | prophet | madman triptych, partitioned by those proverbially thin lines that separate madness from genius and lunacy from prophecy" (21). The resonance here with Pomp regarding lunacy and prophecy is palpable. Questioning such demarcations allows us to see how, as Bruce explains through a reading of Toni Morrison's *Beloved* (1987), "Reason is benefactor of white supremacy," with "merciless cruelty [committed] under the auspices of Reasonable inquiry and scientific method" (19-20). Bruce's reading of Morrison's novelization of the antebellum Margaret Garner story underscores widely held Enlightenment assumptions about uppercase *R* Reason and its ramifications for enslaved and imprisoned Black people in the late eighteenth and nineteenth centuries.

Before and after publication of *The Confessions*, newspapers reported widely on the events and debated or tried to control their meaning. In numerous ways Turner's legacy suggests that his work resisted that control. Within nineteen weeks, from the first killings through to the end of the year 1831, a total of 242 newspaper articles about the revolt were published in Virginia, South Carolina, Maryland, the District of Columbia, New York, Massachusetts, and Rhode Island (Gabrial 363–64). The work of revolt inspired the work of media interpretation and management. Early Black references to the events of 1831 reveal the powerful and complicated impact of the uprising on the imagination. Frederick Douglass, though only making brief mention of the uprising, notes that "the insurrection of Nathaniel Turner had been quelled, but the alarm and terror had not subsided" (*My Bondage* 165). No references to the revolt appear in his first autobiography. If this is a cautious omission, then perhaps it is also indicative of the rippling effects of the events that spilled into the decade following. As literary critic Robert S. Levine points out, Douglass himself regretted that he was unlike John Brown, who was willing to die for Douglass's people: "I could live for my race—John Brown could die for my race" (quoted in Levine 185). Given Turner's inspiring effect on Brown and Douglass's fantasy of himself as the mutinous Madison Washington in his 1852 novella *The Heroic Slave*, we can imagine the impact of the figure of the rebel leader (with Turner a prominent if uncomfortable example) in the mind of one of the nineteenth century's greatest thinkers. Indeed, Douglass caught flack from *New York Age* editor T. Thomas Fortune for suggesting the erection of a monument honoring John Brown and not Nathaniel Turner (see French 152). Harriet Jacobs, William Wells Brown, and Martin R. Delany, among other leading Black thinkers, addressed the revolt throughout the decades following. Brown shifted his position on Turner over the years: in 1863, he noted that those who had condemned Turner in 1831 had begun to applaud his work, and then twenty years later Brown himself depicted Turner as a madman (French 128, 148). The revolt leader's symbolic role fluctuated over time, yet as the Civil War (1861–65) approached, his image signaled the unparalleled bloodshed to come. The intellectual work of the revolt and its articulation in *The Confessions* inspired the belief that the South could fall under armed Black and antislavery resistance and that it was possible that the last should be first after all.

As Brown noted in his first discussion of Turner, the revolt leader's legacy offered hope in the lead-up to the Civil War. Caleb Smith explains, "The struggle, the *Anglo-African* argued, would go on until the system of slavery was abolished: 'The course which the South is now pursuing, will engender in its bosom and nurse into maturity a hundred Nat Turners, whom Virginia is infinitely less able to resist in 1860, than she was in 1831.' Turner had sought 'in the air, the earth and the heavens, for signs which came at last.' More and more, he seemed like the prophet of an irresistible violence that was about to engulf the land" (*Oracle* 176). If antebellum Virginia sought with all its might to deny Turner the status of martyrdom, by the time the Civil War approached it had failed. Fifty-five years after the war, a 1920 assessment of the events of Southampton concluded, "Considered in the light of its immediate effect upon its participants, [the insurrection] was a failure, an egregious failure, a wanton crime. Considered in its necessary relation to slavery and as contributory to making it a national issue by deepening and stirring of the then weak local forces, that finally led to the Emancipation Proclamation and the Thirteenth Amendment, the insurrection was a moral success and Nat Turner deserves to be ranked with the greatest reformers of his day" (Cromwell 232). By the early twentieth century, Turner's intellectual resonance seemed to have influenced watershed moments in US history.

The revolt's one-hundredth anniversary "served as a rallying point for Communist Party organizers, eager to cast their appeal to black Southern workers within the idiom of black folk culture and black history. The Turner centenary coincided with the Communist Party legal defense of 'the Scottsboro boys,' a landmark civil rights case that began in March 1931 and dragged on more than fifteen years" (French 195). The work of Turner, his *Confessions*, and the other rebels has over time influenced law, medicine, literature, art, film, activism, and politics. The intellectual work of the revolt itself and Turner's printed *Confessions* is, perhaps unfortunately, as valuable for understanding injustice today as it was in 1831 and a hundred years later in 1931.

Turner's longer story remains unknown. It's obvious he wanted to tell his tale in much greater detail, almost in literary fashion. After detailing his capture and imprisonment, he concludes his narration to Gray with this: "During my time I was pursued, I had many hair breadth escapes, which your time will not permit you to relate. I am here loaded with chains, and willing to suffer the fate that awaits me" (53). His conclusion in some ways is as dramatic as his revolt. In the next chapter, I turn to *Missouri v. Celia, a Slave* (1855) to consider how enslavement and armed Black resistance reconfigure the tradition of the Black prison intellectual when the individual is a woman.

4

Nearly Six Months Imprisoned

Celia's Textual and Embodied Intellectualism in Missouri's Callaway County Jail (1855)

Celia a slave, belonging to Robert Newsom being sworn says that she killed her master on the night of the 23rd day of June 1855—about two hours after dark by striking him twice on the head with a stick, and then put his body on the fire and burnt it nearly up. Then took up the ashes in the morning after daylight, after breakfast, the bones were not entirely burnt up. I took up the ashes and bones out of the fire place in my Cabin where I burnt the body and emptied them on the right hand side of the path leading from my cabin to the stable

her
Celia   X
mark

State of Missouri v. Celia, a Slave (1855)

As soon as I struck him the devil got into me, and I struck him with the stick until he was dead, and then rolled him into the fire and burnt him up!

Celia, quoted in the *Baltimore Sun* (January 17, 1856)

The long-overlooked case *State of Missouri v. Celia, a Slave* (1855) has since the early 2000s come into scholarly and popular consciousness as a legal window into the sexual politics and economics of US slavery (see A. Davis; Hartman; McLaurin; Stone, *Black Well-Being*; *The Celia Project*).[1] The wealthy, recently widowed farmer Robert Newsom purchased Celia in 1850 when she was approximately fourteen years old.[2] According to trial testimony, Newsom raped Celia on their way back to his home. There she joined five male slaves on Newsom's eight-hundred-acre farm. A Callaway County slave ledger dated August 1, 1850, lists the farmer as owning five slaves, three of whom were identified as being of mixed race and two as Black, their ages ranging from just five years old to thirty-one (Callaway). Once Celia began living at the farm, she resided in a separate brick cabin with the other enslaved inhabitants of the farm. Newsom continued to abuse Celia for five years, until she killed him. Between the ages of fourteen and nineteen, Celia bore two children, at least one fathered by Newsom. She also gave birth to a stillborn child while in jail awaiting trial for the man's murder. Based on trial testimony indicating that another enslaved man on the farm, George, threatened to leave her if she didn't stop seeing "the old man," it has been assumed that they were romantic partners (Callaway). Celia insisted that George had nothing to do with Newsom's killing, but it's unclear whether they were actually romantically involved. On June 23, 1855, Celia—pregnant, sick, and weighed down by George's demands—warned Newsom not to come to her cabin, threatening to hurt him if he did. He disregarded her warning, to his peril. When he entered, she hit him with a stick, killing him with a second blow. According to testimony she rolled him into her fireplace and burned his body, enlisting his grandson to dispose of the ashes the following day.

The two confessions that form the epigraphs to this chapter, as far as we know, contain the only extant directly quoted words from Celia. The first example, her deposition, was taken down shortly after her arrest; the second was voiced on the eve of her execution, almost six months later. This latter quotation was originally published in the *Fulton Telegraph* (not extant), and then reprinted in Baltimore and New York newspapers. Similar to Pomp's and Nathaniel Turner's confessions, Celia's also involve an amanuensis, whose own words guide or interpret hers. We have seen the methods through which Jonathan Plummer and Thomas Gray tried to control the reading of Pomp's and Turner's dying words, particularly in interpreting the two men's mental states as related to their acts of killing. We have far fewer of Celia's own dying words, and by contrast, we also have two presumably different amanuenses (the circuit court employee and the newspaper reporter). Her words in these confessions, though brief and largely overlooked by comparison, actually offer tremendous insight into Celia's character, especially when read in conjunction with study of her time in jail.[3]

To date, most scholarship about the case has focused on the trial; the scraps of information about circumstances leading up to Newsom's killing, his sexual abuse of Celia, and George's potential role in the course of events;

and the harsh daily realities of Black women's enslavement. In this chapter, I want to shift the focus somewhat to an aspect of the narrative of Celia's life that has so far received little attention. From the time of Celia's arrest on June 25, 1855, through to her execution on December 21, 1855, she spent six months in county jail in Fulton, Missouri, apart from two weeks spent at large after escaping. This chapter reads Celia's time in jail along with her two confessions against the broader Black prison intellectual tradition, in order to demonstrate the importance of reading the actions of forerunners of this tradition when we have few of their words. Viewing the illiterate and enslaved Celia as a thinker in light of this book's readings of Pomp and Turner prompts us to consider her actions in enslavement and in jail as a kind of intellectual labor. Conceiving of "Celia, as imprisoned" reveals aspects of her character that readings of "Celia, a slave"—as the court documents identify her—might have overlooked about the woman, her circumstances, and her navigation of mid-nineteenth-century Missouri law and culture. Imagining Celia as both enslaved and imprisoned, as were Pomp and Turner, expands our understanding of midcentury antebellum US conceptualizations of criminals and enemies, particularly regarding race, gender, and domestic violence. The concept of embodied intellectualism highlights the work of Black knowledge, particularly by those convicted of crimes, when it wasn't given the status of intellectual product.

Celia's Case and Context

A June 25, 1855, report from the *Missouri Republican* described what it dubbed the "Fiendish Murder" of Robert Newsom:

> A most violent act was committed on the person of ROBERT NEWSOM, of this county, on Saturday night last, 23d inst., at his residence, eight miles South of this. He was murdered by one of his own slaves, a negro woman, in the kitchen—supposed, some time during the night—and his body entirely consumed by fire in the kitchen fireplace, and the ashes taken up, next morning and deposited in the back yard. His body appears, so far as discovery can be made, to have been entirely consumed, except a few small bones, found in the pile of ashes, including a part of his skull bone and the extremities of some of his fingers. The murder was committed, without any sufficient cause, so far as I can hear. Mr. Newsom was an old citizen of the county, about sixty years of age, and very active and energetic in his business.

He possessed a valuable farm, and had accumulated a very handsome estate. The woman confessed to the murder on Sunday (yesterday) evening, and is in the hands of the law.

This report indicates that Newsom was killed in the kitchen of the main house.[4] This detail has been understood as a fabrication the family likely offered to preempt any suggestion of sexual impropriety on the part of its patriarch. However, there was a kitchen in Celia's cabin. It was likely that she did the cooking for the family, and kitchens were often located in outbuildings for safety reasons (if there were a fire in the kitchen, it would be less likely to spread to the main house). Both trial testimony and an account book, in fact, suggest an "exterior kitchen" (Halpern 130). A separate cookhouse may also explain how Celia was able to burn up Newsom's body. The connection between fire and escape here is one that will come up again while Celia is in jail. When Celia killed Newsom and burned his body, she performed one kind of escape from the immediate sexual abuses of enslavement. Later, she used fire to perform another escape from imprisonment.

Newsom putatively purchased Celia as a domestic servant, but it seems that many knew that the older man had other motives for buying the young woman. The newspaper report also indicates that as far as the writer could tell, there was no "sufficient cause" for Celia having dispatched Newsom, a point that Celia's defense team would later try to refute, arguing that she killed Newsom in self-defense. Much like in ads for capture, the trope of unmotivated Black-on-white attacks we read in white-authored interpretations of Pomp's and Turner's actions and here in newspaper coverage of Celia's action ostensibly deflects attention from the possibility that Black violence occurs in response to white violence. Celia's attorneys would attempt to focus the jury's attention squarely on that scenario of defense. Missouri law at the time afforded women the right to protect themselves from unwanted sexual advances, but with the combination of a prejudiced presiding judge, an increasingly tense battle between pro- and antislavery factions in Missouri, and a slew of other miscarriages of justice, Celia was convicted and sentenced to hang. In the end, she was understood as incapable of occupying the statute's category of "any woman" and therefore rendered legally powerless to defend herself against sexual violence.

After Celia killed Newsom, she was newly freed from the abuses of her enslaver, yet also newly imprisoned in the county jail. Her confinement complicated her status, as she became both enslaved and imprisoned (the latter being easier to escape than the former). In the mid-1800s, alongside the ongoing practice of chattel slavery, the United States saw the rise of the prison system, in which "poor and alien white men constituted the majority of antebellum America's prisoners, North and South" (Ayers 61); the two practices would meld after emancipation in the form of convict leasing programs, which I'll address in the interlude and following chapter. This book has demonstrated how Abraham Johnstone, Pomp, and Turner heralded the Black prison intellectual tradition, which would be taken up by more famous figures in the twentieth and twenty-first centuries. Celia continues in this early tradition. Her case also took on a political significance that extended beyond her subject position as an individual person who had defended herself against rape and as the property of Robert Newsom. In the six-month period she spent in the Callaway County jail, she gave birth to a stillborn child, escaped, and aided two other imprisoned people in their attempts to escape. There is also evidence that she may have plotted her killing of Newsom in advance.

Focus on Celia's time in jail puts her in the company of many imprisoned Black people both before and after her who have better resembled political prisoners than criminals (see Fuentes, esp. ch. 1; Haley). Even though Celia could neither read nor write, she is a leader in what would become the Black prison intellectual tradition for her actions and for what they say about her politically, ideologically, and personally—as an enslaved Black woman, a mother, and a defender of Black human rights. The editors of *Toward an Intellectual History of Black Women* (2015) acknowledge that "the field of intellectual history has until now resisted embracing the implications of the new work on African American women," and the volume itself demonstrates "how ideas have been crucial to Black women in their efforts to navigate both the double jeopardy of race and gender and the uncertain forms of citizenship often accorded to their group" (Bay et al. 4). Celia certainly navigated such terrain, and represents an ancestor from the carceral institution that is the site of so much Black intellectual work. That we don't have as many of her written ideas as we wish we did means that we must trace them through the words we do have in concert with her actions as she strategized to resist and accommodate myriad threats. The previous chapter examined terrorism in the context of Nathaniel Turner and the Southampton, Virginia, revolt of 1831. This chapter contends that Celia lived under the reign of a specific kind of terror while Newsom owned, abused, and raped her. She defended herself from domestic violence—domestic here meaning both within the slave state of Missouri and within the home, sexual abuse in the latter a byproduct of the laws of the former. Celia's act of self-defense;

her confessions, legal defense, and conviction; her conduct in jail, the newspaper coverage; and her state-sanctioned execution reveal that her actions were not only personally necessary but also politically vital. In reading Celia's words and actions, we see the confluence of social history and intellectual history. Many of us have tried to piece together her life on Newsom's farm and gone over the details of her trial and conviction, but we haven't yet considered in much detail her time in the county jail, an important if transitory stage in Celia's all-too-brief life. Through this lens we see another dimension of Celia, one that increases our understanding of the depth and complexity of her character and her legacy as a critique of slavery and criminal justice.

Celia Inside

As I've mentioned, we know that Celia gave birth to a stillborn child while in jail, but it is unclear how far along the pregnancy was when she delivered the baby. The trial testimony indicates that Celia had been sick since February 1855.[5] Newsom's daughter Virginia Winscott explained during her testimony that "Celia had been sick. Took sick in February. Had been sick ever since. Had not been able to work since February" (Callaway).[6] If the illness referred to in Winscott's testimony coincided with the early days of Celia's pregnancy, that would mean that she was approximately four to five months pregnant at the time she killed Newsom, approximately seven to eight months pregnant during her trial, and approximately eight to nine months pregnant around the time she delivered the stillborn child in jail. She would have carried the child nearly to term. This, Celia's third pregnancy, had the potential to delay her hanging, as Missouri law prohibited the execution of pregnant people in prison. Even though it is impossible to know exactly how far into the pregnancy Celia was during the events, what we do know is that she was ill and pregnant for at least part of the time she was in jail. When we consider the horrific conditions of Missouri county jails at the time, we get a sense of the severity of Celia's time inside.

The first common jail in Callaway County was a log building in the original county seat of Elizabeth, completed in May 1828. It was supposed to have been moved to Fulton after the county seat moved there, but the jail burned down before its removal. There is record of four other jails being built in the area, one of them in 1861, but nothing else is known (*History* 118–19). With so little information about the jail in which Celia was imprisoned, we must rely on accounts of contemporaneous US prisons and jails to get a sense of the conditions she faced. Three important works give a more detailed impression of what the Callaway County jail would have been like in the mid-nineteenth century: George Thompson's 1847 memoir of his and two other white men's imprisonment in a Missouri penitentiary after having been convicted for attempting to help enslaved people attain freedom; Blake McKelvey's 1936 history of prisons; and E. C. Wines and Theodore Dwight's 1867 *Report on the Prisons and Reformatories of the United States and Canada*. Of particular importance is the authors' attention to county jails. Penitentiaries and jails differed in midcentury Missouri, and it is perhaps not surprising to know that the jails presented far worse conditions for those imprisoned in them than did the penitentiaries, which were awful enough. Reading these accounts and reports in conjunction with one another facilitates a strong sense of what the conditions of the Callaway County jail might have been like for all those confined there, but in particular for Celia: Black, pregnant, sick, and jailed for defending herself against her enslaver's sexual violence.

To put Missouri penitentiaries and jails in perspective, a broader history of US prisons is helpful. Wines and Dwight refer to government-sponsored reports of American prisons authored by Gustave de Beaumont and Alexis de Tocqueville (1833) of France, William Crawford (1835) of England, Nikolaus Heinrich Julius (1836) of Prussia, and Frédéric-Auguste Demetz and Guillaume-Abel Blouet (1837) of France. Wines and Dwight remark in their chapter on county jails: "The several European commissions, which visited the United States some thirty odd years ago to examine our penitentiary system, while commending American state prisons as at that time far in advance of the same class of institutions in Europe, both in their organization and working, speak of our county jails as among the worst prisons they had ever anywhere seen. From the observations we have made in our own and other states, we fear that there has been little improvement in this class of prisons within the last generation" (314). McKelvey's assessment of the European reports adds that "they were . . . practically unanimous in condemning the neglect of local jails, a phase of penal reform to which England in particular was already devoting careful attention" (17). Compared to facilities in other states, Missouri penitentiaries and jails had particularly dismal conditions. Overcrowding around midcentury in Missouri meant substantially worse circumstances than in Indiana and Illinois: "The convicts of Missouri were crowded into a still more unsatisfactory prison. Early state laws had directed that criminals should be punished with solitary confinement at hard labor, and when the prison was first opened at Jefferson City in 1836, 40 outside cells seemed a reasonable equipment for 46 convicts" (McKelvey 32). Eventually, the state started a program to build "236 small brick cells" in Jefferson City, "but this program was likewise delayed by the war, and Missouri has never been able to boast of possessing a satisfactory prison system" (McKelvey 32). Even the penitentiaries that the European commissions had applauded in the early 1830s only worsened over the next two decades and in the lead-up to the Civil War. "Of all the northern states, Missouri maintained the most diabolical prison conditions" (McKelvey 82). All told, the conditions of penitentiaries and particularly jails in Missouri around the time of Celia's imprisonment were among the worst in the country.

Wines and Dwight, who visited and compared jails in cities such as Detroit, Chicago, and St. Louis, give a sense of the day-to-day conditions Celia would have experienced in the Callaway County jail. Discussing jails in Chicago, they describe how "the cells were dark, without ventilation, and swarming with vermin. Some were so foul that, after a few minutes stay in them, we felt a sickening sensation. Yet in these close and filthy abodes human beings, crowded together are confined for days, weeks, months even, many of whom are afterwards adjudged to be innocent" (316–17). I mention their assessment of Chicago jails because they then turn to the county jail in St. Louis, Missouri, stating that it "is in even a worse condition than that at Chicago. It has been . . . regularly presented as a nuisance, once every two months, by the grand jury of St. Louis, for the last ten years. . . . Not one solitary redeeming feature is found in it" (318). The timing of the report—published in 1867 and assessing conditions over the previous decade—puts the findings very close to the time of Celia's imprisonment in Fulton in 1855. St. Louis boasted a much larger population than Fulton, but conditions in the county jail in the larger city still reveal much about what those imprisoned in Missouri county jails more broadly would have faced. The report continues to detail the particulars of cell size, number of inmates, hygiene, light, and food consumption:

> The cells are eight feet square and ten high; and furnished with a bunk and one stool or chair. At the time of our visit, each of these cells contained from three to six inmates; the average number, we were informed, is about four. All the light and air, admitted for the use of the human beings packed into these apartments, come through a slit in the wall, three and a half inches wide by about five feet high. The bunk may hold three persons, if they are well crowded together;

all beyond that number must sleep on the floor. There is no sewage; everything must be carried out, as well as brought in by hand. There is no water-closet for the prisoners; and only once a day is the slop bucket removed, whatever sickness may prevail; the rest of the time it remains in the cell, covered with a filthy cloth. Two meals a day are handed in tin pans, to be eaten in the cells. (Wines and Dwight 328)

To imagine the darkness, poor ventilation, and raw sewage lingering in an eight-by-ten-foot cell containing several people is miserable; then add to it Celia's illness and pregnancy, and the image is even more horrifying. By no means is this to overlook the conditions Celia experienced during her enslavement on the Newsom farm; rather, my goal is to demonstrate what she likely endured in the shift from the farm to the jail.

Perhaps more representative of jails generally across the state is the jail at Jefferson City, which Wines and Dwight visited in 1865, ten and a half years after Celia's execution. It seems that the smaller the jails, the worse their conditions. Callaway County's would have been smaller than St. Louis's or Jefferson City's, and we can imagine an even worse situation where Celia was than what we read from these accounts:

We visited [the Jefferson City jail] in August 1865, with mingled feelings of horror and disgust. It has but two rooms for prisoners. The largest is only fifteen feet by fourteen, with a ceiling not, we think, exceeding eight feet in height; which gives 1,680 cubic feet. . . . Into this kennel, this dungeon, whenever there happen to be female prisoners, are thrust all the men and boys who are in confinement, each one has just 112 cubic feet of air for his use, and a space on the floor at night two feet wide by seven feet long. . . . This jail at Jefferson city, we were told, is a fair specimen of the county prisons throughout Missouri. It was a relief to be informed that there are many counties in the state, which have no jails. It would be a blessing if what there are could be utterly demolished. (319)

This report's representative impression of Missouri jails gives us much insight into the overcrowding, poor ventilation, and filth people imprisoned there would have experienced.

Wines and Dwight conclude their chapter on Missouri institutions with the assessment that "our state prisons need many and great reforms . . . but the reforms needed in our jails and jail systems are, literally legion" (332). The account here also tells us that in these closed spaces men and women prisoners would be separated—a relatively recent development in part spurred by the 1825 fatal beating of a pregnant woman, Rachel Welch, at the hands of a male guard in Auburn State Prison, New York (Mallicoat 462). Other accounts of jails commensurate with the time of Celia's imprisonment indicate that men and women still were not separated, and furthermore that women were often left in unlocked cells that other imprisoned people or guards could enter, both men and women.

We know only of two Black people in the jail at the time, Celia and Mat, and Celia may well have been the only woman inmate, possibly the only pregnant inmate. The compounding sense of fear, loneliness, isolation, and vulnerability Celia likely experienced offers a bleak picture, to say the least. George Thompson's section titled "Female Prisoners" gives insight into the experience of a white, pregnant incarcerated woman he and his friends met in the Missouri penitentiary where they were imprisoned—as mentioned, by all accounts the penitentiaries in Missouri offered much better conditions than the jails. The woman was arrested for killing her husband, sentenced to five years, and pardoned after nearly two.[7] Thompson explains that the woman was taken outside to work for a Judge B. for approximately four months. He continues:

> In the fall she became the mother of a daughter. The doctor refused to be present at the time of her delivery. Mrs. Brown [the judge's wife] would neither come nor let any one else attend—the overseer told one of the prisoners to assist her—who did so, and he was the only one to wait upon her for some time. Mrs. B. refused to come near her, or to furnish any materials for the child's clothing—so that she remained in her cold cell, with her child, for nearly a week before any thing was done. Nor was she allowed to have any fire during the cold winter weather—but suffered in her damp and chilly cell, till she was pardoned out! The whole is a horrid, disgraceful affair, on all sides. (318)

The abusive treatment of this white woman who allegedly killed her husband and was then was pardoned casts into relief how much worse Celia's situation very likely would have been delivering her stillborn baby in the Callaway County jail as a Black enslaved woman imprisoned for killing her enslaver in the slaveholding state of Missouri.

It is also possible that Celia's sexual abuse did not end with Newsom's death. Accounts of the mixing of sexes in Missouri jails (Wines and Dwight 332) and Thompson's description of the prison system's disregard for sexual abuses inside indicate that Celia may have found herself vulnerable to sexual violence in the jail. Thompson's reflection reads: "The next was a colored women. She arrived in the night, and was locked in a cell with three wicked vile men!" (319). Here the implication is that the "three wicked vile men" in question would have had the freedom to do what they liked with the woman locked in the cell with them, and that certainly the wardens had no concern for her safety or well-being; sexual violence was a possibility. "She was then placed in the wash-house, to work with two wicked men—if in her cell by day, it was unlocked, so that any prisoner could visit her, or any guard by night!" (319). Stressed here also is the woman's Blackness and enslaved status. "Now *why* is she treated in this manner? 'O! she is nothing but a *n——r!*' And what respect is paid to a '*n——r's*' purity in a slave State? Many other things might be mentioned respecting the abominable treatment of these women, but I must pass along" (319, dashes mine). Celia's relation to Newsom and his abuse of her were part of the trial record. Weak, ill, and pregnant in the county jail, Celia may have been subject to any number of abuses and violence—verbal, physical, sexual, or emotional—by guards and other imprisoned people. This context provides an even more substantial motive for Celia to flee the jail.

Celia's Escape

Celia's execution was set for November 16, 1855, and she escaped the Callaway County jail a few days earlier. If the conditions in Fulton were even close to the scenes depicted in St. Louis and Jefferson City, and with her execution looming, it is no wonder that Celia planned or at least participated in an escape. A letter from Celia's defense team requesting a stay of execution refers to this escape:

> Enclosed we send you a copy of the Record in the case of State v Celia a slave which we wish you to examine and if you think it proper order a Stay of Execution until the case can be tried in the Supreme Court, in January next. You will see by the Record that she (Celia) was sentenced to be hung on the 16th of last month (November). But in consequence of her escape from prison, or in other words, taken out by some one a few days before the time set for her execution, and her not being taken until after the 16th Nov another day the 21st of this month has been set for her execution. (Callaway)

The defense attorneys, a Jameson and colleagues, imply that someone outside likely aided Celia's escape as well as her return, and most scholars seem to agree with this assessment. However, newspaper coverage contradicts this assumption, indicating that Celia not only orchestrated the escape, but helped a young boy and a man escape as well. These accounts provide strikingly different images of Celia.

In light of the request for the stay of execution and the conditions of Missouri jails and prisons generally, we can imagine Celia as a sick, pregnant young woman suffering all manner of abuses and inhumane conditions while incarcerated, and then ushered out by some friend in the community just days before her scheduled execution. The image and circumstances are certainly believable, and we can readily imagine Celia's desperation before the murder, as well as the fleeting moments of relief she might have felt at arriving at the jail (perhaps similar to Pomp's experience) and out of Newsom's control, and then again on her removal from the jail. The sense of camaraderie offered by some person or persons in the community in conjunction with the support of her defense team reveals a heartening picture of the network of support Celia received despite her enslaved status, her action of killing an enslaver, and her position as an unmarried pregnant young woman. The newspaper accounts, however, provide a different image of Celia, one much more independently driven to survive, physically capable, strong, smart, and compassionate.[8]

Of all extant Missouri newspapers for the time surrounding Celia's imprisonment, eight refer to her escape or her aid in other people's attempts. Some accounts are reprints of others—some verbatim, some with slight modifications—and others are unique. Most assume that Celia was aided in her escape, but taken together these reports depict Celia as instrumental in the attempted or successful escape of at least three people, including herself. It appears that Celia fled on Sunday, November 11, and was returned to the jail on Sunday, November 25. On Friday, November 9, newspapers reported that Celia also aided in the escape attempt of a man named Thomas Carlisle.

A commonly reprinted account of Carlisle's escape attempt, "Jail Break and a Race," reads:

> Thomas Carlisle, who has been in jail at this place for the last six months awaiting trial under various indictments, made an unsuccessful attempt to escape the punishment of his crimes and thereby defeat the ends of justice. On Friday morning last, while Mr. Anderson, the jailor, was providing for the temporal wants of the prisoners under his charge, Thomas conceived the idea of "creating a space" in the cell appropriated for his benefit. Accordingly, while Mr. A. was procur-

ing some coal, wherewith to warm the "outer man" of the aforesaid Thomas, assisted by the negro woman, Celia, he opened the doors of his cell and decamped. (*Daily Missouri Democrat*, 20 Nov. 1855)[9]

There are at least two ways to read this report: first, that Celia aided the jailor, and second, that she aided Carlisle. It stands to reason that if Celia was the only woman in the jail, she may have had duties such as cooking, similar to the work she did on Newsom's farm, but possibly affording her a different status in the jail, one that might have given her access to areas outside her cell and also meant different sorts of labor. If Anderson is the source of this report, we might read in this an intimation of the ungratefulness of those imprisoned as they attempted an escape while the jailor was tending to their needs. Of course, the likely condition of the jail makes it difficult to read Anderson's "providing for the temporal wants of the prisoners under his charge" as anything more than the provision of the most basic of wants, more likely needs.

Carlisle's effort occurred two days before Celia made her escape. We can speculate that she was inspired by Carlisle's attempt, or that word of Carlisle's near escape motivated Celia's friends on the outside to retrieve her, or that Celia had been plotting her escape for a much longer time and test-drove a method on Carlisle, or some combination of all three. These theories open up possibilities for interpreting Celia's moves in the days leading up to her scheduled execution. Given the appalling state of Missouri jails, the looming day of her hanging, and her and others' belief that she was unjustly and according to her lawyers illegally convicted, it is easy to imagine why Celia would try everything possible and risk what little she had left to flee the jail while her lawyers were seeking a new trial.

The defense attorneys' request for a stay of execution indicates their unwavering faith that Celia was the victim not only of Newsom's sexual violence, but also of an illegal trial. Their letter concludes: "We feel more than ordinary interest in behalf of the girl Celia, believing that she did the act to prevent a forced sexual interference on the part of Newsome. Indeed, the greater portion of the community here are much interested in her behalf, and we feel satisfied that you will upon examination of the Record find that the court gave illegal instructions as well as refused such as were plainly the law, indeed cut out all means of defense—you will please give the matter your earliest attention" (Callaway). This letter suggests that there was community support for Celia, and, combined with the assumption earlier in the letter that someone helped her escape, we have a portrayal of at least part of the larger community that sought to fight the injustices she faced. The rallying around Celia anticipates later campaigns to free Angela Davis, Assata Shakur, Rubin "Hurricane" Carter, and so many others, although Celia's campaign was less formally organized than these later examples. But what they have in common is that they all involved the cooperation of defense attorneys, community activists, and determined, smart, and courageous imprisoned people. This is one way we can see Celia join Johnstone, Pomp, and Turner as a predecessor to this broader tradition of Black prison intellectuals, whom the state conceives of as enemies of the people and whose individual actions take on political significance beyond their own cases. Accounts of Celia's escape point to these very qualities.

The *Fulton Telegraph* report of Celia's escape, which was reprinted in other papers and is quoted in full below, gives a sense of her ingenuity. Regardless of whether she was aided, she was the only one of the three people who escaped on this day to avoid capture, a testament to outside support for her cause, but also to her strategy and determination, either in collaboration with others or on her own. The report, under the heading "Escaped from Jail," explains:

> Two of the prisoners confined in the jail at this place, made their escape on Sunday night last, about 11 o'clock—Matt and Celia. They effected it by burning a hole in the door around the lock. A large quantity of shucks which had been in the woman's bed were found about the door, some of them considerably charred.—These were perhaps used for the purpose of making a light while the door was being burnt with some more solid substance. The boy, Matt, only went a short distance from town, and was brought back by a gentleman at whose house he stayed. The woman has not yet been caught—They were, most likely, assisted in their efforts to escape from the outside. Celia was sentenced to be hung to-day (Friday). (16 Nov. 1855)

Evidence found in her bed in the jail and noted in this report shows that Celia likely orchestrated the escape and the method of burning the door around the lock. Notably, Celia's escape may have been more successful than Carlisle's because she chose to make hers on a Sunday night at eleven o'clock, unlike Carlisle, who attempted to flee midmorning on Friday, while the jailor Anderson was nearby. Additionally, though it is unclear from this report of the escape, the young boy whom Celia helped had also been enslaved and, like Celia, had been convicted of murder. Perhaps there was a sense of camaraderie between the two.

We know from slave narratives and Pomp's and Turner's examples the transformative coming into consciousness of people when they first understand their enslaved condition. Celia and Mat (sometimes spelled Matt) may have shared in the jail a recognition of what their status as both enslaved and imprisoned meant. Mat was the age of the boy on the Newsom farm, and this may have held a particular significance for Celia, the mother of two children and likely a carer for the youngest enslaved person in her company. As well, Celia was only three years older than Mat when Newsom bought her and began to rape and abuse her. Nevertheless, there may have been no real affinity between Mat and Celia. Their relationship in the jail may have been mainly transactional as they helped each other escape. Such a line of thought prompts us to rethink George's role in Newsom's death and the disposal of his body. Perhaps George doesn't represent another layer of Celia's exploitation by men. Maybe she enlisted him to help her and then instructed him to take off so he wouldn't be punished. Celia's charging the grandson with the task of cleaning away the ashes also might represent no more than a pragmatic move to involve someone inculpable.

Testimony from George transcribed in a self-published 1967 history of Callaway County by local judge Hugh P. Williamson offers more details about the circumstances leading up to Newsom's killing.[10] George's deposition implies that Celia may have planned to kill Newsom and thought it through with a friend. George and an enslaved woman Malinda who lived in the same county on the property of her enslaver, Jordan Bush, both faced charges with being accessories to Newsom's murder. The newspaper article that included Celia's printed confession refers to two people as having been exonerated; George and Malinda are presumably these two. The justice found evidence against George insufficient for conviction, and then George was called to testify against Malinda. The grand jury didn't indict Malinda either. Williamson's history transcribes George's testimony in Malinda's examination before the grand jury (27–28), which I will quote in full here:

> George, a Slave of the Estate of Robert Newsom, Deceased, being Produced sworn and examined on the part of the State deposeth, and saith that I am acquainted with Malinda slave of Jordan Bush of Callaway County State of Mizsouri and saw her at Mr. Robert Newsoms about the time of Sheep Sheering last Spring Malinda came here on Tuesday and left on Friday or Saturday following. Malinda stayed in the same room that the girl now charged with murder of Mr. Newsom did while she remained there I stayed in an adjoining room where

Malinda and Celia the girl above mentioned did the rooms we stayed in were seperated by a brick wall the wall did not reach to the roof. I could hear from my room any conversation going on in the room where Malinda & Celia was if there was no noise I heard them talking to each other during several nights they appeared to be talking about something they did not want me to hear. I heard them say they would do something to he or him I was at that time playing my fiddle and when I stoped playing they would say to me play on that they did not want me to hear what they were talking about and said they were not talking about me, the above conversations were going on every night while Malinda was at Mr. Newsoms, these conversations took place about four weeks before Mr. Newsom was killed, the girl there was talking with Malinda is the same girl now charged with the murder of Mr. Newsome. Malinda came back to Mr. Newsoms about one week after the time above mentioned. She stayed untill evening, and I went hohme with her, on the way hohm Malinda said to me that if she was in Celias place she would knock Newsom so dead that he would not know himself further this aefronart saith not

    Sworn to & subscribe before me this 18th day)   his
    of July 1855.   ) George X Newsom
    Wm. Nichols J. P.   )   mark Slave

Through George's words, we see a picture of Celia with the support of another enslaved woman, a picture of a kind of camaraderie perhaps with George as well, and more evidence that Celia was preparing to kill Newsom to protect herself and her unborn child.[11] This image of Celia fits with the woman who conspired to escape the jail and help others do the same.

The case file and reports from the *Telegraph* immediately after Celia's conviction give more information about Mat, who was convicted of the murder of a child and who escaped with Celia. The newspaper report indicates that a "boy, Matt, is now being tried for the murder of a little child. The boy is quite young, perhaps not more than twelve years of age. The child he killed (Mr. W—rmack's) was in its third year" (reprinted in *Weekly Missouri Statesman*, 19 Oct. 1855). Lorenzo J. Greene and colleagues identify this child, spelled "Mat," as "a young slave boy of eleven" who, at his enslaver's request on August 10, went to the adjacent farm, belonging to Allen Womack, to borrow equipment. The story continues that Womack's son died of head injuries later that day, after telling his father that Mat was responsible. "To obtain a confession, three neighbors took Mat into a stable and questioned him about the blood on his shirt. A rope was put around Mat's neck, and he was drawn up some four or five times. Mat was then taken to a nearby barn. There he was stripped naked and whipped until blood ran from his back in several places. Mat confessed to striking the child" (49). There is no implication of any motive for the attack on the child here, and Mat was ultimately charged with first-degree murder and jailed in July 1855. Mat's two court-appointed attorneys attempted to prove that the confession was forced, but failed.

The process of extracting Mat's confession resembles a practice called the slave picket, a torture method drawn from the sixteenth- and seventeenth-century British military. The process involves hanging a person by the wrist while they balance on a small peg or sharp piece of wood. The torturers hoist the person by the wrist so that the only relief for the wrist can come from resting a foot on the sharp object. It seems that in Mat's instance, his torturers tied him by the neck, a potentially even more brutal variation on the practice. Such a method practiced on Mat prompts us to wonder whether this is what Celia feared when she gave her confession after Powell, a neighbor, said that he would get a rope.[12] Perhaps Celia wasn't so much afraid of being hanged on the spot as she was of being tortured into giving a confession. In Mat's case, one of the defense's instructions to the jury read, "The confessions of the prisoner in order to be——— in evidence must be free and voluntary and must not be extracted by way out of threats or violence nor obtained through the influence of hope or fear. And if the jury believe the prisoner induced by fear or terrified by threats of punishment or that the confessions were extracted by actual *torture* ... they will disregard the confessions" (Callaway, emphasis mine). The judge refused to admit this instruction to the jury, but the instruction itself indicates that the process by which the neighbors extracted Mat's confession may have been torturous and therefore illegal. The rejection of this instruction equates to the suspension of the law prohibiting the torture of a suspect, even a child; the practice of torturing enslaved and detained Black people, thus, resembles more the treatment of political enemies than that of those convicted of crimes (see Stone, *Black Well-Being*, ch. 4).

The parallels between Mat's and Celia's cases—the threat or actual experience of torture to produce a confession, the first-degree murder charges, and the judge's disregard for the attorneys' claims of forced confession or self-defense, respectively—may have produced between the boy and the young woman a certain affinity built around their experiences of injustice.

It's not difficult to imagine the two, both sentenced to execution, commiserating over their treatment in slavery and then under the legal justice system as they plotted their escape. Perhaps the twelve-year-old Mat and nineteen-year-old Celia found friends or coconspirators in each other as they faced the horror of the jail in the shadow of the gallows.

Mat was returned very shortly after his escape, indicating that though Celia had helped him out of the jail, the two did not stick together. It's possible that Mat had an idea of where he wanted to go, the house of the man in the report, or that Celia couldn't risk keeping the boy with her during her escape; we may never know. What we can glean from reports, however, is that Celia was instrumental in at least three jailbreaks and that she was thus determined, skillful, resourceful, sharp, and helpful to others, perhaps even acting as a sort of leader among other imprisoned people. Celia refused to acquiesce to her fate on the gallows, to accept her unjust conviction, or passively to await her execution in the county jail. Despite the enormous odds against her, she did what she could to preserve herself and at least two others. Even so, her time "outside" was brief.

Celia's Return

Reports indicate that Celia's two-week stay out of jail after her escape was by far the longest of the three elopements, Mat and Carlisle having been returned on the day of and a day after their respective attempts. What happened between Celia's escape and her return is unclear. Historian Melton A. McLaurin, basing his assumptions on the stay of execution request letter, surmises that she "was hidden by those who engineered her escape until after her original execution date had passed, then returned to her captors" (125). This seems a plausible explanation based on the defense's letter, but the newspaper coverage suggests that there was more to Celia's escape, time at large, and return to jail.

An article from the *Daily Missouri Democrat* dated November 27, 1855, details Celia's return to the jail, reading:

> RECOVERED.—The negro woman, Celia, whose escape from jail was noticed in our last, was brought to town last Sunday by Mr. H. Newsom, to whose house she came on the previous night. She had been out nearly a week, and during that time, as she states, she had lived on raw corn which she gathered from the fields.—She was driven in by

cold and hunger. Being thinly clad and without shoes, and the night very cool, she must have suffered considerably during the time of her absence. The time for her execution has not yet been appointed.[13]

This article offers the image of a strong-willed fugitive from imprisonment and enslavement trying to survive alone in the late autumn in Missouri: barefoot, lightly dressed, cold, and hungry, and under constant threat of capture, punishment, and execution. Given the likely conditions in the jail and the provisions for her clothing and feeding, her time outside the jail may have exacerbated what was presumably her already poor physical condition. We can read Celia's willingness to risk capture as a testament to her will to avoid her execution and remove herself from the brutal conditions of the jail, not to mention her compassion and commitment to helping others avoid the same conditions and eventual fate.

If we think that there is less truth to this account, we can read Celia as possibly protecting the people who helped her, refusing to give them up, just as she may have protected George and Malinda when she insisted that nobody helped her kill Newsom or dispose of his body.[14] We can imagine that she was harbored by community members or some of her legal team and then eventually made her way to one of the Newsoms to return to jail. What were the conversations she had with Harvey Newsom, Robert's son? According to the report, she spent the night at the Newsom farm before Harvey brought her back to the county jail. Who else from the family may have been there? Did she have a conversation with Virginia? Why the decision to go back there? Did she go back to see her children one last time? Did other enslaved people on Newsom's farm, perhaps her friends, help her in hiding? Did Celia think she might actually be able to survive on the sprawling acreage of the Newsom farm by eating what she could find and avoiding capture by hiding in the cornfields? Is that why she tried to sustain herself there? Or did she have some other purpose for going to the farm? Did she have some final words for the man whose father tortured her and whose family looked away? Harvey Newsom owned one of his father's bondspersons, Lewis. Records indicate that Lewis took the Newsom surname, named his first child Harvey, and stayed on with the Newsom family with his own family after emancipation (Halpern 177). It was not uncommon for formerly enslaved people to remain working for their former enslavers. Could Celia have had a friend in Lewis and in his wife, or could she have returned to Harvey because he had been kinder to her than others in his family? Perhaps Celia did stay with supportive community people who hid her from capture, and it was her idea just before returning to jail to first go to the Newsom farm for any of the above purposes or for other reasons I haven't thought of here.

In effect, if the newspaper report is mostly accurate, the Newsom family delivered her twice to the jail, where she awaited both wrongful conviction and then wrongful execution. Perhaps there was a fittingness to this second return by one of the next generation of Newsom men. Could there have been any remorse on the part of the family, any private acknowledgment of the terror that the Newsom patriarch carried out on the young woman? We don't yet (and may never) have any solid answers to these questions, but we do have a much more complex image of Celia.

Celia's Execution

Ultimately, Celia's case did not make it to the Supreme Court. The stay of execution was rejected, and the new date was set for December 21, 1855. Celia hanged on schedule, and delivered a new confession on the eve of her execution. Her deposition after her arrest reads, "I took up the ashes and bones out of the fire place in my Cabin where I burnt the body and emptied them on the right hand side of the path leading from my cabin to the stable," quite a matter-of-fact description. This is the only direct quotation from Celia in the deposition. The eve-of-execution confession, which also appears in the epigraphs to this chapter, builds on her first confession and, as with the deposition, includes only one directly quoted sentence from her. As I mentioned, this confession appeared first in the *Fulton Telegraph* and then was reprinted in the *Baltimore Sun* and the *New York Times*:

> HANGING A NEGRESS.—Celia, a negress, who has been under sentence of death since the 14th of October, for the murder of her master, Robt Newsome, in June last, was executed near this place on the 21 ult. The evening previous to her execution, and while under the gallows, she made what she said was a full confession of the crime. She has, at various times implicated several persons, but by her dying confession all of them are exonerated from any participation in the murder. She said that on the evening of the occurrence she procured a large, stout stick, (much larger and heavier than that before described by her) and took a position behind the door, leaving it slightly ajar; that her master came to the cabin, pushed the door open, and entered; as soon as he entered she struck him with the stick, felling him to

the ground. She did not, at first, intend to kill him, but, she said, "as soon as I struck him the devil got into me, and I struck him with the stick until he was dead, and then rolled him into the fire and burnt him up!" She denied that any one assisted her or aided or abetted in any way. She was hung at 2½ o'clock on Friday, 21st December last. Thus has closed one of the most horrible tragedies ever enacted in our country. (*Baltimore Sun*, 17 Jan. 1856)

This confession exhibits Celia in a similar light to the deposition, especially when we take into account her time in jail. Celia seems strong, independent, and determined. Of course, this could be an example of sensationalistic journalism, but when we take all accounts together—court documents, newspaper coverage, conditions in US and particularly Missouri penitentiaries and jails in the nineteenth century—along with the unspeakable terror of enslaver-enslaved sexual violence and torture and the gross injustices of the nineteenth-century legal system (even in cases with serious, committed legal defense teams), we can see Celia in complicated and varied ways beyond her victimhood.

Celia's Legacy

"Celia, a slave" of the court case documents is a young Black woman, who, between the ages of fourteen and nineteen, suffered repeated sexual abuses and rapes by a man sixty years old. We see her as sick, pregnant, and desperate, driven to commit the act of killing another person. "Celia, as imprisoned" is that same young woman, subjected to the deplorable conditions of a midcentury rural Missouri county jail, vulnerable to physical, sexual, and psychological abuses by guards and other imprisoned people, for four months while she awaits her trial, and then for two more after she's convicted. But we also see in "Celia, as imprisoned" a person who plotted either in concert with others or on her own three jailbreaks: her own and two other people's. We can imagine her conversations with Mat, the twelve-year-old enslaved boy convicted of murder, whose confession was forced through torture. We can picture Celia, unshod, poorly dressed, in the dark, cold months of a Missouri late autumn and in the dim light of a cell, amid the poor ventilation and the stench of the jail, as she collected and stored the shucks in her bed for days, perhaps weeks, perhaps longer, to gather enough to light a fire so that she could see what she and Mat were doing as they burned the wood around the door that locked them in. We can imagine her aided by others, even white Missourians who believed in her and hated the violence, abuses, and injustices that white people, their laws, and local judges perpetuated on Black people—enslaved Black people in particular, and enslaved Black women even more so. We can also imagine her as a sort of rebel outlaw, in the tradition of Nathaniel Turner before her, and Bobby Seale after her. We can see her as a precursor to such unjustly imprisoned Black people as Angela Davis, Assata Shakur, and the Scottsboro Boys.

Celia highlights the contestation of law. She demonstrates how, as legal historian Hendrik Hartog explains, "consciousnesses are never shaped by the content of the law"; law is an "an arena of conflict within which alternative social visions contended, bargained, and survived" (934–35). Perhaps Celia knew that it was illegal for her to kill Newsom, or perhaps she assumed that it was legal for her to defend herself against his sexual abuses and rapes. Perhaps she knew that the legal punishment for rape was the death penalty, and also that as an enslaved woman she had no legal recourse to protect herself against the assault, and so she exacted the punishment herself, in effect sentencing Newsom to that very penalty. In this respect, she performed a kind of intellectual work in asserting her own social vision of the law.

Celia and the Black Prison Intellectual Tradition

Celia, who was illiterate, enslaved, and imprisoned, may not have been an "intellectual" in the traditional sense or an organic manner (to paraphrase Antonio Gramsci), but she was an intellectual all the same. Edward W. Said's *Representations of the Intellectual* is useful here for imagining how Celia fits, if perhaps counterintuitively, into the category and role of the intellectual. Citing Julien Benda, Gramsci, and others, Said asks, "to what extent are intellectuals servants of these actualities [their society, historical situation, etc.], to what extent enemies?" Furthermore, he concedes that his "characterizations of the intellectual [are] as exile and marginal, as amateur, and as the author of a language that tries to speak truth to power" (xv). Celia embodied these characteristics. She was certainly no servant of traditional power structures—she was their enemy. Said refers to James Baldwin and Malcolm X as influences on his ideas about intellectualism, citing their "spirit in opposition, rather than in accommodation . . . because the romance, the interest, the challenge of intellectual life is to be found in dissent against the status quo at the time when the struggle on behalf of underrepresented and disadvantaged groups seems so unfairly weighted against them" (xvii). Celia had neither the capacity nor the access to exercise James Baldwin's or Malcolm X's modes of communication, and yet Said may well have included her in his definition.

Celia's dissent against the status quo is evident in her actions against Newsom and against the jail, and in her efforts to help others "on behalf of underrepresented and disadvantaged groups" when everything was "unfairly weighted against them." Celia was the exact opposite of the sort of intellectual cited by Benda in his attack on "governments [who had] to have as their servants those intellectuals who could be called on not to lead, but to consolidate the government's policy, to spew out propaganda against official enemies . . . [and] disguise the truth of what was occurring in the name of institutional 'expediency' or 'national honor'" (quoted in Said 6). If anything, Celia was the enemy, and her intellectual work exposed the travesty of institutional "expediency" and "national honor." "The purpose of the intellectual's activity is to advance human freedom and knowledge" (Said 17). Celia's actions certainly fulfilled this purpose, revealing the level of enmity with which her enslaver and the state regarded her. "The French biologist, Felix le Tantec, insisted that every social unit from the family to the nation could exist only by virtue of having some 'common enemy'" (Allport 41). As this book reveals, Celia and other enslaved Black people suspected, charged with, or convicted of crimes in the United States served as an internal enemy for many white people, particularly but not exclusively for proslavery people and enslavers themselves. This condition of Black criminal enmity enabled white support of the peculiar institution and rendered it less peculiar to them. The noncitizen status of imprisoned and enslaved Black people—not to mention the double or mixed legal character of enslaved people—enabled some white people to view them as internal enemies, living within the nation's borders, but also politically and socially alien.

Celia—whose death sentence came in the context of her enslavement and imprisonment during the lead-up to the Civil War—differs from those who later faced life sentences or, in the case of Assata Shakur, exile. Escape in each instance means something different. Celia's case in a sense is a slave narrative—and indeed I've read it as such in my comparison of it with Harriet Jacobs's 1861 *Incidents in the Life of a Slave Girl*. The literary here, as in the previous chapter's reading of Turner's *Confessions*, allows us to see Celia's story as a sort of blend of the slave narrative and the dying words genre, to think through the complicated question of what it means to be both enslaved and imprisoned, particularly for a Black woman who defended herself by extreme means against sexual violence. Celia, as do

Pomp and Turner, asks us to read her embodied intellectualism, her actions counting as much as her words in her intellectual work. Celia is an activist/intellectual whose work spoke truth to power. It is up to us to hear as Celia's actions speak.[15] The book's final chapter, following the interlude, proposes a new genre of Black testimony and intellectual work, the parole request letter.

Interlude

Postemancipation Criminality and Enmity in the *Christian Recorder* (1861–1901)

In the intervening years between Celia's execution in 1855 and the letters of James Foster from the turn of the century, the United States erupted into Civil War and then, in its aftermath, saw emancipation; the ratification of the Thirteenth, Fourteenth, and Fifteenth Amendments to the Constitution; the establishment of Jim Crow laws and Black codes; a rise in lynching; the founding of the Ku Klux Klan; and the continuation of convict leasing programs. These are just some of the events that contextualize the Black prison intellectual tradition after slavery. This book's interlude will pause from close readings of the work of Abraham Johnstone, Pomp, Nathaniel Turner, and Celia, and before returning to close readings of James Foster's work. The intervening decades of the latter nineteenth century provide a crucial backdrop for Foster's letters and the literary genre of the parole request letter, vital to our understanding of race and imprisonment in the early part of the twentieth century. Reading Foster in this context, we see how he at once requests parole and offers stiff critique of the justice system and US culture more broadly, making interventions that draw on the earlier Black prison intellectuals' work and anticipating the wave of writing in that tradition to follow.

As this book has considered the dual status of people both imprisoned and enslaved, the Thirteenth Amendment to the Constitution seems a good place to begin thinking about imprisonment of Black people following the abolition of legal slavery in the United States, and to move from a consideration of Celia as a Black prison intellectual to that of James Foster as such. The amendment reads: "Neither slavery nor involuntary servitude, *except as a punishment for crime* whereof the party shall have been duly convicted, shall exist within the United States, or any place subject to their jurisdiction" (emphasis mine). The clause "except as a punishment for crime" left the door open for involuntary servitude through convict leasing programs, which saw a significant increase in their numbers of Black people after emancipation. We can assume that Celia worked while in jail, perhaps cooking or tending to other "domestic" duties, but the leasing system went much further, contracting imprisoned people out to work for private companies. This was not a new system, but, as the next chapter demonstrates, the racial demographics of prisons shifted considerably after the Civil War, from primarily white to primarily Black.

Nomenclature is central to conversations about Black labor in the United States, both pre- and postemancipation. *Slavery* has been invoked to refer to convict leasing, particularly (see Blackmon). This book has tried to distinguish between enslaved and imprisoned statuses, even as they are entwined, and as they ask us to think about the collapse of distinctions between criminal and enemy. This book's focus is of course on how Black prison intellectuals highlight the enmification of Black people convicted of crimes, but it is worth also noting the legal and linguistic demarcations after emancipation that distinguish *slave* and *convict* from *enslavement, peonage, sharecroppers,* and *chain gangs*. This is not to diminish the importance of Douglas Blackmon's work on the "re-enslavement of Black Americans," but to call attention to the complex linguistic distinctions that the people affected most by legal changes had to attend, and that require our consideration as we reckon with and attempt to change the penal justice system as we know it now.

Debates over the Thirteenth Amendment have shaped our understandings of slavery and antislavery in the United States, across generations of historians and activists (see *13th*). This book's interlude draws from these conversations, focusing on how the amendment might have shaped Black people's thinking about criminality/enmity in the postemancipation United States, how convict leasing influenced James Foster's pleas for parole, especially considering the terms of his incarceration, and what the amendment's implications have been for other Black people in prison, generally.

Enslavers' fears of Black people in the lead-up to the Civil War continue to contextualize Foster's letters decades later. Historian Richard S. Newman argues, "Indeed, down to the American Civil War, many slaveholders' greatest fear was not massive slave rebellion but the specter of a 'blackened' republic via universal emancipation and African American equality. In Lincoln's day, these fears took the rather infamous name of 'Black Republicanism.' But they harked all the way back to black founders' vision of revolutionizing the white republic from within" (10). Newman's discussion traces a trajectory of Black intellectualism that extends from the founding of the United States to the American Civil War, encompassing figures like Abraham Johnstone and Pomp, as much as leaders/founders like Richard Allen, Absalom Jones, and Prince Hall.

Examining the role of Black intellectuals amid the Civil War, and especially the identification of Black enmity in this wartime context, historian L. Diane Barnes posits,

> As the Civil War waged on, African American abolitionists and Radical Republicans were spreading the same message [proclaiming "the continuing struggle by African Americans to gain their freedom during the war"]. [Frederick] Douglass focused his energies on waging war for abolition and finding a place for African American soldiers in the Union Army, and his wartime editorials and speeches regularly included reference to the noble group of African American men who fought (and in most cases died) in the struggle for freedom. Most famously, in his recruiting broadside "Men of Color to Arms!" Douglass urged potential recruits to "Remember Denmark Vesey of Charleston; remember Nathaniel Turner of Southampton; remember Shields Green and Copeland, who followed noble John Brown, and fell as glorious martyrs for the cause of the slave." (32)

Examples of Black (and white) armed resistance against slavery demonstrate a continuum of action that likely influenced the US Civil War, which some historians have referred to as a revolution (and a successful one at that, against the institution of US slavery); "martyrs" include those this book calls attention to, even if they were mainly unknown in their time and our own.

Historians continue to contest the meanings of the US Civil War, particularly the relevance of the Thirteenth Amendment and the motivations behind emancipation, incarceration, and convict leasing of Black people. Some believe that the punishment clause of the amendment was intended to facilitate the legal continuation of Black enslavement after emancipation. Rather than wade into the debate about white emancipators' motivations in drafting the amendment, I will focus here on the value of seeing Black reactions to the amendment and on its repercussions beyond its ratification, particularly for Black people in jails and prisons after the Civil War. Black abolitionists, soldiers, and prison intellectuals/writers are central to this discussion and to the undeclared war against Black people in the United States that has continued from the early republic into our own time. They encourage us to consider not how the Thirteenth Amendment acted as "prelude to a long nightmare of white supremacy," as historian Sean Wilentz argues (60), but rather, how it informed white supremacy's foundations, prevalence, and endurance in US culture and the continuation of the nation's undeclared war against Black people.[1] Here we might remind ourselves of the diverse work preceding ratification of the Thirteenth Amendment: the resistance and critique voiced by Johnstone, Pomp, Turner, and Celia (Johnstone free by the time of his imprisonment, the other three enslaved and imprisoned); the writings and urgent calls made by Douglass (enslaved and imprisoned himself), Martin R. Delany, Mary Ann Shadd, Harriet Jacobs, and Jacobs's brother, John Jacobs (also enslaved and imprisoned); and the actions of numerous enslaved individuals who risked everything to flee to free states and Canada, and who helped other people do the same.

In the context of this book and the bridge between Celia's and Foster's times, Wilentz's final arguments in his piece are worthy of note:

> First, American emancipations and abolitions arose not from the enslavers but from their antislavery foes, black and white. Second, the ferocious struggles between these forces produced genuine if partial victories for oppressed blacks and their white advocates. But those victories were subject to dramatic reversal through political reaction, and the conflict has continued for generation after generation, focused, since Reconstruction, on retrieving and expanding on not only the Thirteenth Amendment but also the guarantee of citizenship, equal protection, and political enfranchisement encoded in the Fourteenth and Fifteenth Amendments. (61)

As we see historically in the United States and in our own time, to which Wilentz also refers, every movement and moment against oppression meets with backlash, as well as a response to that backlash. Referring in part to women's prison labor in the Jim Crow South, historian Sarah Haley shows how,

> Black women who sought to protect themselves from domestic violence and exploitation faced the disavowal of their experiences as legal actors and prison authorities reinscribed violation as a normative part of the black female condition. Criminalized women would continue to defend themselves against violence and struggle for bodily autonomy in prison, sabotaging carceral logic and structures.... As

important, black women forged alternative community networks within the carceral regime and developed radical epistemologies of love, life, labor, and freedom. Violent state force was a response to the consistency, complexity, and dynamism of black women's challenges to carceral authority and repression. (194)

We might imagine this history as a postemancipation extension of Celia's actions in 1855. She likely faced similar abuses in jail and also made similar attempts to "sabotag[e] carceral logic and structures" in her own escape and in efforts to help others. Looking ahead to James Foster's work at the turn of the century, we see how he uses his letters to critique prisons from within his own confinement, indeed even writing on penitentiary stationery. As Foster demonstrates, prison correspondence critical of the system, and by implication of its employees and proponents, requires finesse. His attention to labor also features prominently in his requests for parole and his argument that he would be self-sufficient on the outside. His photographs of fellow imprisoned Black men further emphasize the labor that imprisoned Black people performed in the post-Reconstruction United States.

As a preface to Foster's engagement with the state and his incarceration, this interlude takes up the widely read and indeed leading Black newspaper the *Christian Recorder* (which grew out of the *Christian Herald* in 1852), whose opinions and articles bridge the temporal gap between Celia and Foster. This interlude will not attempt a comprehensive examination of the newspaper—for that, see Eric Gardner's excellent study, with its book history methodology—but rather will highlight pieces that provide context for the chapter to come with regard to criminality and enmity postemancipation and post-Reconstruction. These articles speak to concerns about Black involvement in the Civil War, criminality, enmity, imprisonment, and lynching. The interlude culminates with a letter from the editor directed to Alabama, published in the same year as Foster's parole request letters.

There are many instances in the *Recorder* in which we can see traces of thought from intellectual predecessors brought to light in this book. The *Recorder*'s "Advice to Our Young People" from March 23, 1861, at the start of the Civil War, advises honesty among young Black people. The column recalls, if not by name, Johnstone's vitriol against perjury and his comparison of it to pestilence. In this and subsequent columns, the *Recorder* author puts white dishonesty in the context of continual oppression from the earliest days of American "settlement," and advises that being dishonest results in more jail time and impoverishment than does being truthful. Also, the author stresses, just as Johnstone did nearly a century before, that "underhanded[]" people will desert those who trust them.

Two years later, amid the Civil War, an article in the *Recorder* highlights the continued undeclared war against Black people. A correspondent from Louisville, Kentucky, reports that a Black family returning from church met with military personnel who randomly arrested and detained the family, apparently looking for contraband. Free Black people who presented their papers, they were still detained, and one was shot by a guard when the man attempted to leave. The author was understandably critical of the military's behavior (14 Nov. 1863). Another report from that same year in Louisville details abuse of Black people in the Civil War, arrests of escaping enslaved people in Louisville, unsanitary jail conditions, extreme negligence of and hard labor requirements for detainees, and both extortion and physical and verbal abuse by Union soldiers (31 Jan. 1863).

Following the Civil War, P. Houston Murray writes in the *Recorder* to express frustration about white injustice and backlash against Black people in the South. His disappointment in the Emancipation Proclamation comes through in accounts of "rebels" and white hate. He argues: "*Slavery is not dead.* The emancipation proclamation only meant to secure the sympathies of the negro as a soldier, spy, and friend of the Union Army." In the context of Montgomery, Alabama, the subject of this book's next chapter, Murray reports:

> A letter from Montgomery, Alabama, informs me that colored men are coming in from the interior of the state, horribly mutilated. One having his ears cut off, and otherwise inhumanly bruised and hacked. I repeat it, *slavery is not dead.* The emancipation seems only to have been a ruse, a base ruse to secure the triumph of the Union army. As slaves, we had some protection from our masters from the interest they had in us; but as freemen, we have none from the law. We want, first, *complete personal* enfranchisement, and then the civil franchises which indemnify an American *soldier and citizen.* All the ordinary privileges, without the right of suffrage, are as baseless as a shadow.

Referring to the legal system and drawing on previous discourses about enmity between Black and white people, he asks,

> What will avail us the right to sue, testify, and plead in courts, if rebels or our enemies make and administer the law? What can we acquire by having the right to own, buy, and sell property, if virulent prejudice

bars us from all the avenues of industry? Give us the self-protective right, the elective franchise, and we will secure in the law, its makers and executors, the protection against the virulence of the body politic of the state, and against enfranchised traitors that our helplessness and political nudity require, and our labors and patriotism merit. ("Negro Suffering and Suffrage in the South," 1 July 1865)

Murray underscores the continuation of Black oppression after the Civil War and emphasizes the need for Black enfranchisement, which would not see ratification—and even then, only for men—until the Fifteenth Amendment in 1870.

On the flip side, an editorial in the *Recorder* written later that same year discusses enslavers' regret over the war and the abuse and even murder of Black abolitionists in New Orleans:

But the change in it and its inhabitants is very great. Had we made our appearance in its streets four years ago, we would have been arrested and conveyed to jail, as a northern abolitionist; but now every man stands on his own merit, and is free to think, speak and act as he pleases. As for the poor rebels and former slave owners, they look so sheepish and cut, that they are to be pitied more than despised. Had they imagined four years of war would bring about such a change in their social and political status, they never would have rebelled against the government. The time was when, if colored persons were seen out in the street after a certain hour, they were arrested and conveyed to the recking prison,—in the morning to receive for punishment a number of lashes on the bare back. We are credibly informed that many poor unfortunates have been whipped to death in these infernal dens. (25 Nov. 1865)

This article recalls the fear Celia may have felt in jail, even while awaiting execution, and yet, the lynch mobs that would haunt southern jails and prisons in the coming decades demonstrate an unfortunate continuity.

Novelist and activist Frances Harper, whose works were serialized in the *Recorder*, wrote to the paper in 1870 about education and crime after slavery. Harper's comments relate to the next chapter, about Alabama prison education, James Foster, and the question of enmification. She writes:

And yet the want of a proper industrial training is one of the most fruitful sources of crime and pauperism, and of course it is not desirable that our race should be the pauper race of America; to be in the

> midst of our crowded civilization what the Indian has been upon its outskirts. We do not wish to be armed against society, nor society to be armed against us, and if there are causes at work among us that have a tendency to shove toward pauperism and crime, then it becomes us to look our difficulty in the face, and to learn our duty in the light of our danger. Yesterday I found in the report of the prison congress, which has lately been held in Cincinnati, a statement which may well set us to thinking, if we have any interest in the welfare of our race, or of our children, and it is that out of the 17,000 persons confined in our higher penal institutions, 28 percent can not read, and 97 percent have never learned a trade. In the common jails of New York in 1864, 32 percent could not read, and 72 percent were without trades. ("Communications. Our People," 29 Oct. 1870)

The urgency here regarding literacy and industrial training, in light of the continued suppression of education for Black people (as will be discussed in the last letter of this interlude), highlights a fallacy in the white establishment's thinking, which saw educational advancement as linked to Black criminality.

Furthermore, many articles in the *Recorder* take up the subject of the Ku Klux Klan, which was founded in 1865 in Tennessee. One author writes in 1884:

> Are we to understand that these gentlemen of the Klan who are responsible for the cold-blooded, heartless murders of many thousand of republicans against but a few democrats were no respecters of party? That they were not organized and maintained, until they dared not longer, the strong opponents of all the rights of the colored American? In one of their alleged declarations they claim to be, according to Mr. Wilson, "essentially, originally and inherently a protective organization, proposition to execute law instead of resisting it, and to protect all good men, whether white or black, from the outrages and atrocities of bad men of both colors who have been for the past three years a terror to society and an iniquity to us all. The blacks seem to be impressed with the belief that this Klan is especially their enemy. We are not enemies of the blacks so long as they behave themselves, make no threats upon us and do not attack or interfere with us."

This discussion of enmity in the face of justifications for white supremacy and murder resonates through to today. The author reorients the argument:

> We all know what the misbehavior of the Negro was. He refused to remain a slave. He refused to grant many concessions respecting the sidewalk, the pigeon-hole at the Post Office, the uncovered hand, the "masses," etc. It is cheery folly, if not insult, to attempt to make the world agree with Mr. D.L. Wilson respecting the wronged but virtuous K.K.K. How far distant is the day when the whole rebel side of the question will be decided the glorious side, when her chieftains will be covered with laurels for having caused so much bloodshed, starved so many thousands in prisons, robbed homes and submitted graciously to a robbing government snatching from them their slaves, their property, and instructing subordinates to do likewise? ("The 'Ku-Klux Klan,'" 10 July 1884).

This article anticipates a later one that refers to the imprisonment of one of the newspaper's editors for writing negatively about white people.

Three years later, and in the state of Alabama, where James Foster would be imprisoned, an article in the *Recorder* discusses new prison reform in Alabama. The writer gives credit to Julia S. Tutwiler and other women for spearheading these changes. The reforms include opening schools for imprisoned people, requiring the state to fund one teacher for every one hundred imprisoned people, and heating prisons. Still, the writer compares imprisonment to slavery:

> In counties, which have taken advantage of the law permitting them to turn their convicts over to the State, the abuses of the chain-gang system, which is practically without supervision, are said to be much greater than those of the State system. Perhaps the spirit of the authorities is sufficiently shown by the fact that in several counties the Woman's Christian Temperance Union is no longer allowed to hold religious services for their convicts on Sunday. It is singular how many points of likeness there are between this system of slavery and the old one. ("In Alabama a New Prison Code Goes into Effect Next Month," 3 Nov. 1887)

This author highlights the similarities between slavery and imprisonment to critique abuse and a failing/failed legal system postemancipation.

Two years after this article on Alabama prison reform, an editor at the *Recorder* was imprisoned in Alabama for writing disparagingly about white people and Black rights. The newspaper responded by underscoring the different standards applied to Black editors, preachers, and writers:

There is power in the pulpit of the white South and its religious press to change this cruel sentiment, that incarcerates an editor for not being white; for that is the sum of it. A white man writing the same thing concerning black citizens would pass unnoticed. We do feel that our church should be of sufficient power, and wisdom, in faith, in prayer and the diplomacy to observe some influence in behalf of a brother in the case of editor Bryant. We feel that the mighty pens of our bishops, our other ministers, the cause of our pulpit in prayer meetings, all should be engaged for Bryant's safety. ("Editor Bryant in Jail," 5 Sep. 1889)

This article also speaks to the undeclared Black enmity that lingers in the late nineteenth century after emancipation and the passage of due process and voting rights amendments.

Across the next several years, the *Recorder* publishes about lynch mob murders of imprisoned people in different states. The paper highlights "prominent men" who are arrested for lynching (including state representatives in Texas), and for horse stealing, the same crime that will find Foster arrested and convicted in 1901 (Foster will draw on arguments of social standing and education in his pleas for parole). The lynching stories are graphic in detail and account for arrests ("Lynchers Were Inexorable," 1 Mar. 1894; "Prominent Men as Lynchers," 10 May 1894; "'Prominents' as Horse Thieves," 31 May 1894).

On the subject of prominent men, there is also the celebration of prominent Black men, in contrast to those white men mentioned in connection to lynching and horse stealing. Tracing the legacy of eighteenth-century minister and African Methodist Episcopal Church founder Richard Allen (who along with fellow clergyman Absalom Jones published a refutation of accusations of Black impropriety during the Philadelphia yellow fever epidemic of 1793), the editor of the *Recorder* took the anniversary of Allen's birth to call for a celebration of his life and work. One editorial shows how 138 years after Allen's birth, the newspaper was upholding his legacy and fighting against the suppression of Black ideas. The *Recorder* called for memorial services to be held on Sunday, February 13, the day before Allen's birthday ("Allen Day," 3 Feb. 1898). I'll quote this editorial in full:

The 138th anniversary of the birth of Richard Allen; born, February 14, 1760, in Philadelphia, Pa. Happy and blessed are we, the present ministers and the grand old district, to live to-day, this one hundred and thirty-eighth anniversary of the birth of him who made the first effort for Christian manhood in the Methodist Episcopal family, thus leading out the oppressed from their prisons, and organizing the African Methodist Episcopal Church:

I, therefore, call upon you, in all your assemblies, in your respective places of worship, on Sunday, February 13th, 1898, to hold fitting Memorial services in honor of the life and work of our great organizer, and illustrious founder, Rt. Rev. Richard Allen, and that a special collection, throughout the day, for the benefit of our embarrassed Publication Department.

Let this collection be a fitting memorial to our sainted hero, and to our embarrassed Publication Department—our part of the means of lifting that embarrassment. Brethren, sisters, and friends, give a donation on that day worthy of the fame of the grand old Second.

Yours for the Church, this grand old African Methodist Episcopal Church.

JAMES A. HANDY, Bishop.

Baltimore, Md.

Such calls for celebration of Richard Allen and the naming of a day in his honor emphasize his role as an ancestor of those writers, ministers, and activists who follow him in the Black intellectual tradition. Discussion of Allen's "leading out the oppressed from their prisons"—whether these prisons are metaphorical or literal—recalls the early Black prison intellectual work with which this book began. Attention to publishing and ministry and the economic difficulties attending both reminds us of the centuries-old value of print publication for Black communities across the United States.

Moving from celebrations of the life of Richard Allen to the censure of white brutality, two articles published in the *Recorder* in 1901, the year of Foster's parole request letters, are worth noting here. The first of these highlights white violence and "moral depravity" through the report of a violent attack on a young New Jersey woman, "a highly respected person," by four white men, "also respectable." The article focuses on how "many of our enenmies [sic] have been endeavoring to create an impression that only Negros are sufficiently morally depraved to commit certain nameless crimes . . . but hers of one of many cases which completely refutes the charge" ("A Heinous Crime," 10 Jan. 1901). Beyond the crime's commission in New Jersey, Abraham Johnstone's home state of two centuries prior, the piece also recalls his early comments about white people's capacity for violence and his identification of white people as enemies of (Black) freedom—even though this article reports on crime committed by white men on a white woman. It also emphasizes the prevalence of violence against women, recalling Celia's story. The article calls for capital punishment—the fate that Johnstone, Pomp, Turner, and Celia all met with—and underscores the horror and illogic of the indiscriminate lynching of Black people.

The second 1901 article on the topic of white brutality condemns the lynching practice of burning human beings in Texas and focuses on the act's barbarity and illegality, emphasizing the cruel fate of Black people deemed criminal, regardless of whether they've been tried and found guilty. The focus of the piece is on John Henderson, who was taken by a mob from prison and burned to death. This article demonstrates the continuation of the undeclared war against Black people. It reads:

> It was not capable, by reason of its passion blindness, to take in what it was doing when it made a bonfire in front of the temple of justice out of the wretch whose innocence had not been disproved by law. Troops of soldiers, it is claimed, were on their way to protect the prisoner from his mob fate, and so we can't say at this distance that the officers of the law winked at the defeat of justice in the poor man's doom. It is claimed that the victim accused of assault and murder, confessed his guilt. But the accused is put out of the way of self defense, and as dead dogs tell no tale, we refuse to accept the biased and bloody findings of Judge Lynch's court.

The implication, though not substantiated, that "troops of soldiers" may have "winked at the defeat of justice," along with the identification of "Judge Lynch's court," points to the enmification of Henderson, as distinctions between criminal and enemy collapse in law and military actions. The piece continues, "Perhaps the saddest feature of the whole affair is the finding of the coroner's jury, which not only justified the barbarity but declared that it was endorsed by the best people of the country. The claim is a notorious falsehood on its face, which if true, makes the preachers and professing Christians of that section no less notorious and hell-deserving than Judas or Pilate" ("Black Brutality or Caucasian Barbarism," 21 Mar. 1901). This last part reminds us of the words of Johnstone, Pomp, and Turner—and will resonate as well with Foster—in their evocations of religious hypocrisy among white oppressors and liars.

Finally, we arrive at a 1901 letter from the editor of the *Recorder* that reinforces the central concerns of freedom, voting rights, governance, equity, labor, education, and ideas about Black criminality through the ratification of Alabama's massive 1901 Constitution. The Constitution was written to ensure white supremacy by, for example, limiting voting rights of Black men and poor white men through literacy requirements, segregating schools, and reducing education funding. The letter, which is addressed to white Alabamians, traces concerns that predated emancipation and continue through to our time. It sets the stage for Foster; the editor raises many concerns that Foster also outlines from within the confines of the same state's prison system during the same year. The letter—the same literary form through which we learn Foster's ideas—asks for a hearing of the public, similar to the call Foster makes as he requests parole from the state. The injustices, double standards, and implications of criminality and enmity in this letter published in the *Recorder* resonate with Foster's letters to the Alabama governor's office.

I include here as much of the extant letter as possible to provide the writer's take on the political, social, and cultural context affecting Black people at the turn of the century in the state and in Alabama prisons, as we look to the next chapter. The *Recorder* letter, titled "To the White People of Alabama," begins:

> I have served you in slavery and in freedom for over half a century. I have stood with you for "good government" for a quarter of a century. As all of my past life has been devoted to your service and to the welfare of my race, I believe that you will grant me a hearing now.
>
> I love Alabama. I have been true to her at home and abroad. I have never breathed one word against her. I have all along trusted her white people. I revere the names of her long line of noble sons with untarnished honor, who scorned wrong and hated injustice. Their faith in right gave birth to your Confederate monument which stands on Capitol Hill representing what they regarded as truth. But today, I am alarmed! I tremble for the future of my people in Alabama, unless you come to our rescue. The recent campaign was one of bitterness and abuse of my people. Many of the public speakers did not appeal to the highest sentiment in man, but held up the Negro in a manner to make the white masses hostile to him. With all of your best efforts for many years to come, it will be hard to undo the harm which was done to my race by that campaign into which was put so much unkind feeling. Not that you put a premium on suffrage. That was right. Not that the white man become supreme in government. He was that already. But in the sentiment manufactured against us. Was such a cam-

paign necessary? There could have been but one result—ratification—though the press and speakers had held their peace. Then why abuse and mortify the men who are trying hard to please you and serve you every hour? Do not misunderstand me. For God's sake do not misrepresent me. I have never asked for unqualified suffrage. Since a majority of the better element of the white people of Alabama wanted the new constitution and promised better things under it, I was not against it. I am opposed to every phase of social equality so distasteful to us both, and in my opinion, detrimental to Southern society. There is no necessity for it. Ninety-nine thousand, nine hundred and ninety nine (99,999) Negroes in every one hundred thousand (100,000) do not seek social equality, and if every Negro in the State sought it, it would not be. You know all this. Still we were abused, and the hostility of the lower element in your race aroused against us. . . . You got a new constitution, you said, to avoid the necessity of committing fraud in elections. You promised us righteous treatment in educational affairs. Your own statesmen say that the Negro pays taxes and still some men persist in saying that he does not. If you wish a division of the school funds on racial lines, go [illegible] the very bottom of the matter, [illegible] see who pulls the tax money from the bosom of the earth, the only original source of wealth. We do four-fifths of your agricultural labor and add four-fifths to your wealth from that source. Your own record shows that the mass of your Ne[illegible] labor is not only law abiding, but industrious. The proportion of Ne[illegible] wage earners to the entire Ne[illegible] population in Alabama is greater than in any other Southern State except Louisiana. Give us our portion in equity and we will not complain. You promised to do this. You said that with the political matter settled, all else should be fair. I still have faith in you. Though you slay me, yet will I trust you. Present the question fairly to the popular vote of the white people of Alabama alone, I believe they would vote for a division of the school fund on the basis of scholastic enumeration, and they would enumerate fairly, too. Take this matter out of the hands of men who do not like my race. Let it rest on the Golden Rule, then peace, prosperity and happiness will come to all our people, and your waste places will bloom. Leave it with men who hate us, who appeal to prejudice and it will soon take the place of the political question just settled.

It is said that the educated Negro is the criminal Negro. We are in your fields, kitchens and shops at work. We cannot answer you.

But what are the facts as recorded by you in your books? Three million (3,000,000) Negroes can read and write. Only eleven thousand (11,000) Negroes who can read and write are in all the prisons of the country. Just one Negro in every hundred who can read and write is engaged in teaching, preaching and other professional work. That is what your own records tell. Does this show that the educated Negro is the criminal Negro, that all educated Negroes go into the professions and that education unfits the Negro for labor? Two millions, nine hundred and fifty thousand (2,950,000) Negroes who can read and write are working every day for you in all grades of labor. Are not our virtues minimized and our sins magnified by men who do not like us? I do not hesitate to state as a fact that nine out of . . . (19 Dec. 1901)

This interlude will let this letter stand on its own here as a complement to the parole request letters of James Foster, and in hope that critique from within carceral institutions will garner scholarly and popular attention. One of Foster's letters was published in the press, but for many Black prison intellectuals who wrote parole or pardon requests, their work was not published. I hope this book will change this.

5

Dear Governor

The Parole Request as Literary Genre in James Foster's Letters (1901)

The Black prison intellectual tradition includes countless examples of confessions and dying words by incarcerated individuals. Such genres have received extensive academic analysis. But a similar genre that has not garnered the same attention is the parole request letter. This mode of testimony and protest, unlike the confession and dying words, represents a method of negotiating with the state even as it critiques this state. As scholars have brought to our attention the importance of gallows literature as an early mode of Black testimony, I propose here that these letters are also their own genre, which warrants close attention in Black studies. Parole requesters employ a variety of tactical and stylistic approaches and offer another mode of theorizing race and criminal in/justice. Some reveal repeated attempts at securing parole, justifications supporting their release, and the harsh realities for many who, despite seemingly small offenses (possession of a pint of whiskey, for example), routinely saw their requests denied and their sentences to hard labor extended.

As with the other figures studied here, parole request letter writers of the early twentieth century may not readily come to mind as intellectuals, but they produce a kind of intellectual work that, even as it appeals to state power, critiques it, reveals its injustices and its exploitative nature, and highlights those most vulnerable to it. Writers and orators of these letters precede Michel Foucault's assessment of intellectuals' relation to authority: "to sap power, to take power; it is an activity conducted alongside those who struggle for power, and not their illumination from a safe distance"; and "when prisoners began to speak, they possessed an individual theory of prisons, the penal system, and justice. It is this form of discourse which ultimately matters, a discourse against power, the counter-discourse of prisoners and those we call delinquents—and not a theory *about* delinquency" (Foucault and Deleuze 208–9). James Foster, the writer this chapter focuses on, reveals the concerted and brutal political footwork the state had to do to ensure continued Black oppression and exploitation in the postemancipation capitalist South. Foster develops a theory of "prisons, the penal system, and justice" in a genre of writing that demands a form of deference to the state. His use of the genre to appeal for release from prison reveals a deft critique of that very genre, voiced from within the confines of the prison and the request itself.

Since the thirteenth century, the word *request* has enjoyed a fairly consistent definition as "an instance of asking for something, esp. in a polite or formal manner; a petition or expression of wish; a document expressing such a wish; (also) the thing which is asked for"; and "the action, on the part of a specified person, of asking for some favour, service, etc., from another; the expression of one's desire or wish directly addressed to the person or persons able to gratify it" (*OED*, senses 1.a, 1.b). The power differential of the parole request emphasizes the want or need of the individual, private requester and their vulnerability vis-à-vis the individual, public grantor, a representative of the state. Conventions of the request—such as politeness and formality, the concept of the wish, and the expression of desire directly addressed to someone with the power to gratify it—put the post-Reconstruction imprisoned Black letter writer in Alabama into a considerably disadvantaged position in relation to state power, and made the genre a tricky mode of testimony and protest for the negotiation of one's release. Nevertheless, the critique comes through, especially in the case of Foster's letters.

Convict leasing programs, which were initiated during Reconstruction and remained prevalent well after, served as a link between plantation slavery and the modern prison industrial complex, continuing the exploitation of Black labor under capitalism. Many states relied on the practice, but it found its longest run in Alabama. "Virtually from the moment the Civil War ended, the search began for legal means of subordinating a volatile Black population that regarded economic independence as a corollary of freedom and the old labor discipline as a badge of slavery" (Foner 198). For the South, Emancipation signaled the need for a new form of Black subjugation. Southern states enacted Black codes, which "amply fulfilled Radical Benjamin F. Flanders' prediction as Louisiana's legislature assembled: 'Their whole thought and time will be given to plans for getting things back as near to slavery as possible'" (Foner 199). After northern outcry about the prejudicial and severe nature of Black codes in Mississippi and South Carolina, the initiators of this legislation, Alabama followed with its own set of codes, this time omitting overt reference to race. Despite the attempt "to avoid the appearance of discrimination and comply with the federal Civil Rights Act of 1866," however, "it was well understood, as Alabama planter and Democratic politico John W. DuBois later remarked [with regard to the state concern over vagrancy], that 'the vagrant contemplated was the plantation negro'" (Foner 201). During Reconstruction, the South had to work to ensure the continued legal enmification of its imprisoned Black population while simultaneously diverting northern concerns over racial discrimination.

It may be tempting to dismiss the criminal/enemy thesis of this book by saying that convict leasing simply represents the continued systemic (albeit horrific) exploitation and subjugation of Black people in the United States. And yet, the idea that Black people imprisoned in Reconstruction Alabama might occupy an undeclared enemy status throws into relief the complicated desire to continue to subdue and exploit the person deemed criminal and enmified in the New South. Returning here to Paul Kahn's reconception of Carl Schmitt's friend/enemy distinction as criminal/enemy—both thinkers referring to a later twentieth-century time frame—is helpful for thinking through the imaginary that allowed the state's perpetuation of injustices against the Black population accused of criminal activity after the Civil War. Kahn argues, "At stake in the criminal/enemy distinction . . . is the relationship of sovereignty to law. These are not just categories of theory but the organizing principles of political and personal narrative. When we lose control of the categories, we can lose the sense of who we are" (150). Before the Civil War, the scaffold functioned as a display of sovereignty and the sovereign state's right to kill, regardless of the practice's incongruity with republican ideology. After the Civil War, the blurring of political and personal narrative in the South revealed a desperate attempt to maintain demarcations that verged on the chaotic. The South sought to retain a sort of internal sovereignty, operating within the bounds of the Civil Rights Act and yet using Black codes to perpetuate a kind of slave labor through the capitalist exploitation of people convicted of crimes. Black people's consistent rejection of subjugation in all its complex forms realized the enemy distinction for white people, who personally and collectively believed in their racial supremacy and politically and economically believed in their need for and entitlement to a subservient Black labor force. "Both Athens and Jerusalem point us toward the centrality of love to the constitution of the community. A political community founded on love will distinguish enemies from criminals. Think of the analogy to the family; a misbehaving child is metaphorically a criminal, not enemy" (Kahn 152). And yet, we have seen through this book's chapters what happens when imprisoned Black people are not conceived as part of the national family.

In the situation of the undeclared internal enemy in the US context, the Black Other charged with crimes represented from the nation's earliest years a kind of existential difference (physiologically, emotionally, and intellectually) in the realms of medicine, law, religion, and politics. Referring to Schmitt's 1932 *The Concept of the Political*, political theorist Roland Axtmann explains, "The quality of the political resides in the decision through which the 'other,' the stranger or alien, is declared to negate one's own existence and is thus defined as being—in a particularly intense way—existentially different, and hence an enemy against whom battle must be waged, which may—rightly and justifiably—lead to the enemy's extermination" (535). And that Other status, especially in great numbers and amid fear of uprisings, presented a danger to the existence not only of white supremacy but of white lives as well, which were to be protected at all costs (or so the thinking went). As the previous chapters of *Black Prison Intellectuals* demonstrate, exploitation and extermination of the internal enemy in the United States have taken the form of enslavement, torture, discriminating laws, deportation, imprisonment, and legal and extralegal execution.

In practice, Black people charged with criminal offenses after the abolition of slavery remained undeclared enemies of the state in the nation's long-standing war on Blackness (see Engels, *Enemyship*; Engels, "Friend"; Land). Historian Mary Ellen Curtin explains, "The legal history of slavery in Alabama, the ensuing legislation of the Black Codes, and subsequent laws pertaining to larceny, segregation, and disfranchisement warrant a cynical interpretation of southern law as nothing better than 'white law.' Indeed, the fast-rising number of Black prisoners in the 1870s and 1880s and the near absence of incarcerated whites illustrate the racial impact of an increasingly repressive legal system" (33). The Black codes created curfews for Black people and made it illegal for them to possess a gun or swear in the presence of white women. Sentences for such crimes included hard labor, as well as fines, which were very difficult for most imprisoned people to pay. "County convicts worked off this cost by serving extra time in prison at a rate of thirty cents per day," with fines typically set at fifty dollars (Curtin 6). Furthermore, even as Alabama rescinded its law refusing Black testimony against white people (doing so merely in order "to rid the state of military and Freedmen's Bureau courts and to appease Northern public opinion"), "a British barrister noted after observing Richmond's courts early in 1867, with Blacks barred from jury service, 'the verdicts are always for the white man and against the colored man'" (Foner 204). Such practices are reminiscent of the example of Virginia during the time of the 1831 Southampton revolt, when the law served as enemy of the Black population, as we saw in chapter 3. In post-Reconstruction Alabama, the disproportional incarceration of Black people as a result of laws designed to acquit white defendants and convict Black defendants, to protect white people more generally and disenfranchise Black citizens, provided a "solution" to the labor problem of Reconstruction and the New South.

Black codes, contract labor, and convict leasing programs all continued beyond Reconstruction in Alabama, leading to additional developments in the state's prison system. Curtin explains Alabama's postemancipation racial shift in prisons: "Under slavery the prisoners in Alabama's penitentiary were 99 percent white. But after emancipation the vast majority of all prisoners were black" (6). Incarcerated Black people took up the parole request letter as a genre of critique, testimony, and protest. The letter also represented a mode of expression that the writers knew directly addressed the office of the governor.

Alabama passed its first parole legislation in 1897, giving the governor the authority to release imprisoned people prior to the conclusion of their sentences, without needing to grant a full pardon (official forgiveness/absolution). Historically, rigid sentencing laws in the United States had led to overcrowding in jails and prisons. Prior to the institution of parole laws, states needed to grant large numbers of pardons to reduce the prison population. New York instituted the nation's earliest version of a parole law in 1817, when it formalized release from prison as a reward for good behavior with what was termed a "good time" law. "This law authorized a 25 percent reduction in length of term for those inmates serving five years or more who were well behaved and demonstrated industry in their prison work" (Latessa and Smith, *Corrections* 88). Between 1889 (Wisconsin) and 1899 (Colorado), twenty additional states adopted parole laws. Parole request letters from inmates reveal much about the justice system and the people convicted of crimes in the aftermath of Reconstruction in the United States (Letessa and Smith, *Corrections* 161).

Imprisoned people's written correspondence (both personal letters to families and parole requests to authorities) had a psychological effect for the authors, offering them a means to analyze and criticize as well as to hope. Their letters were a connection to the world outside, and "helped many prisoners to endure their incarceration" (Curtin 32). They were not all straightforward appeals expressing hope for release, but were often also a form of state critique, whether implicit or explicit. Parole requests emphasized the person's need to work, especially to get crops in so they could pay the cost of the fines incurred at the time of sentencing. Furthermore, people in prison often had family at home relying on those crops for their survival. As an extension of the dying words, confession, and slave narrative genres of eighteenth- and nineteenth-century Black literature, these letters were pleas for aid, but they also took varying approaches, from calling for sympathy and mercy to expressing frustration and anger to demanding empathy. Somewhat similar to the dying words genre, the requests often included admissions of guilt, references to God, acknowledgments of poor health and disability, and promises not to reoffend. At times, the writers directly encouraged the governor to imagine himself in their position. Unlike printed confessions, parole request letters mostly remained unpublished. Typically, they neither gathered a public audience, nor turned a profit, not even for charity, but they are a window into the world of the leasing program and beyond, representing another important kind of intellectual work, Black expression, and testimony in the racially exploitative continuum of the postbellum United States.

This chapter concentrates on two remarkable letters by the same author, dating from 1901. The first of these is unique in that it *did* find its way to newspaper publication, while the second atypically includes accompanying photographs. Perhaps by comparison to the more straightforward requests I've read, the two letters together showcase the author's literary and rhetorical style. James Foster, the writer of these letters, was sixty-eight years old at the time of writing and imprisoned in Wetumpka, Alabama. Foster uses several tactics of persuasion to demand, rather than request, parole, and reveals his complex and compelling character—slyly deferential, self-consciously tactical, and even a little roguish. His letters appeal to the reader's sense of religion, conscience, guilt, hopefulness, law, religion, and even humor. He also theorizes about the parole process. Written roughly three years into his sentence, Foster's letters date to just four years after the state legislature enacted the parole law. His is an early and notable example of imprisoned Black people's negotiations with the state for their freedom and provides a baseline for comparison with subsequent letters in other contexts.

The state incarcerated James Foster on August 5, 1898, one year after the passage of the parole legislation. His conviction was for grand larceny for stealing a horse, and his sentence was ten years. Foster took the horse of a Dr. Slack and replaced it with his own. From his convict record, we know that at the start of his sentence he weighed 165 pounds, stood five feet eight, and wore a size 7 shoe. He was of fair complexion, with gray hair and brown eyes. Foster had three brothers, Ross, Ash, and Charley Allen. The record describes him as having temperate habits, eyes that were typically half closed—that detail was listed under "peculiarities"—a fair education, one scar in the center of his forehead, two gunshot scars on his back on the shoulder, and two more scars on his left ankle. The scant information available about Foster leaves no indication of whether he had been enslaved, though his age at the time of his imprisonment indicates that he could have been. Shifting gears from the previous chapter about Celia, which involved much speculation, and the interlude, which stepped away from close reading to conceptually bridge the intervening years, this chapter will closely read Foster's words about his relation to the state and state institutions prior to his conviction, in order to glean what we can about him and his ideas.

Of the two extant request letters of Foster's, the first is dated April 28, 1901, and appeared in the *Montgomery Journal* on May 17 (the other one, dated September 5, 1901, is housed in the Alabama Department of Archives and History). I've not been able to locate an extant copy of the newspaper, let alone that issue, and yet, based on an examination of other contemporary Montgomery newspapers, it is clear that Foster's printed parole request is unique. Indeed, the headline expressly refers to it as such. It reads: "An Old Man a Convict Makes a Unique and Remarkable Appeal to Governor for a Pardon." Technically, Foster is appealing for parole, not a pardon, and he names it as such, so it's difficult to account for the mistake in the headline, but what follows is Foster's bold demand for parole, a lively series of justifications, an acknowledgment of his Blackness, and an argument for state deportation of imprisoned people on release. This last part indicates Foster's understanding of his enemy-of-the-state status (recall petit treason, ch. 3).

Foster's letter prepares his primary audience of the governor (and, by extension, newspaper readers) by framing himself as an old man as he begins to justify his request for parole. He attempts to appeal to the governor's sense of reason by providing context for the letter's purpose. Asserting a kind of authority, Foster's opening line commands the governor to read the letter with his age in mind (see figure 5.1). He begins, "Dear Governor:— Bear in mind that this is an old man writing to you at this time." Foster knows he is in a vulnerable position, and he rhetorically overthrows the power dynamic in order to direct the governor's interpretation of the request. Governor William J. Samford would have been fifty-five years old at the time Foster penned his letter. Following up on his command to read with the knowledge that Foster is in advanced years, the next sentence specifies his age and background and then, midway through the line, acknowledges the vulnerability that his first sentence seems to dismiss. He continues, "An old Virginian, 68 years of age, praying for a PAROLE." Foster is not simply requesting a parole; he is praying for it. This gesture toward the prayers of the needy is a seemingly standard deferential move aimed to curry favor and sympathy for an old man, but it also frames the religious analogy Foster uses later in the letter, when he compares himself to King David, who committed adultery and then murder (far worse crimes than Foster's), was pardoned by God, and went on to write sermons that many still preach. This gesture is reminiscent of Abraham Johnstone's reference to his adultery as a way to put into relief the gravity of the crime of perjury, Pomp's discussion that he will do good works preaching if released, and Nathaniel Turner's divine inspiration and self-fashioning as the sacrificial lamb. But to say that Foster's letter is righteous or self-righteous would be misleading, as there is a critical wryness to his work.

Every acknowledgment of guilt, every appeal to religious piety Foster makes, he counters with a sardonic critique of the system that has put him in the extreme situation he is in: a man nearly seventy years old sentenced to ten years for stealing another man's horse (more accurately, exchanging the animal for his own). The rhetorical strategy he employs emphasizes the excessive nature of his punishment. Though making a strong appeal for parole and taking the matter seriously in his prose, Foster refuses an obsequious approach. Describing his sentencing, he aligns himself with the sentencing judge, a Judge Bilbroe, granting himself a certain amount of agency in the decision: "And we, the Judge and I agreed that it was a mean act; an act unbecoming a gentleman of the first water. An act that merited stringent punishment. Therefore he squared himself, and gave me ten years." Here Foster indicates that the two agreed that punitive measures were warranted. In this move, he acknowledges his guilt and his acceptance of some punishment, both noble gestures, which sets up the shock the audience is meant to feel with those last few powerful words, "gave me ten years." The dramatic sentence concludes the paragraph, leaving the reader both potentially surprised at the length of sentence for the crime described and curious about Foster's reaction on hearing he would serve ten years.

As he recounts Judge Bilbroe's words, Foster frames his critique of the state prison system's convoluted and prejudicial sentencing process, which

AN OLD MAN A CONVICT

Makes a Unique and Remarkable Appeal to Governor for a Pardon.

Wetumpka, Ala., April 28th, 1901.
To His Excellency, Gov. W. J. Samford:

Dear Governor:—Bear in mind that this is an old man writing to you this time. An old Virginian, 68 years of age, praying for a PAROLE. And why is it? Because I, James Foster, the old man, have been indurance long enough; have suffered sufficiently for the crime I am charged with—I'm guilty of course. I plead guilty to grand larceny to Judge Bilbroe at the court house in Centre ,Cherokee county, Ala., about the last of July 1898. I told Judge Bilbroe, that I went into Dr. Slack's stable at midnight and exchanged horses with him. I left mine and took his. And we, the Judge and I agreed that it was a mean act; an act unbecoming a gentleman of the first water. An act that merited a stringent punishment. Therefore he squared himself, and gave me ten years.

After pronouncing the sentence, give vent to the following consolatory words, or its substance.

Judge Bilbroe: "It grieves me, Tuster, to send you, an old man to the penitentiary for so long a time, never-the-less, under the surrounding circumstances, I'm compelled to do it. Go now and be a good boy, and it may be the Governor will take a part of it off."

Now Governor, I love Judge Bilbroe some for his soothing words. They have braced me up; engendered a spirit of emulation, The hight of my ambition, from the first day I landed here on August 5th, 1898, until now, have to do my whole duty and at the proper time, put to test the supposition so charitably promulgated in my favor by his honor, the Judge. So far so good. Now we will see. When Warden Perkins took his departure, a few weeks ago, for his native hills in north Alabama, he gave me his hand and said 'good bye Tuster, you've been an excellent prisoner, a good man."

All the officers have been exceedingly kind to me, and with one accord say, "Tuster has been a good prisoner."

Now is there any reward in store for a good prisoner in the Alabama State prison? If not there should be! What is the PAROLE law for Governor if not to meet such cases as mine. A good prisoner without substantial friends or money? Oh, that you were "Our Bob" for about half an hour; My liberty would be sure.

Its a parole, I want, Governor. A parole with the conditions that I leave the state within 24 hours, never to return, else the parole to be forfeited with loss of short time on the 10 years I am now trying to do. Wouldn't it be to the best interest of the state, to have all ex-convicts to leave it? If so then, you should parole me at once; 'twould conform with your oath; you are sworn, if I understand it, to the best interests of the state. Law should be satisfied in my case. I've been here long enough, something over two years and eight months, equivalent to about twenty-five years to a man of 25 or 30 years of age . One year at my time of life is as much to me as ten or 12 would be to a young man.

If you should parole me, Governor, there would be no one to kick. Dr. Slack would not, because he has his own horse, the one I took, and also mine, the one I left in his stable at the time I took his, (took sounds more pleasant to the ear than stole) so you see he's a horse on me, and should not kick. And he may keep it with my best wishes.

I don't live in Cherokee county and do not expect to go back there. Never, Never. You may say. "Tuster, how came you in such a difficulty? Well, I can give no good excuse. I'm not an angel. The flesh is weak. It was a bit of degeneracy that might parallel with similar acts that many well bred men have fallen into; and in many instances where executive clemency was extended, pulled themselves up and became great and serviceable men. King David, with all his advantages through life, with the spirit of Jehovah continually upon him, committed the capital crime of adultry, and followed it with a cold blooded murder long before jack pots and moonshine whiskey was ever invented, and, Jehovah, after inflicting a light punishment, pardoned him, and he became afterwards a great and good man, from whose sublime writings thousands of sermons are preached annually. Christ pardoned the woman caught in the act of capital crime of adultry. "Go and sin no more," John 8-11. Be God-like, Governor. Say to poor old decrepit, repentant Tuster, "Go and sin no more."

Who knows but what, with a sweet parole in my grasp, I may emulate some of the best of king David's life. I've made a good prisoner, and by the everlasting Jupiter, I'll make a good citizen! Please write Governor and tell me what you will do.

Figure 5.1. James Foster's published first letter, "An Old Man a Convict." *Montgomery Journal*, May 17, 1901. Courtesy of Alabama Department of Archives and History.

has left the seemingly reasonable and repentant Foster exceedingly vulnerable. Foster delivers a demonstration of how even the judge thought the sentence may be too harsh, and encouraged him to seek a shorter sentence from the governor: "Judge Bilbroe: 'It grives [sic] me . . . to send you, an old man to the penitentiary for so long a time, never-the less [sic] under the surrounding circumstances, I'm compelled to do so. Go now and be a good boy, and it may be that the Governor will take a part of it off." The newly passed legislation left the option open for the sentencing judge patronizingly to console Foster with the hope of parole, a lesser sentence as a reward for good behavior. The mechanisms of power and control here are obvious. The state sentences a sixty-six-year-old Black man to ten years, which in the penitentiary means hard labor, and if he behaves himself he can maintain hope of an early release. With Foster at the mercy of this faulty justice system, the request letter is his best hope.

Although Alabama did not pass as many Black codes as other states did (due to external reactions to such legislation), it did increase fines and sentences for crimes against property. Legal historian David Martin notes, "Offenses against property contained increased penalties for theft and arson, with a minimum of five years in prison and up to the death penalty. These changes were based upon '. . . the White man's belief that the Negro race had a predilection for theft and arson'" (168, quoting Theodore B. Wilson). Meanwhile, white people generally had to be convicted of more serious crimes to be incarcerated. "Nearly 15 percent of all state prisoners [as of the late nineteenth century] were white males. Their crimes included murder, rape, and theft. If the act was heinous enough, and the perpetrator was unable to pay fines, whites could and did suffer imprisonment in the penitentiary. When it came to the local county system, however, whites were practically immune from prosecution" (Curtin 61). Combining this reluctance to prosecute white men in the county system with the demand that Black people serve hard labor to pay for their own prosecution, we see the capitalist conversion of slavery into convict leasing that many historians have noted. Martin further argues that "the Thirteenth Amendment to the U.S. Constitution and Section 1 of the Civil Rights Act of 1866 attempted to prevent slavery and discrimination, but arguably one effect of these enactments was to simply require Whites to find different methods of treating Blacks the same way as before. . . . A survey of the law and history in Alabama between 1866–1896 indicates that the rule of the law was used to deny the social, political, and economic advancement of Blacks" (187, 196). Those judged as contravening the rule of law were not just denied advancement, however; they were forced to provide a labor base akin to slave labor, with the inclusion of torture in conditions strongly resembling those of political prisoners, state enemies.

In prison, the corporal punishment of slavery continued into Reconstruction:

> Guards and contractors testified in detail how they whipped and tortured prisoners. "We whip with a leather strap or stick about an inch broad and two foot long," said one assistant superintendent. Prisoners were also whipped for "disobeying rules." The state code allowed up to thirty-nine lashes but far more were inflicted for fighting, tearing up bedding and clothes, and "sassing" the guards. If whipping did not cause submission, guards inflicted the torture of "water punishment." A prisoner was strapped down on his back; then "water [was] poured in his face on the upper lip, and effectually stops his breathing as long as there is a constant stream." Contractors wanted prisoners to work, and they maintained control through fear and torture. (Curtin 69)

The practice described here is similar to the controversial torture method we refer to today as waterboarding, which has been used by the United States against state enemies. Waterboarding simulates the experience of drowning and is widely criticized for being inhumane even as a method of torture, which itself is criticized for being inhumane and ineffective in practice. The Black codes, increased arrests of Black people for property crimes, attempts to maintain a virtually unpaid Black labor force through convict leasing, and whipping and torture of imprisoned Black people all represent precisely the legal and historical context during which Foster penned his requests for parole, in which he says as much and more about the state.

Foster makes a number of arguments in his letters that paroling him would fulfill the state's obligations, and he even promises to leave Alabama if paroled. In keeping with his understanding of his unofficial enemy-of-the-state status, he volunteers to deport himself. The author's promise to leave the county and the state for good is intended to reassure the governor that he would not make a mistake by releasing Foster. There is another reason Foster may have wanted to leave upon parole. Curtin explains, "To African Americans, a group that had known the humiliation of slavery, forced labor in postbellum prison mines was especially mortifying. . . . In an age that had supposedly abolished slavery, they had been whipped and abused by whites. They feared the ridicule of Black women and their communities. They dreaded being known as free men turned back into slaves" (201). Furthermore, the governor would not have to concern himself with the possibility of what the state would understand as Foster's recidivism. The racist and exploitative context of early twentieth-century Alabama, the fact that it is not Foster's home state (Foster being an "old Virginian"), and the potential humiliation of returning to the outside as a newly "freed slave" all offer powerful reasons for Foster to want to leave. Adhering to an appeal to the governor as the genre of the parole request requires, Foster's presentation of his proposed departure from Alabama as being in the best interest of the state anticipates and preempts as many counterarguments to his request as possible.

Foster reasons that if the governor accepts his offer, the governor will be fulfilling his oath of office. The author quotes a warden, Perkins, who, before leaving his post, had referred to Foster as an "excellent prisoner and a good man." Having given himself this sort of external reference, Foster then asks the governor to account for the parole law: "Now is there any reward in store for a good prisoner in Alabama State prison? If not there should be! What is the PAROLE law for Governor if not to meet such cases as mine. A good prisoner without substantial friends or money? Oh, that you were 'Our Bob' for about half an hour; My liberty would be sure." Questioning the rationale behind the still-recent parole law and then attempting to get the governor to put himself in Foster's shoes, the author makes his case directly: "It's a parole I want, Governor." Supporting his demand, he also bargains by offering a condition that he will leave the state within twenty-four hours. If he returns, he forfeits his parole.

Foster argues that the governor should require all parolees to leave Alabama. Given that most imprisoned people at this time were Black, perhaps the suggestion is that Foster sees no future for formerly incarcerated Black people in the state of Alabama. Indeed, he seems happy enough at the prospect of leaving for good, which is hardly surprising, in light of the relative seriousness of the crime versus the sentence. We can also recall the deportation that awaited enslaved people convicted of crimes in the early republic. If Foster was familiar with such laws, perhaps he imagined the additional punishment as making a persuasive argument for his release, a continuation of the slave laws that Alabama had been reluctant to forfeit after emancipation. Acknowledging his perceived enmity, his proposed departure from the state probably seemed a reasonable offer to the governor and a welcome solution for himself (see ch. 3 on Turner).

Foster's prose around vacating Alabama is particularly direct, revealing that he thinks beyond his best interests even as he requests their fulfillment.

He uses a rhetorical question to ask the governor whether that wouldn't be to the state's advantage, and then writes, "If so, then you should parole me at once; 't'would conform with your oath; you are sworn, if I understand it, to the best interests of the state." We could read this approach as brazen—risky, even, should the governor read this as too self-assured, "uppity," or presumptuous—but it also demonstrates Foster's knowledge of the duties of the governor's office and his willingness to detail them. He is not passive in his requests, but rather makes his case in the way a lawyer might.

Foster builds on this legal self-representative approach, reassuring the governor through a mathematical conversion of his time served into a younger man's terms: "Law should be satisfied in my case. I've been here long enough, something over two years and eight months, equivalent to about twenty-five years to a man of 25 or 30 years of age. One year at my time of life is as much to me as ten or 12 would be to a young man." If the governor were to do the math, Foster's calculations converting old-age years to young-age years indicate that he's already served double his original sentence. Through this argument—together with his earlier note that the sentencing judge indicated that the governor may lessen his sentence, the warden's comment on his good behavior, the fact that the parole law is meant to reward precisely such conduct, and his advanced age—Foster mounts a compelling case for his release, especially in light of the crime for which the state convicted him.

The force of Foster's argument for parole underscores the modesty of the crime in contrast to his sentencing, so modest that the person whose horse he stole wouldn't even have reason to complain if the state released him. "Dr. Slack would not [kick] because he has his own horse, the one I took, and also mine, the one I left in the stable at the time I took his, (took sounds more pleasant to the ear than stole) so you see he's a horse on me, and I should not kick. And he may keep it with my best wishes." Foster's self-conscious and explicit massaging of the diction he uses to describe his crime both deemphasizes the criminality of his actions (a move that functions in concert with his justification for a lesser sentence) and reinforces the fact that he has never tried to deny that he did take the doctor's horse. He even plays on the word *kick*, as horses kick. Here, Dr. Slack, the doctor's horse, and Foster's horse are all entwined through the word in a scenario that even the offended party has probably forgotten. What's more, through Foster's actions, the doctor came out a horse ahead. The tone is even a bit playful, as Foster explains the events following his arrest and the absurdity of his remaining incarcerated. With Foster's promises to leave the state, not even the doctor can provide the governor with a counterargument to the parole request.

Having attempted to fully justify release and preempt possible counterarguments, Foster broadens his argument with a biblical analogy to explain how the governor, far from making a mistake by paroling him, would be doing a great public service, beyond the state's interests he is sworn to protect. Just as Johnstone, Pomp, and Turner referenced scripture in their theories of race, criminality, enmity, and criminal justice, Foster centers the Bible in his argument against his incarceration and the racist injustices he faces as an unfairly sentenced, incarcerated, leased, and aging Black man. With a nod to humility (and in keeping with Johnstone's confession for having cheated on his wife), Foster acknowledges that he is "not an angel. The flesh is weak. It [the horse theft] was a bit of degeneracy that might parallel with similar acts that many well bred men have fallen into; and in many instances where executive clemency was extended, pulled themselves up and became great and serviceable men." The notion of becoming serviceable through clemency recalls Pomp's turn to preaching while in jail and his argument for the good he could continue to do if not for his impending execution.

Similar also to Johnstone's biblically inspired critique of having been disadvantaged by white supremacy and unjustly sentenced to death for a murder he didn't commit, Foster's parole request enacts a scripturally rhetorical move. In it, Foster elevates the governor and himself as analogous to Jehovah and King David, respectively, yet he still acknowledges that King David had far more advantages and committed far worse acts than he, thereby heightening the intensity of his argument about the unfairness of his incarceration. Through these means, he preempts the possibility that anyone could fairly criticize him as arrogant for imagining himself as occupying the same social status as a king from the Bible. Foster argues:

> King David, with all his advantages through life, with the spirit of Jehovah continually upon him, committed the capital crime of adultery, and followed it with a cold blooded murder long before jack pots and moonshine whiskey was ever invented, and, Jehovah, after inflicting a light punishment, pardoned him, and he became afterwards a great and good man, from whose sublime writings thousands of sermons are preached annually. Christ pardoned the woman caught in the act of capital crime of adultery. "Go and sin no more," John 8–11. Be

God-like, Governor, Say to poor old decrepit, repentant Tuster, [sic] "Go and sin no more."

In this paragraph, Foster underscores the privilege differential (economic and religious) between King David and himself, and acknowledges the difference in severity of the crimes they both committed, his larceny as opposed to David's "capital crime of adultery" and then "a cold blooded murder." Such a move both draws attention to the relatively minor act of stealing a horse and suggests the ways in which laws change over time. For example, by 1901 adultery was no longer a crime at all, let alone a capital crime, though the Alabama legislature that year ratified a Constitution that named larceny as a crime of "moral turpitude" and disenfranchised those convicted for it—the racist intent of the law being widely understood (section 182).[1] Nevertheless, Foster encourages the reader to see that the law's recognition of crimes' severity continually shifts. If sleeping with another person's spouse was a capital crime at one time but not any longer, what are the implications for the turn-of-the-century crime of exchanging another man's horse with one's own, especially in the context of leasing primarily Black people for hard labor?

By comparison, of course, Foster's implicit weighing of the seemingly petty crimes of gambling and making whiskey against two capital crimes in their day—adultery and murder—makes his point both that David for all of his extraordinary privileges still committed serious criminal offenses, and that the sentencing David received from Jehovah (the ultimate judge, no less) was far more lenient than what the disadvantaged Foster received for exchanging a horse. Furthermore, David was pardoned. Foster simply requests parole so that he may "Go and sin no more" and, as David did, potentially do some good upon release: "Who knows but what," he continues, "with a sweet parole in my grasp, I may emulate some of the best of king David's life. I've made a good prisoner, and by the everlasting jupiter, I'll make a good citizen." As we've seen in previous chapters of Black prison intellectuals who anticipate Frederick Douglass's description of his transformation from "a man ... made a slave" into "a slave ... made a man" (*Narrative* 65–66), here Foster's use of parallelism promises a similar transformation upon parole, this time from "good prisoner" to "good citizen." His desire to leave the state implies both that he would be a good citizen elsewhere and that the prospects for Black people in Alabama in his own time are bleak. Perhaps he believes that other states do not perceive the same enmification of

Black people convicted of crimes. We might recall here as well that the low percentage of the prison population who were white had been convicted of much more serious, violent crimes than Foster's, another parallel with the privileged David.

Rhetorically strategic, Foster's parole request letter employs literary tactics of metaphor, irony, analogy, and ventriloquism, to name a few, in order to justify his request to the governor and convince the statesman that parole would be a just move even in an unjust system. Foster both directly and indirectly showcases his talents as a writer and rhetorician as his missive works to persuade the governor to grant him early release.

Ultimately, however, this letter was unsuccessful in its effort to secure parole, as we can surmise from an extant subsequent letter from Foster to Samford's successor. The second letter, handwritten on penitentiary stationery, is dated September 5, 1901, and refers to the published letter, which it encloses as a clipping (see figure 5.2). In this second letter, we can detect Foster's incrementally deflating sense of hope that he will enjoy the early release he seeks. Nevertheless, the second parole request still exhibits the lively character, engaging prose, and sharp wit that we encounter in his first. This letter offers proof that Foster could set up his own photography business if paroled—that is, that he would gainfully employ himself, would not be a financial burden wherever he went, and would not need to rely on white people to hire him. In this letter, Foster underscores the governor's power over him. "To His Excellency Governor W. D. Jelks . . . I write you praying for a Parole." In this letter, he explains that he'd written to the previous governor just before he died, a letter "in which I exhausted near all my witts soliciting a Parole, consequently can say very little here that would add further strength to my case." Foster's frustration at having written already to plead his case for early release only to have his previous addressee die and a new governor take his place becomes evident in this letter. Rather than make his case again, he directs the governor to the clipping from the newspaper.

Foster turns again to the imperative to persuade Jelks and attempts to appeal to the man's position of power, even to flatter him. Frustration and desperation are palpable in this letter. "See inclosed above mentioned letter cliped from the 'Montgomery Journal.' Peruse, cogitate and tell me what you will do for me. I being pennyless it's about all I can offer in my defence. If I had money I would undoubtedly employ a lawyer of influence to present my case before You and the Board of Pardons, But alas I have none: therefore will be compelled to rely solely for executive clemency upon what

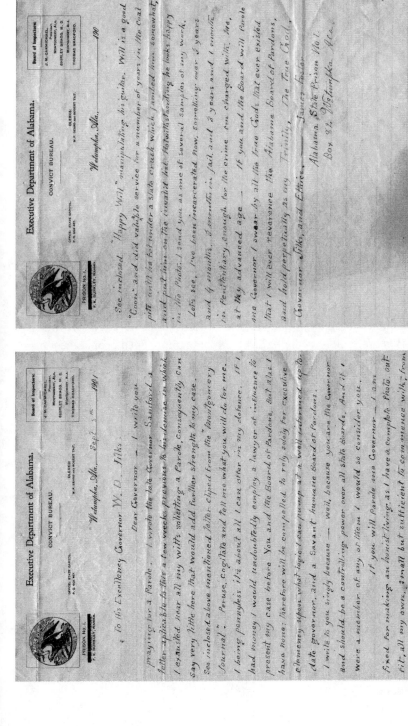

Figure 5.2. Letter from James Foster to the governor on penitentiary stationery, September 5, 1901. Courtesy of Alabama Department of Archives and History.

logic I can pump at a well informed up-to-date governor, and a savant humane Board of Pardons." Foster's strategy here is to imply that if Jelks were "well informed [and] up-to-date" (perhaps as opposed to Governor Samford, whose health allowed him only to serve one interim year, with Jelks serving as acting governor for Samford) and the board "savant humane," they would parole him in accordance with how he laid out his case in the newspaper clipping (as someone of nearly seventy serving ten years for a fairly insignificant crime). He underscores the impossible position he is in as incapable of hiring a lawyer "of influence" to represent him and therefore having to make his case again himself, vulnerable to the rulings of different governors and boards of pardon.

Furthermore, Governor Jelks was an outspoken advocate of white supremacy and lynching. A journalist and co-owner of several Alabama newspapers, William D. Jelks had made his views on such subjects well known. He would publicly if temporarily change his stance on lynching between 1903 and 1905, earning national attention for his antilynching advocacy during those years, but at the time Foster was appealing to him the governor was working on the Constitution that proposed the disenfranchisement of Black, poor, and illiterate people. Nevertheless, Jelks's reform of the convict leasing program is credited with improving imprisoned people's health care and living conditions (Alsobrook). It is likely that Foster would have been well familiar with Jelks's ideas about Black people.

It is perhaps worth noting here that penitentiaries not only leased inmates to coal mines for work, but also offered some formal education. As Curtin points out, though, "By no means did prisoners have access to regular education; and after spending a day at the mines, an evening in a classroom may not have appealed to all" (31). However, she also explains, "state prisoners gained the benefits of state-funded stationery" (31). I mention this because Foster authored his letters in the penitentiary. Wherever he learned to write, he employs various rhetorical tactics that fulfill the purpose of the parole request letter but that also critique the injustice of his situation, and he used state stationery to do so. There is an added layer of admonishment, perhaps, in reading Foster's implicit critique of the Black codes and the state's justice system more broadly when this critique is lodged on the state's own paper (see figure 5.2). When we think back to Celia's case and her actions as a reminder of the contestation of law—the idea that "consciousnesses are never shaped by the content of the law"—we can see something similar happening here in writing (Hartog 934–35; see ch. 4).

Foster makes the case for his early release by appealing to Jelks's power and explaining that he would be able to support himself and not be a burden to his community: "I write to you simply because—well, because you are the Governor and should be a controlling power over all state Boards [perhaps a suggestion of Jelks's role in the board's being 'savant humane']. And if I were a member of any of them I would so consider you." Putting himself in the imagined position of state board member may have been a poor strategy for appealing to a racist governor such as Jelks, and we do not know whether the governor paroled Foster; however, the tactic might have come across as flattery. Foster argues that he would immediately upon release be able to sustain himself financially with his photography business. "If you will Parole me governor—I am fixed for making an honest living as I have a complete Photo Outfit, all my own, small but sufficient to commence with, from which I am making a few pictures at periods when not at work." This line indicates that though he is working as part of the lease program, he is practicing photography in his spare time. In fact, in this letter he also includes examples of his photography, the artistic pursuit through which he previously earned a living. Through this, he offers a glimpse into the world of imprisoned Black people, highlighting his talent and his potential to support himself on release.

As Foster did in the first letter, in his second he uses an imperative statement, this time compelling the governor to "See inclosed 'Happy Will' manipulating his guitar" (figure 5.3). Foster's approach here is to emphasize his artistic work, offer a visual image of an imprisoned Black man who is also artistic (musical), and underscore Will's Blackness as well as the physical dangers of the convict leasing program: "Will is a good 'Coon' and did valuable service for a number of years in the coal pits until he fel under a slate crush which jambed him somewhat, and put him on the invalid list. Notwithstanding he looks happy." This last sentence, as well as the opening reference to the nickname "Happy Will," is curious in that it draws on racial stereotypes of the "happy coon," who remains gleeful under the pressures of hard physical labor or injury. I read it as an attempt to appeal to the governor's assumed racism, but also as a way to make the image appealing to the governor despite the irony I think Foster uses in his description, particularly in the single quotation marks he inserts around the racial slur. In the photograph, Will looks almost defiant. Even in his prison clothing, he is stylish: hat tipped to the side, cigarette in the corner of his mouth, posture relaxed, and eyes directed at Foster's lens, with a look that is calm,

Figure 5.3. *Happy Will*, photograph by James Foster, 1901. Courtesy of Alabama Department of Archives and History.

almost rebellious. Though the Jamaican rebel outlaw Vincent "Ivanhoe" Martin (also known as Rhyging, 1924–48), who would inspire Jimmy Cliff's Ivan in the 1972 Jamaican film *The Harder They Come*, would not be born for another two decades, Will is nearly his spitting image. Perhaps Will is "happy" having his guitar, cigarette, and rocking chair, but this image does not match the "happy coon" stereotype that Foster's letter conveys. I read this as Foster's attempt to both conjure and explode the stereotype as the governor regards the image of Will.

With reference to folk culture, Curtin refers to anthropologist Lawrence W. Levine's explanation:

> Black folklore did not idolize prisoners, outlaws, or criminals. Despite popular songs that told the story of "Stagolee" and other "bad men,"

according to Levine, "Black folk refused to romantically embellish or sentimentalize" such characters. As he points out, Black folklore lacks a criminal hero such as Robin Hood or Jesse James, bad men who nevertheless were chivalrous to women and gave riches to the poor. No "noble" outlaws exist in Black folk culture. Instead, these "negro bad men" preyed on everyone: rich, poor, male, and female. They were to be feared and their acts resulted in prison or death—decidedly undesirable, antisocial outcomes. As Levine trenchantly observed, "The situation of Negroes in the United States was too complex for nostalgia." This was especially true in the Alabama Black Belt, where Black people suffered criminal acts at the hands of both whites and Blacks. (184)

Foster's photograph of "Happy Will" evokes this image of Black outlaw culture. Will appears in the photograph as the sort of rebel outlaw that, as I argued in chapter 4, is a lens through which we might also see Celia.

Figure 5.4. Untitled photograph by James Foster, 1901. Courtesy of Alabama Department of Archives and History.

Figure 5.5. Untitled photograph by James Foster, 1901. Courtesy of Alabama Department of Archives and History.

Furthermore, the composition of the photograph demonstrates Foster's skill as an artist and professional, offering more dimensions to his character than the category "convict" reveals.

The other portraits are similarly compelling, and offer a window into the world of Black people imprisoned at the Alabama State Penitentiary in Wetumpka (see figures 5.4, 5.5, and 5.6). In them we can note slight differences in clothing, the relative prevalence of the guitar, evidence of a cigarette allowance, styles of kerchief tying and haircuts, and, most importantly, facial expressions we can interpret as signaling frustration, dejection, hopelessness, even depression. Though these photographs are in keeping with the style of early twentieth-century photography, in which subjects did not smile, there is still something precisely visible of the harsh realities of state prison life for Black men imprisoned in Alabama.

According to Foster's convict record, he was paroled, date unknown, but this parole was revoked on November 4, 1904. He then escaped on November 17, 1904, was recaptured on October 28, 1909, and paroled again on July

Figure 5.6. Untitled photograph by James Foster, 1901. Courtesy of Alabama Department of Archives and History.

23, 1914 (*Alabama*). His second letter's desperate tone and the determined character we glean from reading his letters together recalls Celia, who escaped the Missouri jail nearly fifty years before Foster. The timing of Foster's eventual parole puts him at the age of approximately eighty-one at the time of his release. These details leave us with many questions about why his parole was revoked, whether he initially left the state as he promised he would, whether he continued to photograph, how he escaped, and why he was paroled eventually in 1914. Did he do any more writing?

Similar to study of Celia's story in antebellum Missouri, regardless of the answers to the many questions still lingering about Foster's time in and out of prison, his letters provide tremendous insight into the aftermath of Reconstruction in Alabama, convict leasing, sentencing, the parole process, and the man Foster himself. His letters offer a basis from which we can read and compare others' practices in this genre of writing as another mode of

Black testimony, protest, and critique. I wonder whether Foster enjoyed the life he sought after incarceration or perhaps whether, even at his advanced age, he participated in the Great Migration. In a state that was determined to continue the exploitation of Black people after emancipation, that supported lynching, and that enjoyed the rise of the Ku Klux Klan and its influence on Alabama politics, I'm not sure he did find the life he sought.[2]

Parole request letters from the 1920s and 1930s exhibit a similar sense of urgency, as well as the frustration and hopelessness that come with multiple rejections in the New South, reminiscent of the more famous correspondence of the Scottsboro Boys (Kinshasa). The next decades would see the second rise of the Ku Klux Klan, campaigns to end convict leasing, and the Great Depression, all providing context for the next generation of Black parole request letter writers from the Deep South. Many requesters penned their own letters, while in other instances, family members wrote to attorneys appealing for their help to secure parole for loved ones. A primary justification for parole in the 1930s is from farmers concerned about getting in their crops. The Depression era and missed crops could spell starvation for farming families. Similar to Foster's multiple appeals, Black-authored parole request letters held in the collections of the Alabama Department of Archives and History report offenses such as "unlawful train riding" (which received a sentence of "45 days hard labor") and reveal parolees unable to find work to pay the balance of their sentences (Alexander). There are not many requests from imprisoned women, but they certainly exist. I tried in vain to track down a twenty-six-page letter from Julia Ann May, an approximately fifty-year-old Black woman, to her lawyer, laying out her argument for parole in July 1899. Unfortunately, the letter itself seems to have been lost. Her convict record indicates that she was sentenced to life on March 29, 1892, and her attorney R. B. Smyer's letters to the governor indicate that she was convicted for the murder of her twelve-year-old daughter's baby on the testimony of a "negro girl (10 yrs old)."

Continued exploration of these letters gives us another literary genre to study, as hard labor meets intellectual labor. The letters also offer a series of personal histories of incarceration, contributing to our understanding of the foundational trajectory of Black prison intellectuals from the earliest years of the United States, as they theorized and experienced the realities of enmification in the unofficial war against them. The letters, too, offer firsthand insight into the history of US prison culture. These requests reveal much about the nation's transition from slavery to the internationally unparalleled and inhumane incarceration of Black people, a situation seemingly unceasing and still growing in the United States, despite painstaking efforts by activists, writers, intellectuals, artists, social workers, and friends and family of those imprisoned. The figures of the mid- to late twentieth century we think of when we think of the Black prison intellectual tradition have their roots in the nation's inception. As letters and confessions from the gallows are now a much studied and valued contribution to American letters and history, I hope the parole request letter will find a similar place of importance in the canon, and that close study of such letters might help change the attitudes and works of those who would continue the injustice.

Conclusion

Early Black Prison Intellectual Legacies

The figures centered in *Black Prison Intellectuals* represent what might seem like a prehistory. The intellectual history of imprisoned Black people in the United States—and not only their criminalization, but their enmification—continues to this day and throws into stark relief the white supremacy that governs US institutions and the ideas that bolster them. The forerunners of the tradition of thought that threatens the reign of white supremacist thinking provide the foundation for those central to more recent articulations of Black intellectual critique coming from within carceral institutions. In short, what we see in Black intellectual critique in the twentieth and twenty-first centuries—from criticism of the prevalence of police violence to white assumptions of Black guilt to the association of Blackness with state enmity—is nothing new, not by a long shot. It's as old as the history of the United States, and a product of colonialism.

Without question, it is not difficult to list the names of those more recent figures who would populate a second volume of this book: Mumia Abu-Jamal; Reginald Dwayne Betts; Susan Burton; Rubin "Hurricane" Carter; Eldridge Cleaver; Angela Davis; Malcolm X; Chester Himes; George Jackson; Bobby Seale; Angelo Herndon; Olen Montgomery, Clarence Norris, Haywood Patterson, Ozie Powell, Willie Robertson, Charles Weems, Eugene Williams, Andrew Wright, and Leroy "Roy" Wright (the Scottsboro Boys); Assata Shakur; the writers from *Inside This Place, Not of It* (Levi and Waldman); and the writers of *The Sentences That Create Us* (Meissner), to name just a few. There are countless people less well known from the twentieth- and twenty-first centuries who could also feature in a second volume and who reveal the continued criminalization and enmification of Black people in the United States. They offer important criticism of the interrelation of incarceration, racism, and sexism in their time. Further study of their ancestors beyond what I have done here in looking at the eighteenth and nineteenth centuries of imprisonment in the United States and its relation to Blackness is central to this larger project.

Black prison intellectuals Abraham Johnstone, Pomp, Nathaniel Turner, Celia, and James Foster critique injustice—from slavery to incarceration—and reveal enduring truths about systemic and individual violence as foundational to US cultures of oppression. The work of their contemporary imprisoned Black authors—such as Fortune (1762); Bristol (1763); Arthur (1768); Joseph Mountain (1790); Edmund Fortis (1795); Stephen Smith (1797); John Joyce and Peter Matthias (1808); Madison Henderson, Alfred Amos Warrick, James W. Seward, and Charles Brown (1841); William J. Anderson (1857); and William Walker (1892)—as well as the numerous unpublished authors of postbellum parole request letters, and those who did not leave their own written record and whose actions resulted in their incarceration, all warrant closer reading. Such analysis would focus on what their actions reveal about their motivations and shed important light on their individual histories and the deep histories of the crises we face today.

Black Prison Intellectuals not only underscores the literary, critical, and historical relevance of different genres of prison writing; it also reveals the forms of testimony that navigated complicated publishing practices and produced witness accounts outside racially restricted courtrooms. Such work provides a window into the world of incarceration during the period of legal slavery and convict leasing programs, which continued efforts to target and silence Black people and their critique in and of the United States.

This ancestry of Black prison intellectuals is important in its own right, and provides crucial insight into the foundations of the mass incarceration that flourishes today. Arrests and convictions of women and girls are rising in the United States, particularly for women and girls of color (see *Sentencing Project*). COVID-19 infection and death rates in prison have underscored the reality of what it means to be "inside," with the understanding that the distinction between inside and outside is as arbitrary as it is fictitious. The treatment of pregnant Black and Indigenous peoples and people of color, including under COVID-19, highlights the reproductive injustices carceral systems and their supporters perpetrate against an already racially skewed population ("COVID-19"). Shortages of books and print materials in prisons, partly due to the proliferation of "public-facing" online publication and restrictions on works by anti-incarceration activist authors, mean that access to information for imprisoned people is severely limited. Additional barriers to information access exist once incarcerated individuals have "done their time." Upon release, many people who have been incarcerated discover the difficulty of navigating our technological world; practices from cell phone etiquette to more advanced yet more ubiquitous uses of technology can be barriers for formerly incarcerated people, barriers that even the most well-intentioned friends, relatives, and potential employers might not understand or anticipate.

Comprehending the crises we face today requires analysis of this deep US history of race, racism, and incarceration. That was part of the inspiration for writing this book: the false association of Blackness with criminality and enmity dates back to the nation's roots, visible in Abraham Johnstone's and Pomp's eighteenth-century republican/revolutionary rhetoric of Blackness and Britishness.

Johnstone's pamphlet reassigns revolutionary rhetoric to expose hypocrisies in the politics of New Jersey and, by extension, the new republic in general. He argues that the true enemies of the state are white supremacist people and that they are threats to state and national security. Pomp's critique of slavery in Massachusetts demonstrates how his legal personhood, achieved through his arrest for committing a crime, translates him into an early national enemy requiring expulsion from the social body. Both men, each in his own way, refute associations between Blackness and enmity and expose the workings of white racism in the late eighteenth-century northeastern United States.

In the nineteenth century, Nathaniel Turner's and Celia's works reveal how the color line factors in distinctions between revolution and terrorism in the "official" narratives of the South and Black resistance. Turner's Southampton revolt, confession, newspaper coverage, trial, and execution call into question contemporaneous explanations for the Virginia revolt and demonstrate how the law functioned as an enemy to Black people, especially Black people who rebelled. Similarly, Celia's physical violence in response to myriad forms of violence white people enacted on her, her escapes from Missouri county jail, her attempts to help other people escape, newspaper coverage of Celia, her confessions, and her ultimate execution all add more dimensions of character and context to her case. Turner's and Celia's works also exhibit the ways in which legal systems cast them as enemies of the state. Each represents a kind of outlaw who is rebellious, even revolutionary.

James Foster's early twentieth-century exposure of the transfer of structures of enslavement to those of convict leasing programs in Alabama, too, tells the critical story of Blackness and incarceration in the United States.

His work invites us to see the realities of prison work, the hypocrisies of pardon and parole laws, and the racially motivated injustices of post-Reconstruction law. Foster uses an important mode of testimony—the parole request letter—to call attention to his case and critique it. I believe that the parole request letter is a revealing form of writing and a compelling literary genre in its own right, worthy of further in-depth study and analysis.

More than a century later, the United States continues to imprison more people than anywhere else in the world. If we are to understand the dire situation we are in today—the stark and violent racial lines on which incarceration is based; the people whom the war on drugs and tough-on-crime legislation continue to target; and the long-standing violence of policing against Black communities—we must reckon with centuries-deep histories, and listen to the people who tell these stories from the start.

I'll conclude with a few profound words from poet, novelist, and scholar Ian Williams: "Because we can't realistically know everything, humility is the best companion to ignorance" (32).

NOTES

Introduction

1 Four key scholars analyze the ancestral knowledge and the Black prophetic tradition central to this book. The first is Jennifer C. James, who observes about "the relationship between [Old Testament] religious tradition and African Americans' attitudes toward war: first, that blacks have developed a notion of 'just war' in light of their own historical experiences of oppression; second, that those experiences have made it correspondingly difficult to abandon collective violence as a tool of liberation and justice; and third, that the centrality of sacred warfare in the black prophetic tradition's mythologies has led to a tolerance of secular war, however unintentionally" (168). I read her work particularly in light of Turner and my criminal/enemy thesis more broadly. The next scholar is Devonya N. Havis, who argues that "Spirituals, Work Songs, Blues, and other forms of Black expressive culture operationalize 'thick' conceptions of Blackness and Black cultures generated in those sacred liminal sites of Black Ancestral Discourses. Such 'thick' conceptions transpose the racialized, gendered economy of the weary oppression trope, making it possible to hear Blackness in a different register—beyond the limited possibilities available when conceiving blackness as mere oppressed opposition or counterpoint to whiteness" (154). All the figures I study in this volume anticipate this conception through the forms available to them—dying words, confessions, depositions, and letters. The third scholar is David G. Holmes, who points out that "historically, African American prophetic rhetoric was rarely just about reaching heaven; it was mostly about renouncing the hell on earth that Black folk encountered. Over the years Blacks—enslaved and segregated—interpreted their struggle through their racial and cultural experiences, and mined those experiences into discursive strategies and brilliance of Black ways of knowing and being" (244). All narratives of the book do this; *Black Prison Intellectuals* reveals this ancestral knowledge and prophetic tradition. And the fourth scholar I want to acknowledge is Erroll A. Henderson, who contends through W. E. B. Du Bois that "the US Civil War and its immediate aftermath was a revolution that transformed the USA—if only until the end of Reconstruction: It radically transformed the polity by recognizing the citizenship rights of former slaves—and blacks, in general; the economy by outlawing slavery; and the society by establishing a *de jure* basis for black social equality. Thus, it was a political, eco-

nomic, and social revolution" (194). To these four, I'll add my own essay "Ancestors and the Ivory Tower."

2 In keeping with my theory to follow that literacy is not a requisite feature of intellectualism, I refer to the figures studied in this book as authors, even when amanuenses transcribed their accounts.

3 These ideas build on the work of my previous book, *Black Well-Being: Health and Selfhood in Antebellum Black Literature* (2016), in which I argue that the physical, intellectual, and emotional are all components of selfhood; that Frederick Douglass, for one example, refuses to de-emphasize the body because of fear that attention to the intellect will suffer as a result; and that the use of violent and unlawful acts can function as intellectual work (162, 166, 172).

4 To date, I have not been able to discern how or where Foster died.

5 It is also noteworthy that hooks distinguishes between intellectuals and the professional class (hooks and West 119).

6 Dylan Rodríguez makes the point that "the terms 'prison intellectual,' 'prison writer,' or 'radical prisoner' (terms that I freely used until the last revisions of this manuscript) tend to reinscribe and naturalize the regime of imprisonment, as if it were a natural feature of the social landscape and an irreducible facet of the 'prisoner's' identity and historical subjectivity" (3). I understand this position, but here and with reference to the much-earlier period I am studying, I want to emphasize the imprisoned person as well as the jail and prison as sites of intellectual work for incarcerated Black people. I hope that my use of *prison intellectual* does not naturalize carceral regimes, but rather underscores the continuing relevance of the work of the people in this book.

7 This book's centralization of the category of the enemy encompasses considerations of humanity and processes of dehumanization important to individual, community, and state creation of "the enemy." My preoccupation here is less with the constitution of the human and beyond and more with the Black prison intellectuals' legal and literary articulations of enmity, with the understanding that they occupy the legal category of human, even if when they are enslaved the state only understands them as legal persons in the context of criminal law and the commission of crime.

8 As a brief note on chronology: the book begins with Johnstone's 1797 pamphlet to introduce the genres of dying words and confessions as it is an anomalous example. The next chapter will draw on the generic introductions laid out in this chapter and look toward the Black prophetic tradition we see in the third chapter about Nathaniel Turner and the Southampton revolt.

9 My research at the American Antiquarian Society uncovered much new information about Pomp's amanuensis and Pomp himself—information that is often impossible to find in the genre of gallows literature. A version of this chapter appeared in a special issue of *Early American Literature* on disability (see Stone, "Lunacy").

Chapter 1. Gallows Death and Political Critique

1 I'd like to acknowledge and thank my colleagues from the Conference on Problematizing the Self in Eighteenth-Century Autobiographical Writing in English, at the Université de Paris Diderot 7, November 2014, for their valuable thoughts and insights about this work in its early stages.
2 It is worth noting that Philadelphia was the new nation's temporary capital during the time of Johnstone's publication.
3 Contextualizing the apex of people writing from prison in the 1790s, Jodi Schorb argues, "With an apparatus designed to encourage and facilitate readers' trust in Johnstone's authority and reliability, the *Address* reveals the potential of writing prisoners to repurpose confession narratives into platforms for radical social critique" (69).
4 Samuel Otter notes that in Johnstone's period, "In the case of black criminals, authorities sometimes implied that merely to be an African in America was to have violated the law" (41).
5 My reading of Johnstone extends and, perhaps more optimistically, somewhat contrasts Ajay Kumar Batra's analysis, which argues that "gallows texts such as Johnstone's functioned, on the one hand, to naturalize the historically persistent link between blackness and moral degeneracy and, on the other, to persuade readers of the need for black subjects to submit to the disciplines associated with divine salvation and civic inclusion" (335).
6 This book's first and last chapters emphasize the endurance of this fear of Black idleness/slothfulness from early eighteenth-century enslavement to early twentieth-century imprisonment.
7 Otter notes, paraphrasing Mathew Carey's 1793 *Short Account* of Philadelphia's yellow fever epidemic, that "in a New Jersey town, the residents establish[ed] a patrol to guard against Philadelphians," a measure that Philadelphian readers of Johnstone's pamphlet four years later might well have remembered (56). Johnstone's pamphlet amplifies the era's political connections or parallels between New Jersey and Philadelphia at the time of his life, death, and publication.
8 Banner notes that the addresses condemned people gave served as warnings and "tended like the sermons to reinforce hierarchies of race and gender" (42). Johnstone's subversion of this convention of the genre makes use of active double-voiced discourse in appearing to address Black people, but functioning to critique white spectators and readers and the injustice of his conviction and condemnation.
9 The last word is somewhat illegible, but it looks as though it reads *lamb*.
10 Schorb quotes Sarah Pearsall's work on transatlantic missives: "'Letter-writers, men and women, measured each other's credit, in domestic and economic terms, as much through their letters as through their behavior.' Thus, cautions Pearsall, letters were unreliable indicators of '"real" or "private" feelings,' but instead they were 'dialogic,' seeking equally to fashion others' behavior along with a self. Above all, letters expressed the writer's insistent desire to establish credibility during an era of intense anxiety over whom to trust, an anxiety itself generated by the spread of print" (62). Referring to Pearsall's argument about how letter-writers relied on "artifice and

convention," Schorb asserts that "even the most conventional exchanges between prisoners and their spouses, children, or supporters could function as conveyors of truth and models of authenticity to a reading public familiarizing themselves with the new art of letter writing" (63). Schorb's excellent reading of Johnstone's letter focuses on "familial disintegration" as a thread of his "wider social critique," whereas this book concentrates on the missive's political critique (67). The social and political implications of Johnstone's mostly neglected *Letter to His Wife* are coming into relief. Furthermore, religious allusions feature prominently and function similarly in James Foster's parole requests two hundred years after Johnstone's letter.

Chapter 2. Lunacy and Liberation, Black Crime and Disability

1 I would like to thank the graduate students of the Harvard University American Studies Workshop for their invitation to present an early version of this paper and for their helpful insights and questions. I also extend thanks to participants of the International Interdisciplinary Scientific Symposium on the Birth of Mental Illness, at Jagiellonian University, Kraków, Poland, as well as Michael Thurston, the anonymous reviewers, and issue editors Sari Altschuler and Cristobal Silva of *Early American Literature*'s special issue on disability (vol. 52, no. 1, 2017) for their most useful comments and suggestions on the article version of this chapter, "Lunacy and Liberation: Black Crime, Disability, and the Production and Eradication of the Early National Enemy."

2 Another note on chronology, following the last chapter: this chapter travels back in time two years from Johnstone's *Address, Dying Confession, and Letter to His Wife* (1797) to build on the confession and dying words genres introduced in the previous chapter and, then, frame the next chapter, about the Southampton revolt, Black prophetic tradition, and ideas about madness/lunacy and what we now refer to as disability. Pomp's text demonstrates a connection between genre, tradition, and legacy in Black prison intellectual work.

3 Jennifer Barclay offers a reading on the connection between disability and minstrelsy (126–86). The emergence of minstrel shows and freak shows in the United States coincides historically with the Southampton revolt in Virginia, the subject of the next chapter.

4 John Sekora and Sheila J. Nayar offer readings that emphasize the influence of Plummer on Pomp's confession. Thinking about Pomp's narrative and confession and beyond, however, I position my analysis more in the tradition of literary scholar Frances Smith Foster's work on early crime narratives and the origins of African American print culture, and legal historian Christopher Tomlins's readings of Black consciousness. I remain inspired by Foster's foundational argument, mentioned in the previous chapter, that in crime narratives "the black person as statistic or subject gave way to the black person as narrator," particularly when Black testimony was inadmissible (*Witnessing* 36). Furthermore, Foster's "leer[iness] of claims to 'comprehensive' or 'definitive' narratives," combined with recovery work that understands how "with African-American texts, as with other cultural materials produced by and for other devalued groups, so much has already been lost, gone

astray, or been stolen that complete restoration is impossible," suggests the need for continued recovery work that requires close reading for what the "black person as statistic or subject" turned narrator might be telling even with or through, for example, white amanuenses ("Narrative" 714). Tomlins more recently contends that "for too many years, historians of slavery disdained as untrustworthy the glimpses of slave consciousness available in autobiographical testimonials, gallows confessions, abolitionist sponsored slave narratives, folklore, and ethnographic interviews . . . prefer[ring] actuarial records, plantation ledgers, planters' diaries, and the observations of northern travelers" (xi–xii). Aware of the fraught and complicated context of the late eighteenth-century publication of Black-authored/orated texts, this book reads for what it may glean about what these authors/orators desired to tell.

5 I see Pomp's creative resistance as complicating Shoshana Felman's contention that "quite the opposite of rebellion, madness is the impasse confronting those whom cultural conditioning has deprived of the very means of protest or self-affirmation" (quoted in Jarman 21), because I understand his articulation of his condition as a combination of messily, mutually influential biological and social experiences.

6 Sheila J. Nayar offers a compelling argument that Pomp/Plummer may have inspired Edgar Allan Poe's "The Tell-Tale Heart," "with its own unhinged narrator who murders the old man with whom he shares his abode." She continues: "Conceivably, then, there is a multidirectional flow when it comes to fugitive slave narratives and other indigenously American literary genres" (203). Some scholars (Frances Smith Foster and George Elliott Clarke, just to name two) have disputed the notion that the slave narrative is, as Nayar defines it, an "indigenously American literary genre"; however, the possibility that Poe's story and perhaps the horror/mystery/detective genre more generally found their origins in the increasingly secular and sensationalized genre of the criminal confession (and, for Poe, specifically in Pomp's account) seems plausible and worth further consideration.

7 Here I use *mental distress* in lieu of *mental illness* in the way Michelle Jarman does. She writes, "In order to destabilize the dominant medical/psychiatric discourses around mental illness, which frame the experience in terms of 'individual pathology' or 'disorder,' I often refer to mental distress, which attempts to challenge the static nature illness diagnoses tend to impose" (11). In the context of the early national period, the subject of my discussion, I hope that my use of *mental distress* will remind us of the pathologization of the experience in Pomp's own time, as well as its continuation in our own time.

8 Indeed, Rebecca Tannenbaum explains that even prior to Pomp's time, "people of Colonial America recognized several neurological disorders: stroke (or apoplexy), paralysis, and epilepsy (also known as the falling sickness, or just 'fits')" (137).

9 See Jeannine Marie DeLombard, as quoted in chapter 1: "Of the roughly two hundred works offering 'sermons, moral discourses, narratives, last words, and dying sayings, and poems written for, by, and about persons executed for criminal activity' published from 1674 to the Civil War, at least sixty featured criminals of African heritage" ("Apprehending" 95). Also see Lennard J. Davis, who notes, "The loose association between what we would now call disability and criminal activity, mental

incompetence, sexual license, and so on established a legacy that people with disabilities are still having trouble living down" (37).

10. *The History of Mary Prince* (1831), *Narrative of the Life of Frederick Douglass* (1845), and Harriet Jacobs's *Incidents in the Life of a Slave Girl* (1861) are prominent examples.

11. The conventions of the crime narrative genre in the latter half of the century typically involved the confessor's admission of guilt, description of the crimes, conviction for sinful nature, and repentance for sins. Later in the period, as the dying words genre became more secular, the figure of the criminal rogue or picaresque emerged.

12. La Marr Jurelle Bruce discusses how white supremacy benefits from the disputable value of Reason/rationality (speaking in the context of Toni Morrison's 1987 novel *Beloved*) (18–19). I'll return to this concept in the next chapter, regarding Nathaniel Turner and the Southampton revolt.

13. I have left all (mis)spellings and indications of the broadside's illegibility as they appear in the transcription.

14. Douglass declares in his 1845 *Narrative*, "You have seen how a man was made a slave; you shall see how a slave was made a man" (65–66).

15. We will see this interrelation in the following chapter in Turner's *Confessions* as well.

16. It is also possible that Furbush understood that most "distracted Massachusetts residents who needed attention . . . were probably cared for by their own families" because "there was little alternative for those who were not paupers" (Jimenez 27). Pomp's condition likely would have made it difficult for Furbush to sell him.

17. Though Mary Ann Jimenez doesn't explicitly state how this plea resolved, the title of the document she references here—"Pardons Issued by the General Court of Massachusetts," in the Massachusetts State Archives—suggests that the layman's plea was successful.

18. They are also the only aspects of the confession that Plummer explicitly doubts as true.

19. We will see in chapter 4 that Celia imagined the same scenario for herself in 1855.

20. Pomp's desire, perhaps even promise, to go out into the world as a valuable contributor to society now that his fits have left him anticipates James Foster's 1901 parole requests, analyzed in chapter 5. In each man's writings, there is at the very least the implication (and in Foster's work a direct argument) that society not only would benefit from the man's release, but also would deprive itself of his useful participation in the intellectual life of the community if the state were to execute Pomp or continue to incarcerate Foster.

21. The laws indicate a fear of Black uprising in the time leading up to the reprint of the pamphlet in Massachusetts: "Slaves were to be whipped for having weapons or meeting in groups of three or more, and in 1738 and 1751, Boston issued orders that slaves out after 9 p.m. without permission from their masters would be sent to the House of Correction" (Ryan 89–90). Of course, the reprint might speak generally to a fear of loss of order as the colony edged toward revolution, but the racialization of that anxiety is evident in the creation of laws to maintain the order of the Massachusetts Black (and particularly enslaved) population.

22 The Naturalization Act of 1790 reads: "Be it enacted by the Senate and House of Representatives of the United States of America, in Congress assembled, That any Alien being a *free white person*, who shall have resided within the limits and under the jurisdiction of the United States for the term of two years, may be admitted to become a citizen thereof on application to any common law Court of record in any one of the States wherein he shall have resided for the term of one year at least, and making proof to the satisfaction of such Court that he is a person of good character, and taking the *oath* or affirmation prescribed by" (emphases mine).

23 Henri-Jacques Stiker observes, "Paradoxically, [disabled people] are designated in order to be made to disappear, they are spoken in order to be silenced" (quoted in Shildrick, "Critical" 38).

Chapter 3. Nineteenth-Century Counter/Terrorism

1 Douglass proclaimed in 1852: "There is more protection there for a horse, for a donkey, or anything, rather than a colored man—who is, therefore, justified in the eye of God, in maintaining his right with his arm."

2 Recently, historian Patrick H. Breen has disputed these numbers. I have chosen to use the numbers from the greatest number of sources, but footnote Breen's findings. This is not to say that I dispute his findings; I'll leave it to historians to determine what the most accurate numbers are. Next, two notes on naming, terminology, and capitalization. First, I am convinced by Celeste-Marie Bernier's decision to use Nathaniel Turner's full name when referring to him, and have decided to do the same. Bernier notes, "Nat. 'Ol' Prophet Nat.' 'General Nat.' The 'Great Bandit.' These are just a few of the names used to identify Turner within white mainstream racist and popular historical and political archives. I adhere to 'Nathaniel Turner' on the grounds that Frederick Douglass, Henry Highland Garnet, and many other Black radicals recuperated his full name in a political condemnation of racist naming practices" (93). Second, I am following literary critic Eric J. Sundquist's lead in calling the events in Southampton a *revolt*, and not a *revolution* (as Bernier does), *rebellion*, or *insurrection*. Sundquist explains his logic as building on the work of historian Henry Irving Tragle,

> who chooses *revolt* over *rebellion* because of the limited scale of the Turner event (although a full-scale, successful political revolution, as in Haiti, might suggest the opposite usage), and over *insurrection*, which was typically applied to instances of treason, with which slaves, as chattel, could not legally be charged. Both rebellion and insurrection nevertheless have connotations that are of particular value—the former because it points to the fluid state of resistance in which many slaves could be said to live; the latter because it highlights the fact that the ideology of Turner's revolt, like that expressed in David Walker's or Frederick Douglass's writings, was grounded in a belief that what was to be overthrown was not the entirety of democratic government but the immoral institution of slavery. Moreover, revolt has the added significance of referring implicitly to the Haitian Revolution, with its extension of French principles, and

explicitly to the American revolutionary tradition, with which Turner would align himself. (40)

3. Among those examples that predate Turner's *Confessions* are Arthur, *The Life, and Dying Speech of Arthur, a Negro Man* (1768); James Albert Ukawsaw Gronniosaw, *A Narrative of the Most Remarkable Particulars in the Life of James Albert Ukawsaw Gronniosaw, an African Prince* (1770); Venture Smith, *A Narrative of the Life and Adventures of Venture, a Native of Africa* (1798); John Jea, *The Life, History, and Unparalleled Sufferings of John Jea, the African Preacher* (1811); William Grimes, *Life of William Grimes, the Runaway Slave* (1825). Published in the same year as Turner's *Confessions* was Mary Prince, *The History of Mary Prince, a West Indian Slave* (1831).

4. This thinking intersects with the theory of *bodymind* in critical disability studies (see Price; Schalk).

5. I mention Douglass's novella *The Heroic Slave* (1852) later in this chapter, but I want to remind readers of what I suggest in my previous book, *Black Well-Being* (2016): Douglass characterizes Madison Washington as *the* heroic slave, not one of many. Turner's self-characterization seems to prefigure Douglass's hero in terms of the uniqueness/exceptionalism he occupies.

6. Turner's intellect, dedication to reading, and devotion to prayer remind one of Malcolm X's transformation from Malcolm Little—while doing time for a larceny conviction and after research—to one of the most engaging and influential, if also often maligned, leaders of the movement.

7. Tomlins reads Turner's translation of faith and violence as a creation of a "politics of action." He argues, "To translate faith into action in which others could share required that he invent a politics that could enunciate faith's intentions but in a distinct language, that could supply a way to understand the objectives of the action for which he called that might be comprehended by all those who decided to follow" (xiv).

8. New Testament and ancient culture scholar Sean A. Adams distinguishes between "the historical/Pauline Luke . . . the Gospel of Luke . . . and the purported author of Luke-Acts" (125). That these three Luke figures may not all be the same person seems to be a relatively recent scholarly inquiry. It is likely that Turner and Johnstone would have imagined Luke as one person and the writings as his. For my purposes here in the discussion of Turner and Johnstone (and to avoid confusion), I will follow what I believe is their lead and not distinguish between what may be three different biblical Lukes.

9. In this continuum, it's important to also acknowledge the racism undergirding current voter suppression laws.

10. It is worth noting here that under eighteenth-century coverture laws, "petit treason" also applied to women charged with murdering their husbands, as well as white servants charged with murdering their employers (see Ryan 143–44).

11. Land traces the category of the "enemy of humanity" back to Roman law, which defined pirates as "enemies of the human race" (6).

12. Celia, the subject of chapter 4, expressed what Bruce calls "willful womanhood."

Chapter 4. Nearly Six Months Imprisoned

1. Part of the Celia Project's aim is to reveal research about Celia and her case that has followed Melton A. McLaurin's 1991 book. Still, historians and literary scholars rely heavily on McLaurin's research.
2. James Adam Halpern posits that "it is . . . theoretically possible that Celia was procured from Audrain County closer to the September 1852 enumeration of the Missouri State Census, when she would have been approximately sixteen years old" (130).
3. This chapter responds to a call that Kali N. Gross and Cheryl D. Hicks made in their 2015 "Gendering the Carceral State," a special issue of *Journal of African American History*: "We need more information on how enslaved black women ended up in courts of law and imprisoned during slavery and the Civil War" (362). I'll add that Sowande Mustakeem notes in the same issue that "five women—four African American and one white female—were executed in and by the state of Missouri between 1828 and 1855" (395). Celia's execution was the last of these five.
4. I've written about Celia's case twice, first in an article in the 2009 special issue "Technologies of Enslavement and Liberty" of the journal *American Literature* ("Interracial"), and again in a chapter of my book *Black Well-Being* (2016). As a member of the Celia Project ("a research collaboration on the history of slavery and sexual violence"), I utilize methods of speculation in my discussion of Celia (see Sichtermann, 90–91; Peterson).
5. As recently as 2021, Leah Wang, writing for the Prison Policy Initiative, lamented that "historically, the [US] government has not collected data about carceral pregnancy on a regular basis, meaning no national effort has been made to understand maternity care for thousands of incarcerated pregnant women." She applauded the Pregnancy in Prison Statistics project for "shed[ding] light on a common but rarely discussed experience," through an effort "spearheaded by Dr. Carolyn Sufrin of the Johns Hopkins University School of Medicine and School of Public Health."
6. The trial records spell the name "Wainscott," but census records and Virginia's gravestone spell it "Winscott."
7. Several times, Thompson observes how often imprisoned people suffer abuses while awaiting trial, only to be acquitted.
8. Of course, Celia's lawyers and the newspapers could have had different motives for how they portrayed her actions while she was imprisoned. Nevertheless, together they offer a richer picture of her, and as we have so few of her words through which to imagine her it is important to compare all available accounts.
9. Dates are tricky to sort out when newspapers are reprinting one another's stories. Obviously, news traveled slower in the 1850s than it does today. At any rate, the date I've been able to secure for Carlisle's attempted escape is November 9. At first it had appeared to me that Celia had assisted in this attempt on November 16 (if I'm counting correctly from the date of the article), but that would have made it the day of her scheduled execution, and I find it highly unlikely that she would have returned

to the jail for any reason on that day. Also, another newspaper source lists Carlisle's escape attempt as being on November 9.
10 This testimony is no longer part of the extant court documents that I've been able to locate, but also appears in part in Halpern's thesis (137).
11 Compared with other testimony, George's reads as though it includes court clarification, with phrases such as "above mentioned." As I rely on Williamson's transcription, the exact changes are not certain, but we can definitely detect another voice at points in this transcript.
12 Pomp also assumed he would be hanged on the spot after killing Furbush.
13 The newspaper reports that Celia was out of jail for one week, but evidence suggests she was out for two weeks.
14 Of course, if Celia had implicated Malinda as knowledgeable of the plan, the prosecution would have had evidence of intent, further substantiating the murder charge.
15 Perhaps, with her 1988 essay "Can the Subaltern Speak?," Gayatri Chakravorty Spivak helps us read the significance of Celia's actions. I'll note here as well Rudolph T. Ware III's example of what he calls embodied knowledge in Islam. While it's not quite the same thing as the embodied intellectualism I discuss here, the idea that the physicality of Islam makes it an embodied knowledge is worth noting.

Interlude

1 Writing in 2022 for the *New York Times*—both commenting on our current moment and clarifying the amendment's effects—Nicholas Bogel-Burroughs notes that "in Alabama, for example, the State Constitution would be amended to remove an exception that allows involuntary servitude 'for the punishment of crime.'" He continues: "Courts have at times referenced the amendment in denying prisoners the same rights as other workers, but they have more often relied on other laws and justifications to do so. A group of federal lawmakers has proposed a bill to remove the clause, but the lawmakers have not won enough support to pass it. Sharon Dolovich, a law professor at the University of California, Los Angeles, said that even if the 13th Amendment was not the primary justification for allowing mandatory prison labor, its existence in the Constitution most likely weighs on the mind of judges who evaluate prisoners' claims. 'The 13th Amendment, as it's currently written, and the state's analogues to the amendment, form a backdrop that infuses the legal regime governing incarcerated people,' said Ms. Dolovich, who leads the Prison Law and Policy Program at U.C.L.A. 'It forms the moral atmosphere around which we treat incarcerated workers.'"

Chapter 5. Dear Governor

1 In 2017, the governor of Alabama signed a bill restoring voting rights for those who had been disenfranchised under this section of the 1901 Constitution (Ebenstein).
2 Klan influence on Alabama politics began during Reconstruction, even though politicians attempted to deflect attention from the group's power: "Even Alabama Gov. Robert Lindsay, who sought to discourage violence after his election in 1870, could declare, 'I do not think there ever was a political motive in any outrage committed

on a colored man.' Both 'white line' and New Departure party leaders put up bail for arrested Klansmen, spoke of the 'good' the organization accomplished despite its 'excesses,' and strongly opposed federal intervention. Rather than dissociate themselves from the campaign of terror, prominent Democrats either minimized the Klan's activities or offered thinly disguised rationalizations for them. Some denied the organization's existence altogether, dismissing reports of violence as electoral propaganda, products of a Republican 'slander mill.' Others sought to discredit the victims, portraying them as thieves, adulterers, or men of 'bad character' who more or less deserved their fate" (Foner 434).

WORKS CITED

13th. Directed by Ava DuVernay, Netflix, 2016.
Adams, Sean A. "The Relationships of Paul and Luke: Luke, Paul's Letters, and the 'We' Passages of Acts." *Paul and His Social Relations*, edited by Stanley E. Porter and Christopher D. Land, Brill, 2012, pp. 125–42.
Alabama, U.S., Convict Records, 1886–1952. Entry for James Foster-Watson.
Alexander, Jesse. Letter, 6 June 1933. Correspondence Relating to Convict Paroles, 1916–1934, SG009681, *Alabama Department of Archives and History.*
Alkalimat, Abdul. *The History of Black Studies.* Pluto Press, 2021.
Allmendinger, David F., Jr. *Nat Turner and the Rising in Southampton County.* Johns Hopkins UP, 2014.
Allport, Gordon W. *The Nature of Prejudice.* 1954. Basic Books, 1979.
Alsobrook, David E. "William D. Jelks (1901–1907)." *Encyclopedia of Alabama*, 22 Jan. 2008, www.encyclopediaofalabama.org/article/h-1438.
Anderson, William J. *Life and Narrative of William J. Anderson, Twenty-four Years a Slave; Sold Eight times! In Jail Sixty Times! Whipped Three Hundred Times!!! Or the Dark Deeds of American Slavery Revealed. Containing Scriptural Views of the Origin of the Black and of the White Man. Also, a Simple and Easy Plan to Abolish Slavery in the United States. Together with an Account of the Services of Colored Men in the Revolutionary War—Day and Date, and Interesting Facts.* Chicago, 1857.
Arthur. *The Life, and Dying Speech of Arthur, a Negro Man, Who Was Executed at Worcester, October 20th 1768. For a Rape Committed on the Body of One Deborah Metcalfe.* Boston, 1768.
Axtmann, Roland. "Humanity or Enmity? Carl Schmitt on International Politics." *International Politics*, vol. 44, 2007, pp. 531–51.
Ayers, Edward L. *Vengeance and Justice: Crime and Punishment in the 19th-Century American South.* Oxford UP, 1984.
Bakhtin, Mikhail. *Problems of Dostoevsky's Politics.* Edited and translated by Caryl Emerson, U of Minnesota P, 1984.
Banner, Stuart. *The Death Penalty: An American History.* Harvard UP, 2003.
Barclay, Jennifer. *The Mark of Slavery: Disability, Race, and Gender in Antebellum America.* U of Illinois P, 2021.
Barnes, Albert. "Commentary on Jeremiah 4." *Barnes' Notes on the Whole Bible*, 1870,

StudyLight.org. www.studylight.org/commentaries/eng/bnb/jeremiah-4.html. Accessed 1 July 2024.

Barnes, L. Diane. "Insurrection as Righteous Rebellion in *The Heroic Slave* and Beyond." *Journal of African American History*, vol. 102, no. 1, 2017, pp. 21–34.

Barton, John Cyril. "The American Prison, 1786–1860." *The Routledge Research Companion to Law and Humanities in Nineteenth-Century America*, edited by Nan Goodman and Simon Stern, Routledge, 2017, pp. 242–56.

Batra, Ajay Kumar. "Reading with Conviction: Abraham Johnstone and the Poetics of the Dead End." *Early American Literature*, vol. 55, no. 2, 2020, pp. 331–54.

Bay, Mia, et al. Introduction. *Toward an Intellectual History of Black Women*, edited by Mia Bay et al., U of North Carolina P, 2015, pp. 1–14.

Baynton, Douglas. "Disability in History." *Perspectives*, vol. 44, no. 9, 2006, pp. 5–7.

Beaumont, Gustave de, and Alexis de Tocqueville. *On the Penitentiary System in the United States, and Its Application in France; with an Appendix on Penal Colonies, and also, Statistical Notes*. Translated by Francis Lieber, Philadelphia, 1833.

Benda, Julien. *The Treason of the Intellectuals*. Translated by Richard Aldington, W. W. Norton, 1969.

Bernier, Celeste-Marie. *Characters of Blood: Black Heroism in the Transatlantic Imagination*. U of Virginia P, 2012.

Berry, Daina Ramey. *The Price for Their Pound of Flesh: The Value of the Enslaved, from Womb to Grave, in the Building of a Nation*. Beacon Press, 2017.

Blackmon, Douglas A. *Slavery by Another Name: The Re-Enslavement of Black Americans from the Civil War to World War II*. Anchor Books, 2008.

Blain, Keisha N., et al. Introduction. *New Perspectives on the Black Intellectual Tradition*, edited by Keisha N. Blain et al., Northwestern UP, 2018, pp. 3–16.

Bogel-Burroughs, Nicholas. "Why a Question about Slavery Is Now on the Ballot in 5 States." *New York Times*, 22 Oct. 2022.

Boster, Dea H. "An 'Epeleptick' Bondswoman: Fits, Slavery, and Power in the Antebellum South." *Bulletin of the History of Medicine*, vol. 83, no. 2, 2009, pp. 271–301.

Boudreau, Kristin. *The Spectacle of Death: Populist Literary Responses to American Capital Cases*. Prometheus Books, 2006.

Breen, Patrick H. *The Land Shall Be Deluged in Blood: A New History of the Nat Turner Revolt*. Oxford UP, 2016.

Bristol. *The Dying Speech of Bristol*. Boston, 1763.

Bruce, La Marr Jurelle. *How to Go Mad without Losing Your Mind: Madness and Black Radical Creativity*. Duke UP, 2021.

Byrd, Brandon R. *The Black Republic: African Americans and the Fate of Haiti*. U of Pennsylvania P, 2020.

Callaway County Circuit Court Record. "State of Missouri vs. Celia, a Slave." Case file 4496, 1855. *Missouri Digital Heritage*, 3 Mar. 2009. cdm16795.contentdm.oclc.org/digital/collection/mocases/id/33/.

Cameron, Christopher. "Haiti and the Black Intellectual Tradition." *Modern Intellectual History*, vol. 18, no. 4, 2021, pp. 1190–99.

Carr, Robert. *Black Nationalism in the New World: Reading the African-American and West Indian Experience*. Duke UP, 2002.

The Celia Project. U of Michigan, sites.lsa.umich.edu/celiaproject. Accessed 15 Apr. 2024.

Chaison, Joanne Danaher. "Early American Street Literature: The Broadsides of Jonathan Plummer." 1985, typescript, American Antiquarian Society, Worcester, MA.

Christian Recorder. 1861–1901.

Clarke, George Elliott. "'This Is No Hearsay': Reading the Canadian Slave Narratives." *Directions Home: Approaches to African-Canadian Literature*, by George Elliott Clarke, U of Toronto P, 2012, pp. 19–29.

Cohen, Daniel A. *Pillars of Salt, Monuments of Grace: New England Crime Literature and the Origins of American Popular Culture, 1674–1860*. Oxford UP, 1993.

———. "Social Injustice, Sexual Violence, Spiritual Transcendence: Constructions of Interracial Rape in Early American Crime Literature, 1767–1817." *William and Mary Quarterly*, vol. 56, no. 3, 1999, pp. 481–526.

"COVID-19: A Curated Collection of Links." *The Marshall Project*, www.themarshallproject.org/records/8793-covid-19. Accessed 15 Apr. 2024.

Crawford, William. *Report of William Crawford, Esq., on the Penitentiaries of the United States Addressed to His Majesty's Principal Secretary of State for the Home Department*. London, 1835.

Cromwell, John W. "The Aftermath of Nat Turner's Insurrection." *Journal of Negro History*, vol. 5, no. 2, 1920, pp. 208–34.

Currier, John J. *History of Newburyport, Mass., 1764–1905*. Newburyport, MA, 1906.

Curtin, Mary Ellen. *Black Prisoners and Their World, 1865–1900*. U of Virginia P, 2000.

Dagbovie, Pero Gaglo. Introduction to part 3. *New Perspectives on the Black Intellectual Tradition*, edited by Keisha N. Blain et al., Northwestern UP, 2018, pp. 133–38.

Davis, Adrienne. "'Don't Let Nobody Bother Yo' Principle': The Sexual Economy of American Slavery." *Still Brave: The Evolution of Black Women's Studies*, edited by Stanlie M. James et al., Feminist Press, 2009, pp. 215–39.

Davis, Lennard J. *Enforcing Normalcy: Disability, Deafness, and the Body*. Verso, 1995.

Deleuze, Gilles, and Félix Guattari. *Anti-Oedipus: Capitalism and Schizophrenia*. Translated by Robert Hurley, U of Minnesota P, 1983.

———. *A Thousand Plateaus: Capitalism and Schizophrenia*. Translated by Brian Massumi, U of Minnesota P, 1987.

DeLombard, Jeannine Marie. "Apprehending Early African American Literary History." *Early African American Print Culture*, edited by Lara Langer Cohen and Jordan Alexander Stein, U of Pennsylvania P, 2012, pp. 93–106.

———. *In the Shadow of the Gallows: Race, Crime, and American Civic Identity*. U of Pennsylvania P, 2012.

———. "The Very Idea of a Slave Is a Human Being in Bondage." *Routledge Research Companion to Law and Humanities in Nineteenth-Century America*, edited by Nan Goodman and Simon Stern, Routledge, 2017, pp. 20–34.

Demetz, Frédéric-Auguste, and Guillaume-Abel Blouet. *Rapports a M. le Comte de Montalivet, Pair de France, Ministre Secrétaire d'État au Département de l'Intérieur, sur les Pénitenciers des États-Unis*. Paris, 1837.

Derrida, Jacques. *The Politics of Friendship.* Translated by George Collins, Verso, 2005.

Douglass, Frederick. "The Fugitive Slave Law." Speech to the National Free Soil Convention, Pittsburgh, PA, 11 Aug. 1852.

———. *The Heroic Slave. Autographs for Freedom,* edited by Julia Griffiths, vol. 1, John P. Jewett, 1854, pp. 174–239.

———. *My Bondage and My Freedom.* New York, 1855.

———. *Narrative of the Life of Frederick Douglass, an American Slave.* Boston, 1845.

Downes, Paul. *Hobbes, Sovereignty, and Early American Literature.* Cambridge UP, 2015.

Drewry, William Sidney. *The Southampton Insurrection.* Neale, 1900.

Ebenstein, Julie. "The Alabama Governor Just Signed a Bill That Will Restore Voting Rights to Thousands of Alabamians." *American Civil Liberties Union,* 26 May 2017, www.aclu.org/blog/voting-rights/voter-restoration/alabama-governor-just-signed-bill-will-restore-voting-rights.

Egerton, George. "Politics and Autobiography: Political Memoir as Polygenre." *Biography,* vol. 15, no. 3, 1992, pp. 221–42.

Engels, Jeremy. *Enemyship: Democracy and Counter-Revolution in the Early Republic.* Michigan State UP, 2010.

———. "Friend or Foe? Naming the Enemy." *Rhetoric and Public Affairs,* vol. 12, no. 1, 2009, pp. 37–64.

Erevelles, Nirmala, and Andrea Minear. "Unspeakable Offenses: Untangling Race and Disability in Discourses of Intersectionality." *Journal of Literary and Cultural Disability Studies,* vol. 4, no. 2, 2010, pp. 127–45.

"Escaped from Jail." *Fulton Telegraph,* 16 Nov. 1855.

"Fiendish Murder." *Missouri Republican,* 25 June 1855.

Finseth, Ian. "Irony and Modernity in the Early Slave Narrative: Bonds of Duty, Contracts of Meaning." *Journeys of the Slave Narrative in the Early Americas,* edited by Nicole N. Aljoe and Ian Finseth, U of Virginia P, 2014, pp. 17–46.

Foner, Eric. *Reconstruction: America's Unfinished Revolution, 1863–1877.* Harper and Row, 1988.

Fortis, Edmund. *The Last Words and Dying Speech of Edmund Fortis, a Negro Man, Who Appeared to Be between Thirty and Forty Years of Age, but Very Ignorant. He Was Executed at Dresden, on Kennebeck River, on Thursday the Twenty-Fifth Day of September, 1794, for a Rape and Murder, Committed on the Body of Pamela Tilton, a Young Girl of about Fourteen Years of Age, Daughter of Mr. Tilton of Vassalborough, in the County of Lincoln.* Exeter, ME, 1795.

Fortune. *The Dying Confession and Declaration of Fortune, a Negro Man, Who Was Executed in Newport, (Rhode-Island) on Friday the 14th of May, 1762, for Setting Fire to the Stores on the Long Wharf.* Boston, 1762.

Foster, Frances Smith. "A Narrative of the Interesting Origins and (Somewhat) Surprising Developments of African-American Print Culture." *American Literary History,* vol. 17, no. 4, 2005, pp. 714–40.

———. *Witnessing Slavery: The Development of Ante-Bellum Slave Narratives.* U of Wisconsin P, 1994.

Foster, James. "An Old Man a Convict Makes a Remarkable Appeal to Governor for a

Pardon." *Montgomery Journal*, 28 Apr. 1901. Alabama Department of Archives and History, digital.archives.alabama.gov/digital/collection/voices/id/2920.

———. "To His Excellency Governor W. D. Jelks." 5 Sep. 1901. Alabama Department of Archives and History, digital.archives.alabama.gov/digital/collection/voices/id/3468.

Foucault, Michel. *Discipline and Punish: The Birth of the Prison*. Translated by Alan Sheridan, Pantheon Books, 1977.

Foucault, Michel, and Gilles Deleuze. "Intellectuals and Power." *Language, Counter-Memory, Practice: Selected Essays and Interviews*, edited by Donald F. Bouchard, translated by Donald F. Bouchard and Sherry Simon, Cornell UP, 1977, pp. 205–17.

France, Anatole. *The Red Lily*. Translated by Winifred Stephens, 6th ed., John Lane, 1921.

Free, John. *An Anniversary Sermon, Preached in the Parish Church of St. Mary, Newington-Butts, in Surry; on Whitsunday, 1769; Being the Sequel to That Occasioned by the Murder of Mr. William Allen the Younger, on the Bloody 10th of May, 1768, and Published at the Request of his Friends as a Remembrancer, to prevent the Continuation of Political Murder*. London, 1768; Boston, 1773.

French, Scot. *The Rebellious Slave: Nat Turner in American Memory*. Houghton Mifflin, 2004.

Fuentes, Marisa J. *Dispossessed Lives: Enslaved Women, Violence, and the Archive*. U of Pennsylvania P, 2016.

Gabrial, Bryan. "From Haiti to Nat Turner: Racial Panic Discourse during the Nineteenth Century Partisan Press Era." *American Journalism*, vol. 30, no. 3, 2013, pp. 336–64.

Gardner, Eric. *Black Print Unbound: The Christian Recorder, African American Literature and Periodical Culture*. Oxford UP, 2015.

Gigantino, James J., II. *The Ragged Road to Abolition: Slavery and Freedom in New Jersey, 1775–1865*. U of Pennsylvania P, 2014.

Gramsci, Antonio. *Selections from the Prison Notebooks*. Edited and translated by Quintin Hoare and Geoffrey Nowell Smith, International, 1971.

Greene, Lorenzo J., et al. *Missouri's Black Heritage*. U of Missouri P, 1993.

Griffith, Lee. *The Fall of the Prison: Biblical Perspectives on Prison Abolition*. William B. Eerdmans, 1993.

Grimes, William. *Life of William Grimes, the Runaway Slave. Written by Himself*. New York, 1825.

Gronniosaw, James Albert Ukawsaw. *A Narrative of the Most Remarkable Particulars in the Life of James Albert Ukawsaw Gronniosaw, An African Prince, As related by Himself*. Edited by Walter Shirley, Bath, England, 1770.

Gross, Ariela J. *Double Character: Slavery and Mastery in the Antebellum Southern Courtroom*. Princeton UP, 2000.

Gross, Kali N., and Cheryl D. Hicks. "Gendering the Carceral State: African American Women, History, and the Criminal Justice System." *Journal of African American History*, vol. 100, no. 3, 2015, pp. 357–65.

Haley, Sarah. *No Mercy Here: Gender, Punishment, and the Making of Jim Crow Modernity*. U of North Carolina P, 2016.

Hallevy, Gabriel. *The Matrix of Insanity in Modern Criminal Law*. Springer, 2015.

Halpern, James Adam. *Archeological and Historical Investigations of the Robert Newsom Farmstead (23CY497), Callaway County, Missouri*. 2015. Michigan State U, master's thesis.

Halttunen, Karen. *Murder Most Foul: The Killer and the American Gothic Imagination*. Harvard UP, 2000.

"Hanging A Negress." *Baltimore Sun*, 17 Jan. 1856.

The Harder They Come. Directed by Perry Henzell, New World Pictures, 1972.

Hartman, Saidiya V. *Scenes of Subjection: Terror, Slavery, and Self-Making in Nineteenth-Century America*. Oxford UP, 1997.

Hartnett, Stephen John. *Capital Punishment and the Making of America, 1683–1807*. Michigan State UP, 2010.

Hartog, Hendrik. "Pigs and Positivism." *Wisconsin Law Review*, 1985, pp. 899–935.

Havis, Devonya N. "Black Ancestral Discourses: Cultural Cadences from the South." *Thinking the US South: Contemporary Philosophy from Southern Perspectives*, edited by Shannon Sullivan, Northwestern UP, 2021, 153–61.

Henderson, Errol A. "Slave Religion, Slave Hiring, and the Incipient Proletarianization of Enslaved Black Labor: Developing Du Bois' Thesis on Black Participation in the Civil War as a Revolution." *Journal of African American Studies*, vol. 19, no. 2, 2015, 192–213.

Henderson, Madison, et al. *Trials and Confessions of Madison Henderson, alias Blanchard, Alfred Amos Warrick, James W. Seward, and Charles Brown, Murderers of Jesse Baker and Jacob Weaver, as Given by Themselves; and a Likeness of Each, Taken in Jail Shortly after Their Arrest*. St. Louis, 1841.

Higginbotham, A. Leon, Jr., and Anne F. Jacobs. "The Law Only as an Enemy: The Legitimization of Racial Powerlessness through the Colonial and Antebellum Criminal Laws of Virginia." *North Carolina Law Review*, vol. 70, no. 4, 1992, pp. 969–1070.

History of Callaway County, Missouri, Written and Compiled from the Most Authentic Official and Private Sources, Including a History of Its Townships, Towns and Villages. St. Louis, 1884.

"History of Richmond." *Southern Literary Messenger*, Jan. 1852.

Holmes, David G. "Black Religion Matters: African American Prophecy as a Theoretical Frame for Rhetorical Interpretation, Invention, and Critique." *Reinventing (with) Theory in Rhetoric and Writing Studies: Essays in Honor of Sharon Crowley*, edited by Andrea Alden et al., UP of Colorado, 2019, 243–55.

hooks, bell, and Cornel West. *Breaking Bread: Insurgent Black Intellectual Life*. South End Press, 1991.

Hunter, Donna. *Dead Men Talking: Africans and the Law in New England's Eighteenth-Century Execution Sermons and Crime Narratives*. 2000. U of California, Berkeley, PhD dissertation.

———. "Race, Law, and Innocence: Executing Black Men in the Eighteenth Century." *Studies in Law, Politics, and Society*, edited by Austin Sarat and Patricia Ewick, vol. 20, Emerald, 2000, pp. 71–97.

Hunt-Kennedy, Stefanie. *Between Fitness and Death: Disability and Slavery in the Caribbean*. U of Illinois P, 2020.

Jackson, Jonathan. Manumission letter, 19 June 1776. *History of Newburyport, Mass. 1764–1905*, by John J. Currier, Newburyport, MA, 1906, p. 71.

Jacobs, Harriet. *Incidents in the Life of a Slave Girl*. Boston, 1861.

"Jail Break and a Race." *Daily Missouri Democrat*, 20 Nov. 1855.

James, Jennifer C. "Blessed Are the Warmakers: Martin Luther King, Vietnam, and the Black Prophetic Tradition." *Fighting Words and Images: Representing War across the Disciplines*, edited by Elena V. Baraban, U of Toronto P, 2012, pp. 165–84.

James, Joy. Introduction. *Imprisoned Intellectuals: America's Political Prisoners Write on Life, Liberation, and Rebellion*, edited by Joy James, Rowman and Littlefield, 2003, 3–28.

Jarman, Michelle. "Coming Up from Underground: Uneasy Dialogues at the Intersections of Race, Mental Illness, and Disability Studies." *Blackness and Disability: Critical Examinations and Cultural Interventions*, edited by Christopher M. Bell, Michigan State UP, 2012, pp. 9–29.

Jea, John. *The Life, History, and Unparalleled Sufferings of John Jea, the African Preacher. Compiled and Written by Himself*. Portsea, England, 1811.

Jimenez, Mary Ann. "Madness in Early American History: Insanity in Massachusetts from 1700 to 1830." *Journal of Social History*, vol. 20, no. 1, 1986, pp. 25–44.

Johnstone, Abraham. *The Address of Abraham Johnstone, a Black Man, Who Was Hanged at Woodbury, in the County of Glocester, and State of New Jersey, on Saturday the the [sic] 8th Day of July Last; to the People of Colour, to Which Is Added His Dying Confession or Declaration Also, a Copy of a Letter to His Wife, Written the Day Previous to His Execution*. Philadelphia, 1797.

Jones, Martha S. *Birthright Citizens: A History of Race and Rights in Antebellum America*. Cambridge UP, 2018.

Joyce, John, and Peter Matthias. *Confession of John Joyce, alias Davis, Who Was Executed on Monday, the 14th of March, 1808. For the Murder of Mrs. Sarah Cross: with an Address to the Public, and People of Colour, Together with the Substance of the Trial, and the Address of Chief Justice Tilghman, on His Condemnation. Confession of Peter Matthias, alias Matthews, Who Was Executed on Monday, the 14th of March, 1808. For the Murder of Mrs. Sarah Cross; with an Address to the Public, and People of Colour, Together with the Substance of the Trial, and the Address of Chief Justice Tilghman, on His Condemnation*. Edited by Richard Allen, Philadelphia, 1808.

Julius, Nikolaus Heinrich. *Amerika's Besserungs System und Dessen Anwendung auf Europa*. Berlin, 1836.

Kahn, Paul. "Criminal and Enemy in the Political Imagination." *Yale Review*, vol. 99, no. 1, 2011, pp. 148–67.

Kilgore, John Mac. "Nat Turner and the Work of Enthusiasm." *PMLA*, vol. 130, no. 5, 2015, pp. 1347–62.

Kinshasa, Kwando M., editor. *The Scottsboro Boys in Their Own Words: Selected Letters, 1931–1950*. McFarland, 2014.

Land, Isaac. Introduction. *Enemies of Humanity: The Nineteenth-Century War on Terrorism*, edited by Isaac Land, Palgrave Macmillan, 2008, pp. 1–20.

Latessa, Edward J., and Paula Smith. *Corrections in the Community*. Routledge, 2011.

Lejeune, Philippe. *Le Pacte autobiographique*. Seuil, 1975.

Levi, Robin, and Ayelet Waldman, editors. *Inside This Place, Not of It: Narratives from Women's Prisons*. McSweeney's, 2011.

Levine, Robert S. *The Lives of Frederick Douglass*. Harvard UP, 2016.

Levy, La TaSha. "Beyond the 'Great Men' Canon of Black Intellectual History." *Black Perspectives*, 11 June 2019. www.aaihs.org/beyond-the-great-men-canon.

Madison, James. "Federalist no. 54: The Apportionment of Members among the States." *The Federalist Papers*, New York, 1788.

Mallicoat, Stacy L. *Women and Crime: A Text/Reader*. Sage, 2014.

Marshall, I. Howard. *Luke: Historian and Theologian*. IVP Academic, 1988.

Martin, David. "The Birth of Jim Crow in Alabama 1865–1896." *National Black Law Journal*, vol. 13, no. 1, 1993, pp. 184–97.

Mather, Cotton. *Tremenda. The Dreadful Sound with which the Wicked are to be Thunderstruck. In a Sermon delivered unto a Great Assembly, in which was present, a Miserable African, just going to be Executed for a most Inhumane and Uncommon Murder. At Boston, May 25th. 1721. To which is added, a Conference between a Minister and the Prisoner, on the Day before his Execution*. Boston, 1721.

Mbembe, Achille. "Necropolitics." Translated by Libby Meintjes, *Public Culture*, vol. 15, no. 1, 2003, pp. 11–40.

McKelvey, Blake. *American Prisons: A Study in American Social History prior to 1915*. U of Chicago P, 1936.

McLaurin, Melton A. *Celia, a Slave*. 1991. Avon, 1999.

McRuer, Robert. *Crip Theory: Cultural Signs of Queerness and Disability*. New York UP, 2006.

———. "Disability Nationalism in Crip Times." *Journal of Literary and Cultural Disability Studies*, vol. 4, no. 2, 2010, pp. 163–78.

———. "Submissive and Non-Compliant: The Paradox of Gary Fisher." *Blackness and Disability: Critical Examinations and Cultural Interventions*, edited by Christopher M. Bell, Michigan State UP, 2012, pp. 95–112.

Meissner, Caits, editor. *The Sentences That Create Us*. Haymarket Books, 2022.

Michael, John. *Identity and the Failure of America: From Thomas Jefferson to the War on Terror*. U of Minnesota P, 2008.

Mills, Charles W. *The Racial Contract*. Cornell UP, 1997.

Morrison, Toni. *Beloved*. Alfred A. Knopf, 1987.

Mountain, Joseph. *Sketches of the Life of Joseph Mountain, a Negro, Who Was Executed at New-Haven, on the 20th Day of October, 1790, for a Rape, Committed on the 26th Day of May Last*, edited by David Daggett, New Haven, 1790.

Muhammad, Khalil Gibran. *The Condemnation of Blackness: Race, Crime, and the Making of Modern Urban America*. Harvard UP, 2010.

Mustakeem, Sowande. "'Armed with a Knife in Her Bosom': Gender, Violence, and the

Carceral Consequences of Rage in the Late 19th Century." *Journal of African American History*, vol. 100, no. 3, 2015, pp. 385–405.

Nayar, Sheila J. "The Enslaved Narrative: White Overseers and the Ambiguity of the Story-Told Self in Early African-American Autobiography." *Biography*, vol. 39, no. 2, 2016, pp. 197–227.

Nelson, William E. *Americanization of the Common Law: The Impact of Legal Change on Massachusetts Society, 1760–1830*. Harvard UP, 1975.

New American Standard Bible. Lockman Foundation, 1960.

Newman, Richard S. *Freedom's Prophet: Bishop Richard Allen, the AME Church, and the Black Founding Fathers*. New York UP, 2008.

Newman, Sara. "Disability and Life Writing: Reports from the Nineteenth-Century Asylum." *Journal of Literary and Cultural Disability Studies*, vol. 5, no. 3, 2011, pp. 261–78.

Otter, Samuel. *Philadelphia Stories: America's Literature of Race and Freedom*. Oxford UP, 2010.

Parkinson, Robert G. *The Common Cause: Creating Race and Nation in the American Revolution*. U of North Carolina P, 2016.

Pearsall, Sarah. *Atlantic Families: Lives and Letters in the Later Eighteenth Century*. Oxford UP, 2008.

Peterson, Carla L. "Subject to Speculation: Assessing the Lives of African-American Women in the Nineteenth Century." *Women's Studies in Transition: The Pursuit of Interdisciplinarity*, edited by Kate Conway-Turner et al., U of Delaware P, 1998, pp. 109–17.

Pomp. *Dying Confession of Pomp, a Negro Man, Who Was Executed at Ipswich, on the 6th August, 1795, for Murdering Capt. Charles Furbush, of Andover, Taken from the Mouth of the Prisoner, and Penned by Jonathan Plummer, Jun*. Newburyport, MA, 1795.

"Pregnancy in Prison Statistics (PIPS)." *Advocacy and Research on Reproductive Wellness of Incarcerated People*, Johns Hopkins School of Medicine, arrwip.org/projects/pregnancy. Accessed 15 Apr. 2024.

Price, Margaret. "The Bodymind Problem and the Possibilities of Pain." *Hypatia*, vol. 30, no. 1, 2015, pp. 268–84.

Prince, Mary. *The History of Mary Prince, a West Indian Slave. Related by Herself. With a Supplement by the Editor. To which is added, the Narrative of Asa-Asa, a Captured African*. London: F. Westley and A. H. Davis, 1831.

"Recovered." *Daily Missouri Democrat*, 27 Nov. 1855.

Reid-Pharr, Robert. *Conjugal Union: The Body, the House, and the Black American*. Oxford UP, 1999.

Rodríguez, Dylan. *Forced Passages: Imprisoned Radical Intellectuals and the U.S. Prison Regime*. U of Minnesota P, 2006.

Rommel-Ruiz, Bryan. "Vindictive Ferocity: Virginia's Response to the Nat Turner Rebellion." *Enemies of Humanity: The Nineteenth-Century War on Terrorism*, edited by Isaac Land, Palgrave Macmillan, 2008, pp. 63–78.

Ryan, Kelly A. *Everyday Crimes: Social Violence and Civil Rights in Early America*. New York UP, 2019.

Said, Edward W. *Representations of the Intellectual*. Vintage Books, 1996.

Schalk, Samantha Dawn. *Bodyminds Reimagined: (Dis)Ability, Race, and Gender in Black Women's Speculative Fiction.* Duke UP, 2018.

Schmitt, Carl. *The Concept of the Political.* 1932. Translated by George Schwab, U of Chicago P, 1996.

Schorb, Jodi. *Reading Prisoners: Literature, Literacy, and the Transformation of American Punishment, 1700–1845.* Rutgers UP, 2014.

Sekora, John. "Black Message/White Envelope: Genre, Authenticity, and Authority in the Antebellum Slave Narrative." *Callaloo*, no. 32, 1987, pp. 482–515.

The Sentencing Project. www.sentencingproject.org. Accessed 15 Apr. 2024.

Shildrick, Margrit. "Critical Disability Studies: Rethinking the Conventions for the Age of Postmodernity." *Routledge Handbook of Disability Studies*, edited by Nick Watson et al., Routledge, 2012, pp. 30–41.

———. *Dangerous Discourses of Disability, Subjectivity, and Sexuality.* Palgrave Macmillan, 2009.

Sichtermann, Barbara. "Woman Taking Speculation into Her Own Hands." *The Politics of the Essay: Feminist Perspectives*, edited by Ruth-Ellen Boetcher Joeres and Elizabeth Mittman, Indiana UP, 1993, pp. 87–94.

Smith, Caleb. *The Oracle and the Curse: A Poetics of Justice from the Revolution to the Civil War.* Harvard UP, 2013.

———. *The Prison and the American Imagination.* Yale UP, 2011.

Smith, Stephen. *Life, Last Words and Dying Speech of Stephen Smith, a Black Man, Who Was Executed at Boston This Day Being Thursday, October 12, 1797 for Burglary.* Boston, 1797.

Smith, Venture. *A Narrative of the Life and Adventures of Venture, a Native of Africa: But Resident above Sixty Years in the United States of America. Related by Himself.* New London, CT, 1798.

Smyer, R. B. Letters to governor, 1890s. Applications for Pardon, Paroles, or Remission of Fines, 1870–1915, SG010304, *Alabama Department of Archives and History*.

Spires, Derrick R. *The Practice of Citizenship: Black Politics and Print Culture in the Early United States.* U of Pennsylvania P, 2019.

Spivak, Gayatri Chakravorty. "Can the Subaltern Speak?" *Marxism and the Interpretation of Culture*, edited by Cary Nelson and Lawrence Grossberg, U of Illinois P, 1988, pp. 271–313.

Stone, Andrea. "Ancestors and the Ivory Tower: Reflection on Keynote." *Black Perspectives*, 12 Nov. 2019, www.aaihs.org/ancestors-and-the-ivory-tower.

———. "The Black Atlantic Revisited, the Body Reconsidered: On Lingering, Liminality, Lies, and Disability." *American Literary History*, vol. 24, no. 4, 2012, pp. 814–26.

———. *Black Well-Being: Health and Selfhood in Antebellum Black Literature.* UP of Florida, 2016.

———. "Interracial Sexual Abuse and Legal Subjectivity in Antebellum Law and Literature." *American Literature*, vol. 81, no. 1, 2009, pp. 65–92.

———. "Lunacy and Liberation: Black Crime, Disability, and the Production and Eradication of the Early National Enemy." *Early American Literature*, vol. 52, no. 1, 2017, pp. 109–40.

Sundquist, Eric J. *To Wake the Nations: Race in the Making of American Literature.* Belknap Press of Harvard UP, 1998.
Tannenbaum, Rebecca. *Health and Wellness in Colonial America.* Greenwood, 2012.
Taylor, Alan. *The Internal Enemy: Slavery and War in Virginia, 1772–1832.* W. W. Norton, 2013.
Thompson, George. *Prison Life and Reflections: Or a Narrative of the Arrest, Trial, Conviction, Imprisonment, Treatment, Observations, Reflections, and Deliverance of Work, Burr and Thompson, Who Suffered an Unjust and Cruel Imprisonment in Missouri Penitentiary, for Attempting to Aid Some Slaves to Liberty.* Oberlin, OH, 1847.
Tomlins, Christopher. *In the Matter of Nat Turner: A Speculative History.* Princeton UP, 2020.
Turner, David M. *Disability in Eighteenth-Century England: Imagining Physical Impairment.* Routledge, 2012.
Turner, Nathaniel. *The Confessions of Nat Turner and Related Documents.* 1831. Edited by Kenneth S. Greenberg, Bedford, 1996.
Vimalassery, Manu. "Counter-Sovereignty." *J19: The Journal of Nineteenth-Century Americanists*, vol. 2, no. 1, 2014, pp. 142–48.
Walker, David. *Appeal to the Coloured Citizens of the World.* 1829, rev. 1830. Edited by Peter P. Hinks, Pennsylvania State UP, 2003.
Walker, William. *Buried Alive (behind Prison Walls) for a Quarter of a Century: Life of William Walker.* Edited by Thomas S. Gaines, Saginaw, MI, 1892.
Wallace, Maurice O. *Constructing the Black Masculine: Identity and Ideality in African American Men's Literature and Culture, 1775–1995.* Duke UP, 2002.
Wang, Leah. "Unsupportive Environments and Limited Policies: Pregnancy, Postpartum, and Birth during Incarceration." *Prison Policy Initiative*, 19 Aug. 2021, www.prisonpolicy.org/blog/2021/08/19/pregnancy.
Ware, Rudolph T., III. *The Walking Qur'an: Islamic Education, Embodied Knowledge, and History in West Africa.* U of North Carolina P, 2014.
"Which Countries Still Use the Death Penalty?" *Week*, 2 Aug. 2018, www.theweek.co.uk/91736/which-countries-still-have-the-death-penalty.
White, Ashli. *Encountering Revolution: Haiti and the Making of the Early Republic.* Johns Hopkins UP, 2010.
Wilentz, Sean. "The Emancipators' Vision." *New York Review of Books*, vol. 69, no. 20, 2022, 58–61.
Williams, Daniel E. "Rogues, Rascals and Scoundrels: The Underworld Literature of Early America." *American Studies*, vol. 24, no. 2, 1983, pp. 5–19.
Williams, Ian. *Disorientation: Being Black in the World.* Europa Editions, 2021.
Williamson, Hugh P. *The Kingdom of Callaway.* Fulton, MO, 1967.
Wines, E. C., and Theodore W. Dwight. *Report on the Prisons and Reformatories of the United States and Canada, made to the Legislature of New York, January, 1867.* Albany, NY, 1867.
Wood, Marcus. *The Horrible Gift of Freedom: Atlantic Slavery and the Representation of Emancipation.* U of Georgia P, 2010.

X, Malcolm. "Message to the Grass Roots." Northern Negro Grass Roots Leadership Conference, 10 Nov. 1963, King Solomon Baptist Church, Detroit, MI.

Zur, Ofer. "The Love of Hating: The Psychology of Enmity." *History of European Ideas*, vol. 13, no. 4, 1991, pp. 345–69.

INDEX

Page numbers in *italics* refer to figures

Abu-Jamal, Mumia, 1, 14, 167
Abuse: physical, 48, 55, 58, 62; sexual, 12–13, 103–7, 111–12, 122–23
Academia, 4–6, 15
Acquittals, 144–45, 179n7
Adams, Sean A., 178n8
Address, Dying Confession, and Letter to His Wife (Johnstone), 2–3, 11, *19*, 21, 41–44, 57, 84–85, 89, 173n3, 173n10; on capital punishment, 33–34; as a declaration of innocence, 17–18, 22; use of irony in, 23, 28, 31–32, 39–40
Admissions of guilt, 36, 40, 53, 146, 148, 175n1
Adultery, 154–55
"Advice to Our Young People" (*Christian Recorder*), 130–31
African American print culture, 2–3, 14, 51–52, 174n4
African American soldiers, 128, 131–32
African Methodist Episcopal Church, 135–36
Age, 79, 122, 163–64; parole request letters addressing, 147–48, *149*, 150, 153–54
Agency, 37, 50, 148
Agricultural labor and, 53, 139, 146, 164
Alabama, 134–35, 144, 180n1; Black codes in, 142–45, 150; Constitution, 137–40, 155, 158, 180n1; convict leasing programs in, 2–3, 13–14, 142, 145, 158–59, 169–70; Foster J., imprisoned in, 146–48, *149*, 150–57, 159–61, *160*, *163*; Ku Klux Klan influence in, 164, 180n2; Wetumpka, 146, *160*, *161*, *162*, *163*
Aldridge v. Commonwealth, 92–93
Alexander, Michelle, 8

Alien enemy, 92, 94
Alkalimat, Abdul, 4
Allen, Richard, 127–28, 135–36
Allen, William, the Younger, 63
Allmendinger, David F., Jr., 88
Amanuenses, 103, 172n2; for Pomp, 11–12, 46–47, 50, 60–61, 66–71, 78, 172n9; for Turner, 12, 69, 77–80, 89–90, 98–99, 101
Americanization of the Common Law (Nelson), 27–28
Ancestry, ancestral knowledge and, 1, 48–49, 73, 168, 171n1
Antebellum era, 12, 14, 51–52, 91–97, 100–101
Appeal to the Coloured Citizens of the World (Walker), 10, 74
Arrests, 8, 32, 131–32, 135, 151; of Celia, 103–4; of Pomp, 169
Auburn State Prison, 110–11
Autobiographies, 6–7, 18, 78, 100, 174n4
Axtmann, Roland, 144

Baldwin, James, 123–24
Baltimore Sun (newspaper), 102
Banner, Stuart, 32, 43, 173n8
Barbarism, 63, 90, 136–37
Barclay, Jennifer, 174n3
Barnes, L. Diane, 128
Batra, Ajay Kumar, 173n5
Bay, Mia, 6, 106
Beaumont, Gustave de, 108
Beccaria, Cesare, 50
Beloved (Morrison), 99
Benda, Julien, 4, 123–24
Bernier, Celeste-Marie, 177n2
Berry, Daina Ramey, 98

The Bible, 41–43, 63, 65, 82–87, 154–56; New Testament, 83, 85, 178n8
Bilbroe (Judge), 148, 150
Bill of Rights, US, 93
Bill of Rights, Virginia, 92–93
Black abolitionists, 74, 128, 132
Black civic authority, 2, 51
Black civility, 11, 20, 24
Black codes, 126, 142–43, 157–58
Black freedom, 25–26, 74–75, 136–37
Black labor, 49, 127, 142–43, 151
Blackmon, Douglas, 127
Blackness, 1, 70–71, 99, 112, 144, 171n1, 173n5; criminality and, 3, 7–8, 14–16, 47, 49, 51, 137–38; enmity associated with, 167, 169; Foster, J., acknowledging his, 147, 159, *160*; incarceration and, 5–6, 167–70; Slotkin on, 28; Turner on, 84, 90
Black-on-white violence, 69, 77, 105
Black political exclusion, 20, 28, 40
Black prison intellectuals. *See specific topics*
Black prophetic tradition, 12, 45–47, 171n1, 172n8, 174n2; Turner and, 73, 79–86, 99–101
Black rebel outlaws, 13, 123, *161,* 161–62, *162*
Black Republicanism, 127
Black resistance, 12, 45–46, 95, 101, 169
Black revolts, 12, 75–77. *See also* Southampton revolt
Black studies, 4, 6, 141
Black subjugation, 142–43, 150–52
Black violence, 9, 28, 32–33, 76–77, 91, 95–96; white supremacy prompting, 12, 105
Black violent resistance, Black revolutionary violence and, 47, 69, 72, 74–77, 96
Black women, 6, 103–4, 110–11, 151, 164, 168; prison labor of, 129–30. *See also* Celia
Blouet, Guillaume-Abel, 108
Bogel-Burroughs, Nicholas, 180n1
Bondsman, bondswoman, 24, 37–39, 65
Boster, Dea H., 58
Boston Massacre, 63
Boudreau, Kristin, 34
Breen, Patrick H., 177n2
Britain, 21, 23–26, 34, 40, 42, 118, 169
Brown, John, 100
Brown, William Wells, 100
Bruce, La Marr Jurelle, 99, 176n12

Bush, Jordan, 116
Byrd, Brandon R., 74–75

Callaway County jail, 12–13, 102–3, 106–12, 116
Cameron, Christopher, 74
Capital crime, 36–37, 154–55
Capitalism, 142–43, 150
Capital punishment, 17, 33–35, 44, 64, 66, 137
Carceral institutions, 7, 17, 140, 167. *See also specific institutions*
Carlisle, Thomas, 113–14, 179n9
Carter, Rubin "Hurricane," 14, 115
Cary, Mary Ann Shadd, 81
Celia (enslaved woman), 1, 6–7, 168, 176n19, 178n12, 179n2, 180n14; actions in Missouri county jail, 2–3, 12–13, 104–21, 129–30, 158, 169; confessions by, 2–3, 13, 102–4, 116–17, 121–22, 169; depositions by, 2–3, 13, 103, 121–22; execution of, 13, 110, 121–22, 126, 169; jailbreaks by, 86, 104, 112–19, 122, 163; Newsom, R., murdered by, 102–5, 116–17; newspaper coverage of, 113, 115–17, 119–22, 179n8, 180n13; prison labor by, 127; stay of execution request by, 112–14, 119, 121
Chaison, Joanne Danaher, 66–68
Childhood, 52, 80–81
Christ, 22–23, 41–43, 79, 82–86
Christianity, 20, 36–37, 41, 53, 74, 80–82
Christian Recorder (newspaper), 13, 126, 130–40
Citizenship, 20, 24, 28, 93–94, 171n1
Civic responsibility, 28
Civil Rights Act of 1866, US, 143, 150
Civil rights movement, US, 12, 14, 17, 81, 101
Civil War, US, 3, 13, 124, 171n1, 175n9, 179n3; African American soldiers and, 128, 131–32; *Christian Recorder* during, 130–31; convict leasing programs following the, 126–27, 142–43; Southampton revolt and, 100–101
Cleaver, Eldridge, 14
Clemency, executive, 154, 156, 158
Cliff, Jimmy, 160
Cognitive disabilities, 57–61, 65, 72
Cohen, Daniel A., 20
Colonialism, colonial period and, 6, 23–24, 62, 64–66, 167; England and, 49; execution sermon during, 51; on mental disability, 55

Common Sense (Paine), 10
The Concept of the Political (Schmitt), 144
Confession genre, criminal, 16, 54, 65, 77–78, 171n1, 172n8, 174n2; dying confession, 36–41; Johnstone, A., and, 26–27, 40, 85–86, 89, 173n3; parole request letters compared to, 141, 146; printed confessions in, 2–3, 12–13, 61–62, 146
Confessions: by Celia, 2–3, 13, 102–4, 116–17, 121–22, 169; Johnstone, A., and, 26–27, 40, 85–86, 89, 173n3; by Pomp, 11–12, 45–47, 50, 62–63, 68, 71–72, 89, 174n4
The Confessions of Nat Turner, 2–3, 12, 48, 73, 76–92, 99–100, 124; introduction by Gray to, 86–87
Constitution, Alabama, 137–40, 155, 158, 180n1
Constitution, US, 13–14, 28, 101, 126, 128–29, 132, 150. *See also specific Amendments*
Constitutional Whig (newspaper), 95
Continental army, 67–68
Convictions, 8, 24, 37, 40, 44, 45, 59–60
Convict leasing programs, 126–27, 146, 150–51, 164, 168; in Alabama, 2–3, 13–14, 142, 145, 158–59, 169–70
Corporal punishment, 24–25, 64, 151
Countersovereignty, 87–89
Counterterrorism, 87, 91
COVID-19, 168
Craig, James, 18
Crawford, William, 108
Crime narrative genre, 51, 176n11
"Criminal and Enemy in the Political Imagination" (Kahn), 9
Criminal / enemy distinction, 2–3, 8–9, 11–15, 17, 85–87, 143–44, 172n7; Johnstone A., on, 10–11, 20–26, 28, 34–35, 37–41; Pomp and, 45–47. *See* Criminal
Criminality, criminalization of Black people and, 2, 5, 9–11, 167, 169, 173n4; Black, 3, 7–8, 14–16, 47, 49, 51, 137–38; Black codes facilitating, 143–44; of Black women, 129–30; fines and, 144–46, 150, 154; noncitizen status and, 24
Criminal law, 27–28, 32, 52–53, 172n7
Crip theory, 49–50
Crucifixion of Christ, 42, 79, 84, 86
Cuffee (enslaved man), 37

Curfews, 144
Currier, John J., 66–68
Curtin, Mary Ellen, 144, 160–61

Dade (Judge), 92–93
Dagbovie, Pero Gaglo, 6–7
Daily Missouri Democrat, 119–21
Davis, Angela, 1, 8, 14, 115, 123
Davis, Lennard J., 175n9
Death rates in prison, 169
Deaths, 24, 63–64, 88, 111, 132, 135, 156; Southampton revolt related, 12, 76–77, 87, 91, 99; state sanctioned, 5, 9, 37, 57, 106–7; yellow fever related, 26. *See also* Executions; Murders
Death sentences, death penalty and, 43–44, 78, 94, 112–13, 117–24, 150, 154; abolitionist support for, 25
Declaration of Independence, US, 35
Dehumanization, 97–98, 172n7
Delany, Martin R., 81, 100, 129
DeLombard, Jeannine Marie, 2, 51–52, 68, 87, 97–98, 175n9; on criminalization, 11; on gallows literature, 18, 20; on Johnstone, A., 27–28; on printed confessions, 61–62
Demetz, Frédéric-Auguste, 108
Deportation, 91–92, 94, 151–55
Depositions, 2–3, 13, 103, 121–22, 151–55, 171n1
Derrida, Jacques, 10–11
Dexter, Timothy, 66–67, 67
Disability, 12, 47, 88, 174nn2–3, 175n9, 177n23, 178n4; cognitive, 57–61, 65, 72; of Pomp, 45–46, 48–63
Dolovich, Sharon, 180n1
Domestic violence, 104, 106, 129–30
Douglass, Frederick, 81, 128–29, 155, 172n3, 176n14, 177nn1–2, 178n5; on Haitian Revolution, 74–75; on the Southampton revolt, 100
Downes, Paul, 90–91
Drewry, William Sidney, 98
DuBois, John W., 143
Du Bois, W. E. B., 171n1
Dwight, Theodore, 108–9
Dying Confession (Johnston, A.), 22, 36–41
Dying Confession of Pomp (1795), 45–49, *46*, 56, 66, 71, 77, 89

Dying words genre, 11–12, 16–17, 124, 171n1, 174n2, 175n9, 176n11; of Celia, 103; of Green, 31; of Johnstone, A., 21, 36–41, 50; parole request letters compared to, 141; of Pomp, 61, 69, 71; slave narrative genres and, 78–79

Education, 6–7, 40, 132–34, 137–40, 158
Edwards, Jonathan, 79
Emancipation, 3, 13, 23, 126–27, 131–32; form of Black subjugation following, 128, 142–45, 150–52
Emancipation Proclamation, US, 101, 131
Embodied intellectualism, 3, 104, 124–25, 180n15
Enemies of the state, 42, 44, 66, 95–97, 144, 169; Foster, J., on status as, 147, 151–52
Engels, Jeremy, 10–11
Enlightenment rhetoric, 22, 33, 99
Enmification of Black people, 3, 5, 7–8, 64, 155–56, 167; in New Jersey, 23–26, 37–38; post Civil War, 14; postemancipation, 126–27, 131–32; Reconstruction era, 143; Turner underscoring, 90; in Virginia, 91–92. *See also* Criminal/enemy distinction
Enslavers, 10, 75–76, 82–84, 127, 132; murders of, 8–9, 12–13, 37, 45, 52, 56–60, 70–71, 73, 87, 94, 102–5, 113, 121–22
Epilepsy, 51, 55
Erevelles, Nirmala, 62
Escapees, jailbreaks and, 13; by Carlisle, 113–15, 119; by Celia, 86, 104, 112–19, 122, 163; by Foster, J., 162–63
Europe, 73, 90
Executions, 7, 17–18, 43–44, 50, 65–66, 92, 179n3; of Celia, 13, 110, 121–22, 126, 169; execution sermons preceding, 21–22, 26–27, 29, 30, 36, 46, 51, 63, 70; of Johnstone, A., 21, 24, 26, 43–44, 73; of Pomp, 66; Southampton revolt related, 76–77, 79, 94; as state-sanctioned deaths, 5, 9, 37, 57, 106–7. *See also* Hangings
Executive clemency, 154, 156, 158

False oath taking, 18, 22, 36, 39–41, 44, 64
False white civility, 11, 20
"Familial disintegration," 173n10
Fanaticism, religious, 69, 76, 89–90, 95–96, 98

Felman, Shoshana, 175n5
Fifteenth Amendment, US Constitution, 132
Fines, criminalization and, 144–46, 150, 154
Finseth, Ian, 32
Flanders, Benjamin F., 142
Florida. *See specific regions*
Fortune, T. Thomas, 100
Foster, Frances Smith, 36, 174n4
Foster, James, 1, 5, 24, 126, 168, 172n4; on convict leasing programs, 169–70; imprisoned in Alabama, 146–48, 149, 150–61, 160, 163; parole request letters by, 2–3, 14, 86–87, 136, 138, 141–42, 147–48, 149, 150–56, 157, 158–64, 170, 173n10, 176n20
Foucault, Michel, 4, 8, 65, 141
Fourth Amendment, US Constitution, 28
France, Anatole, 93–94
Francis, Will, 88
Franklin, Bruce, 8
Free, John, 62–64
Freedman, freedwoman, freedpeople, 20, 23–25, 74–75, 91–92, 131, 151
Freedom of the press, 92
Free speech, 92–93
French Revolution, 76
Friend/enemy distinction, 66, 143
Fugitive Slave Act of 1850, US, 74, 76
Fugitive Slave Law (1793), US, 20
Full pardons, 145
Fulton Telegraph (newspaper), 103, 115–17, 121–22
Furbush (Captain, enslaver), 45–47, 176n16, 180n12

Gabriel's Rebellion, 76
Gallows literature, prison writing and, 1, 11–12, 14, 27, 45, 52, 141; DeLombard on, 18–20; genres of, 168, 172n8, 174n2. *See also specific genres*
Gardner, Eric, 130
Garrison, William Lloyd, 90
Gender segregation of prisoners, 110–11
George (enslaved man), 103–4, 116–17, 120
Gigantino, James J., II, 25, 36
Good behavior, parole rewards for, 145, 150, 153
Goodell, William, 91

Index · 199

Governors, authority of, 138, 145–48, *149*, 150–56, 158–59
Gramsci, Antonio, 4, 123
Grand larceny, 92, 146–47
Gray, Thomas, 12, 77–80, 84–85, 89–91, 96–99, 101, 103
Great Depression, 164
Great Migration, US, 164
Green, Johnson, *31*
Greenberg, Kenneth S., 87
Greene, Lorenzo J., 117
Griffith, Lee, 85–86
Gross, Kali N., 179n3

Haitian Revolution, 12, 26, 28, 73–74, 177n2
Haley, Sarah, 129–30
Hall, Prince, 127–28
Halpern, James Adam, 179n2, 180n11
Hangings, 27, 60–61, 84, 107, 121–22; of Johnston, A., 37, 43; of Pomp, 71–72
"Happy coon" stereotype, 159–60, *160*
Happy Will photograph, 159–60, *160*
The Harder They Come (film), 160
Hard labor, 13–14, 108–9, 131, 141, 144, 150, 164
Harper, Frances, 132–33
Hart, Daniel, 37
Hartnett, John, 43
Hartog, Hendrik, 123
Havis, Devonya N., 171n1
Henderson, Erroll A., 171n1
Henderson, John, 137
The Heroic Slave (Douglass), 100, 179
Hicks, Cheryl D., 179n3
Hierarchy, 49, 173n8
Higginbotham, A. Leon, Jr., 91
History of Newburyport (Currier), 66–67
Holland, Edwin C., 90
Holmes, David G., 171n1
hooks, bell, 4–5, 172n5
Huffsey, Samuel, 18
Human, concepts of, 97–98
Human rights, 2, 106
Hutchinson, Anne, 59

Identity, 20; national, 10, 17, 47, 51; sovereign, 33, 66
Illiteracy, 104, 123, 158

Incarceration, carcerality and, 1, 129–30, 167–70, 172n6, 179n3; Black intellectual labor and, 2–8, 15, 104, 164; education and, 132–34, 158; fines and, 144–46, 150; pregnancy and, 13, 103, 107–8, 110–11, 113, 122, 179n5; of white women, 111. *See also* Jails; Prisons; *specific prisoners*
Incidents in the Life of a Slave Girl (Jacobs, H.), 124
Individual freedom, 23, 25–26
Individual violence, 99, 168
Infanticides, 88
Injustices, 168; racial, 7, 44, 141, 143, 154, 170
Insanity, 12, 45, 59–60, 72. *See also* Madness/lunacy and
Intellectuals, intellectualism and, 1–8, 15, 16–17 164–165, 123–25, 172n2, 175nn5–6; disability and, 12; Foucault on, 141
Internal enemy, Black people as the, 2, 76, 87, 124, 144
Involuntary servitude, 126–27, 180n1
Irony, 23, 28, 31–32, 39–40
Ivens, Henry, 40

Jackson, George, 14
Jackson, Jonathan, 66–67
Jacobs, Anne F., 91
Jacobs, Harriet, 100, 124, 129
Jacobs, John, 129
Jails, 2–5, 7, 17, 61–63, 107–10
James, Jennifer C., 57, 171n1
James, Joy, 4
Jarman, Michelle, 175n7
Jefferson, Thomas, 11
Jelks, W. D., 156, *157*, 158–59
Jim Crow laws, 126
Jimenez, Mary Ann, 176n17
Johnstone, Abraham (Benjamin), 1, 57, 127–28, 168–69, 172n8, 173n10, 273n8; appeals to religion by, 154; confessions and, 26–27, 40, 85–86, 89, 173n3; on criminal/enemy distinction, 10–11, 20–26, 28, 34–35, 37–41; declaration of innocence by, 17–18, 20–22, 31–32, 34; execution of, 21, 24, 26, 43–44, 73; Foster, J., compared to, 148, 154; on perjury, 18, 22, 27, 32–36, 39–41, 66, 75–76, 86, 130–31; Pomp compared to, 45–47, 70;

Turner compared to, 73, 86–87. *See also* Address, Dying Confession, and Letter to His Wife
Johnstone, Sarah (Sally), 18, 41–42, 44, 85
Jones, Absalom, 127–28, 135
Judgment day (biblical), 82–84
Julius, Nikolaus Heinrich, 108

Kahn, Paul, 9, 26, 33, 44, 65–66, 143–44
Kettner, James H., 93
Ku Klux Klan, 13, 126, 164, 180n2

Labor, 3; agricultural, 53, 139, 146, 164; Black, 49, 127, 142–43, 151; Black intellectual, 2–3, 5–6, 15, 104, 164; hard, 13–14, 108–9, 131, 141, 144, 150, 164; prison, 114, 129–30, 145, 170, 180n1; slave, 143, 150–51
Land, Isaac, 97
Larceny laws, 92, 144, 146–47, 155
Legal personhood, 51–52, 56–57, 65, 169
Le Lys Rouge (*The Red Lily*) (France), 93–94
Letter writers, 41–42, 85, 173n10. *See also* Prison correspondences
Levine, Lawrence W., 160–61
Levine, Robert S., 100
Levy, La TaSha, 6
Lewis (bondsperson), 120–21
Liberator (newspaper), 90, 96
Lincoln, Abraham, 127
Lindsay, Robert, 180n2
Literacy, 3, 81, 133, 140, 172n2
Little, Malcolm, 178n6. *See also* X, Malcolm
Louisiana, 139, 142
Love, 44, 57, 70
Luke (apostle), 41–43, 83–86, 178n8
Lynchings, lynch mobs and, 61, 132, 135, 137, 158, 164; Jelks supporting, 13; Jim Crow laws and, 126

Madness/lunacy and, 11–12, 80, 95–100, 174n2, 175n5; Pomp and, 45–46, 48–63, 70–72. *See also* Mental distress
Malinda (enslaved woman), 116–17, 120, 180n14
Manumission, 18, 39, 67–68, 79
Marshall, I. Howard, 83
Martin, David, 150
Martin, Vincent "Ivanhoe," 160

Massachusetts, 44, 55, 59–60, 63–64, 92, 176n17; slavery in, 52–53, 169, 176n21
Mat (escapee), 111, 115–19, 122
Mather, Cotton, 36
May, Julia Ann, 164
Mbembe, Achille, 9–10
McKelvey, Blake, 108
McLaurin, Melton A., 119, 179n1
McRuer, Robert, 50
Mental distress, 12, 77, 89, 97, 175n7; of Pomp, 45–46, 48–63, 70–72
"Message to the Grass Roots" (X), 1
Mills, Charles W., 6–7, 53–54
Minear, Andrea, 62
Minstrelsy, 174n4
Mississippi, 142–43
Missouri, 107, 153, 179n3
Missouri Republican (newspaper), 104–5
Missouri v. Celia, a Slave, 12–13, 101, 102
Montgomery Journal, 147, 156, *158*
Morrison, Toni, 99
Muhammad, Khalil Gibran, 2, 8
Murders, 3, 22, 35, 118; of enslavers, 8–9, 12–13, 37, 45, 52, 56–60, 70–71, 73, 87, 94, 102–5, 113, 121–22; of Furbush, 45–47, 180n12; of Newsom, R., 102–5, 116–17
Murray, P. Houston, 131
Mustakeem, Sowande, 179n3

National enemy, 20, 43, 169
National identity, 10, 17, 47, 51
National security, 11, 20, 34–35, 44, 63, 169
Naturalization Act of 1790, US, 66, 177n22
Nayar, Sheila J., 174n4, 175n6
Nelson, William E., 27–28
Neurological disorders, 55, 175n8
New Jersey, 17, 22, *38*, 84, 86, 136–37, 173n7; enmity in, 23–26, 37–38; revolutionary government in, 40; yellow fever epidemic in, 34
New Jersey Journal, 25
Newman, Richard S., 127–28
New Perspectives on the Black Intellectual Tradition (Dagbovie), 6–7
Newsom, Harvey, 119–20
Newsom, Robert, 102–5, 112, 114, 116–17
Newspapers, newspaper coverage and, 169, 179nn8–9; of Carlisle, 113–14, 119–20; of

Celia, 113, 115–17, 119–22, 179n8, 180n13; of parole request letters, 146–47, *149,* 156, 158; of Southampton revolt, 95–97, 99–100; of Turner, 12, 90, 95, 99–100. *See also specific newspapers*
New Testament, Bible, 83, 85, 178n8
New York, 110–11, 145
New York Age (Fortune), 100
Noncitizen status, 9, 12, 66, 94–95, 124
Notes on the State of Virginia (Jefferson), 11

Oath taking, 43, 86; false, 18, 22, 36, 39–41, 44, 64
"Old Man a Convict, An" (Foster), 147–48, *149,* 150
Orality, orators and, 3, 6, 14, 16, 50, 141
The Other, 47, 144
Otter, Samuel, 34, 173n4, 173n7
Overcrowding of jails and prisons, 108, 110, 145

Pacifism, 74
Paine, Thomas, 10
Paratexts, 47–48, 69, 77, 96
Pardons, 59–60, 111, 145, 170. *See also* Parole laws
Parkinson, Robert G., 93
Parole laws, Alabama, 14, 145–46, 152
Parole request letters, 13, 126–27, 145–46, 168; by Foster, J., 2–3, 14, 86–87, 136, 138, 141–42, 147–48, *149,* 150–56, *157,* 158–64, 170, 173n10, 176n20
Pathologization, 9, 75–76, 97–98, 175n7; insanity and, 12, 45, 59–60, 72
Pauperism, 132–33
Pearsall, Sarah, 173n10
Perjury, 21–22, 27, 32–36, 39–41, 66, 75–76, 130–31, 148
Petit treason, 92, 94, 147, 178n10
Philadelphia, Pennsylvania, 11, 84, 136, 173n2; yellow fever epidemic in, 18, 26, 62, 75–76, 135, 173n7
Physical abuse, 48, 55, 58, 62
Pleasants, John Hampden, 95
Plummer, Jonathan, *67,* 98, 103, 174n4, 175n6, 176n18; as amanuensis for Pomp, 11–12, 46–47, 50, 60–61, 66–71, 78, 172n9
Poe, Edgar Allan, 175n6

Political prisoners, 14, 150–51
Pomp (enslaved man), 1, 116, 127–28, 168–69, 175nn5–6, 176n20; appeals to religion by, 59–61, 154; confession by, 11–12, 45–47, 50, 62–63, 68, 71–72, 89, 174n4; enslaved by Furbush, 48, 52–57, 176n16; Foster, J., compared to, 148, 154; Furbush killed by, 73, 180n12; manumission letter for, 67–68; Plummer as amanuensis for, 11–12, 46–47, 50, 60–61, 66–71, 78, 172n9; as public enemy, 63–72; Turner compared to, 73, 86–87
Porter, Henry, 88
Postemancipation era, 126–27, 130–32, 142, 145
Post-Reconstruction era, 7, 13–15, 130, 142, 145, 170
Power, 39, 79, 83–84, 85; parole requests and, 142, 147–48, 150, 154–56, 158–59; of religion, 79, 135; sovereign, 21, 65–66, 68; state, 9, 141–42
Pregnancy, 168; carceral, 13, 103, 107–8, 110–11, 113, 122, 179n5
Print culture, 16, 21–23, *31,* 37, 44; African American, 2–3, 14, 51–52, 174n4. *See also* Newspapers, newspaper coverage and
Prison correspondences, 1, 13, 130, 145–46, 158. *See also* Parole request letters
Prisons, penitentiaries and, 2–5, 7, 17, 107–8, 134, 141; early release from, 150, 156, 159; Foster, J., critiquing, 130, 148, *149,* 150; labor in, 114, 129–30, 145, 170, 180n1; racial shift in, 126–27, 144–45, 156
Property, enslaved people considered, 52–53, 56
Prophecy, 12, 47, 57; disability and, 48–49; madness and, 99. *See also* Black prophetic tradition
Prosser, Gabriel, 74
Proto-national enemy, 24
Public enemy, 12, 47, 55, 63–72, 98
Puritan settlers, 75

The Racial Contract (Mills), 6
Racial injustices, 7, 44, 141, 143, 154, 170
Racialization, 8, 14–15, 27–28, 44, 97, 176n21; Black disability and, 47; of citizenship, 20, 28; exclusion from political participation and, 40

Racial stereotypes, 27–28, 51, 54, *80,* 159–60, 160
Racism, 8, 32–33, 152, 159, 169, 177n2, 178n9; Black violent resistance in response to, 76; revolutionary, 26
Rape, 25, 28, 102–3, 116, 122–23
Read, Thomas (Tom), 18
Reason, rationality and, 147–48, 152–56, 158
Recidivism, 131, 151–52
Reconstruction era, 1, 9, 129, 143, 151, 171n1, 180n2
Religion, 26–28, 35, 76, 79, 80–81, 134–36; parole request letters appealing to, 146, 148, 154–56
Religious fanaticism, 69, 76, 89–90, 95–96, 98
Religious hypocrisy, 85–86, 137
Report on the Prisons and Reformatories of the United States and Canada (Wines, Dwight), 108–9
Representations of the Intellectual (Said), 123
Republican ideology, 22–23, 49, 54, 127–28, 143
Revolutionary rhetoric, 11, 18, 25, 49, 54, 143, 169
Revolutionary War, US, 2, 48, 57, 60, 66–68, 90, 96; African American soldiers, 128, 131–32; Black enmity following, 23–24
Richmond Enquirer (newspaper), 95
Rights, 98, 131–32, 171n1, 180n1; civil, 2, 14, 17, 81, 91, 93, 101, 143, 150; human, 2, 106; to kill, 9, 44, 143; voting, 135, 137–38, 180n1
Rodríguez, Dylan, 172n6
Rommel-Ruiz, Bryan, 97
Rush, Benjamin, 62

Said, Edward W., 4, 53, 123–24
Samford, William J., 147
Schizophrenia, 51
Schmitt, Carl, 10, 66, 143–44
Schorb, Jodi, 173n3, 173n10
Scottsboro Boys, 101, 123, 164
Seale, Bobby, 123
Secularization, 27, 37
Segregation, 62, 110–11, 138, 144
Sekora, John, 174n4
Self-defense, 9, 105–7, 118
Self-governance, 75–76
Self-representation, legal, 153, 156, 158

Sémelin, Jacques, 87
Sentences, severity of sentencing and, 40–41, 60–61, 111, 127, 164; death, 35, 78, 94, 112–13, 117–24, 150, 154; Foster, J., addressing, 147–48, *149,* 150, 152–55
Sentencing laws, 145
Seven Years' War, 63
Sexual abuse, 12–13, 103–7, 111–12, 122–23
Sexuality, 57, 70
Sexual violence, 102–5, 108, 111–12, 114, 116, 122, 124–25
Shadd, Mary Ann, 129
Shakur, Assata, 1, 11, 14, 123–24, 167
Skinner, Richard, 40
Slack (horse owner), 146–47, 153
Slave laws, salve codes and, 9, 24–25, 152
Slave narratives, 6–7, 55–56, 71, 78–79, 116, 124, 174n4, 175n6; childhoods addressed in, 52, 80
Slave picket (torture method), 118
Slave revolts, 11–12, 24, 74–75, 99, 127
Slavery, enslavement and, 2, 5, 23–24, 172n7, 173n6, 174n4, 176n14; abolition of, 126–27, 171n1; armed resistance to, 128; of Black women, 123, 179n3; convict leasing programs and, 142, 164–65, 169; Emancipation Proclamation and, 131; Engels on, 11; imprisonment compared to, 61–63, 134–35; Johnstone on, 18; in Massachusetts, 169; mental distress and, 77; noncitizen status and, 9, 12, 66, 94–95, 124; Pomp on, 12, 48, 52; significance of Haitian Revolution on, 74–75; Turner on, 82, 87, 90–91; in Virginia, 92–93. *See also* Emancipation
Slotkin, Richard, 28
Smith, Caleb, 2, 50, 100
The Southampton Insurrection (Sidney), 98
Southampton revolt, 90, 94–96, 169, 172n8, 174n2, 177n2; as Black violent resistance, 74–77; deaths related to, 12, 76–77, 87, 91, 99; is an example of countersovereignty, 87–89; Virginia during, 145
South Carolina, 142–43
Sovereign identity, 33, 66
Sovereign power, 21, 65–66, 68
Sovereignty, 26, 33–36, 65–66, 88–91, 143
Spivak, Gayatri Chakravorty, 180n15

Starvation, 164
State: power, 9, 141–42; sovereignty, 65–66, 143; violence, 27, 130
State-sanctioned death, 5, 9, 37, 57, 106–7
Stay of execution, 112–14, 119, 121
Stereotypes, racial, 27–28, 51, 54, *80*, 159–60, *160*
Stewart, James Brewer, 21
Stiker, Henri-Jacques, 177n23
Stillbirth, 103, 106–7, 111
Suffrage, 131–32, 138–39
Sufrin, Carolyn, 179n5
Sundquist, Eric J., 90, 96, 177n2
Sun Tzu, 23
Surveillance, 97
Sympathy, 43, 58, 69, 146

Tannenbaum, Rebecca, 55, 57–58, 62, 65, 175n8
Tantec, Felix le, 124
"The Tell-Tale Heart" (Poe), 175n6
Terrorism, production of terror and, 87–91, 97
Testimony, 168, 180nn10–11; Black, 14, 16, 51–52, 125, 141, 144–45, 163–64, 174n4; trial, 102–3, 105, 107, 116–17. *See also specific forms of testimony*
Thirteenth Amendment, US Constitution, 13–14, 101, 126, 128–29, 150
Thompson, George, 108, 111–12, 179n7
Tocqueville, Alexis de, 108
Tomlins, Christopher, 79, 83, 87, 174n4, 178n7
Torture, 9, 76–77, 92, 118, 150–51
To the Free Africans and Other Free People of Color in the United States (1796), 21, 27
"To the White People of Alabama" (*Christian Recorder*), 138–40
Toward an Intellectual History of Black Women (Bay), 6, 106
Treason, 34–36, 40–42, 92, 94, 177n2, 178n10
Tremenda (Mather), 36
Turner, Nathaniel, 9, 123, 168–69, 172n8, 177n2, 178nn6–7; appeals to religion by, 12, 76, 80–87, 154; confession by, 77–79, 85–86, 169; Foster, J., compared to, 148, 154; Gray as an amanuensis for, 12, 69, 77–80, 89–90, 98–99, 101; Haitian Revolution, 74–75; newspaper coverage of, 12, 90, 95, 99–100; Pomp compared to, 45, 59; production of terror invoked by, 87–89. *See also The Confessions of Nat Turner*; Southampton revolt
Tutwiler, Julia S., 134

Union Army, 128, 131–32
United States, US, 35, 74–77, 151; antebellum era, 12, 14, 51–52, 91–97, 100–101; postemancipation era, 126–27, 130–32, 142; post-Reconstruction era, 7, 13–15, 130, 142, 145, 170; Reconstruction era, 1, 9, 129, 143, 171n1, 180n2; Revolutionary War, 2, 23–24, 48, 57, 60, 66–68, 90, 96; undeclared war against Black people in, 2, 14, 128–29, 131, 137. *See also* Civil War; Emancipation; Slavery, enslavement and; *specific legislation*; *specific states*

Vesey, Denmark, 74, 76, 90
Violence, 20, 89, 156, 169–70, 171n1, 172n3, 180n2; Black, 9, 12, 28, 32–33, 76–77, 91, 95–96, 105; Black-on-white, 69, 77, 105; Black revolutionary, 47, 69, 72, 74–77, 96; domestic, 104, 106, 129–30; individual, 99, 168; sexual, 102–5, 108, 111–12, 114, 116, 122, 124–25; state, 27, 130; white, 69, 77, 105, 136–37
Virginia, Commonwealth of, 76–78, 81, 90, 144–45; antebellum, 12, 91–97, 100–101. *See also* Southampton revolt
Voting rights, 135, 137–38, 180n1

Walker, David, 10–11, 74, 177n2
Wang, Leah, 179n5
Ware, Rudolph T., III, 180n15
War on drugs, 170
Washington, Madison, 178
Waterboarding, 151
Welch, Rachel, 110–11
West, Cornel, 4–5
Wetumpka, Alabama, 146, *160*, *161*, 162, *162*, *163*
Whippings, 94, 118, 132, 151, 176n221
White, Ashli, 75
White abolitionists, 23, 71
White brutality, 136–37
White civility, false, 11, 20
White fears, 24, 37, 75–77

Index · 203

Whiteness, 11, 171n1
White supremacy, 2–3, 6–8, 90, 98–99, 167, 169, 176n12; Alabama Constitution reinforcing, 137–38; Jelks supporting, 158; Johnstone, A., on, 154; Ku Klux Klan and, 133–34; Other status threatening, 144; on the perception of Black people as threats, 10–11; Thirteenth Amendment and, 128–29
White violence, 69, 77, 105, 136–37
White women, 28, 111
Wilentz, Sean, 128–29
Williams, Ian, 170
Williams, Rebecca, 88
Williamson, Hugh P., 116–17
Wines, E. C., 108–9
Winscott, Virginia, 107, 179n6
Womack, Allen, 117–18
Woman's Christian Temperance Union, 134
Wood, Marcus, 59, 69

X, Malcolm, 1, 5, 12, 123–24, 178n6

Yellow fever epidemic, 18, 20, 26, 34, 62, 75–76, 135, 173n7

Zur, Ofer, 10–11

Andrea Stone is professor of English language and literature at Smith College. She is the author of *Black Well-Being: Health and Selfhood in Antebellum Black Literature,* which was awarded the Canadian Association for American Studies Robert K. Martin Book Prize.

Printed in the United States
by Baker & Taylor Publisher Services